God as Creator in Acts 17:24

Africanus Monograph Series

The *Africanus Monograph Series* is published by the Africanus Guild, based at Gordon-Conwell Theological Seminary's Boston campus, the Center for Urban Ministerial Education (CUME). Like the *Africanus Journal*, it strives to promote academic work by men and women that is globally evangelical in the historically orthodox, multiethnic, multicultural sense, with a commitment to biblical fidelity, in conversation with the realities of the world in which we live.

The journal is named in honor of Julius Africanus, a Christian scholar born around AD 200. He probably was born in Jerusalem; studied in Alexandria, Egypt; and later became bishop of Emmaus. He was considered by the ancients a man of consummate learning and sharpest judgment, a careful historian who sought to defend the truth of the Bible.

The journal may be read online at http://www.gordonconwell.edu/boston/africanusjournal.

The *Africanus Monograph Series* publishes academic dissertations and books by scholars who agree with its goals and have earned research degrees.

God as Creator in Acts 17:24

An Historical-Exegetical Study

JENNIFER MARIE CREAMER

WIPF & STOCK · Eugene, Oregon

GOD AS CREATOR IN ACTS 17:24
An Historical-Exegetical Study

Africanus Monograph Series, 2

Copyright © 2017 Jennifer Marie Creamer. All rights reserved. Except for brief quotations in critical publications or reviews, no part of this book may be reproduced in any manner without prior written permission from the publisher. Write: Permissions, Wipf and Stock Publishers, 199 W. 8th Ave., Suite 3, Eugene, OR 97401.

Wipf & Stock
An Imprint of Wipf and Stock Publishers
199 W. 8th Ave., Suite 3
Eugene, OR 97401

www.wipfandstock.com

PAPERBACK ISBN: 978-1-5326-1536-8
HARDCOVER ISBN: 978-1-5326-1538-2
EBOOK ISBN: 978-1-5326-1537-5

Manufactured in the U.S.A.   AUGUST 11, 2017

Contents

List of Tables | vii
Preface | ix

1 Introduction | 1

2 Literary Setting and Context of Acts 17:24 | 6

    2.0 Introduction
    2.1 Literary Setting
    2.2 Literary Context
    2.3 Conclusion

3 Semantic Study of "The God Who Made the Heaven and Earth" in Biblical and Extra-Biblical Jewish Literature | 42

    3.0 Introduction
    3.1 Semantic Study of Key Phrases Related to Acts 17:24
    3.2 Analysis: Comparison With Acts 17:24
    3.3 Conclusion

4 Greek Views of the Creation of the Universe as it Relates to the Deity or Deities in Philosophical Writings Influential in the First Century A.D. | 97

    4.0 Introduction
    4.1 Summary of Scholarship
    4.2 Methodology
    4.3 Introduction to the Athenian Philosophical Setting

Contents

    4.4 Origins of the Cosmos
    4.5 Relationship of the Gods to the Cosmos
    4.6 Summary

5 Conclusion | 148

    5.1 Summary of Findings
    5.2 Theological Reflection

Appendix: Greek Text and Translation of Acts 17:16–34 | 157
Bibliography | 161
Subject Index | 173
Ancient Document Index | 177

List of Tables

Table 1. Structure of the Areopagus speech | 28

Table 2. Comparison of speeches in Lystra and Athens | 35

Table 3. Semantic Category A (θεός or κύριος + ποιέω + 2 (or more) of οὐρανός, γῆ, κόσμος) | 45

Table 4. Semantic Category B (θεός or κύριος + ποιέω + 1 of οὐρανός, γῆ, κόσμος) | 46

Table 5. Semantic Category C (θεός or κύριος + 1 of οὐρανός, γῆ) | 46

Table 6. Six classifications of literary type | 47

Table 7. Comparison of Acts 17:24 with Genesis 1:1 | 90

Table 8. Structural similarities between Acts 17:24–30, Isaiah 45:18–22, and Jeremiah 10:12–16 | 92

Table 9. Structural similarities between Acts 17:19–34 and Jonah 1:6–16 | 93

Table 10. Philosophers, work cited, and connection to Athens | 102–3

Table 11. Passages as divided by branch of philosophy articulated | 109

Table 12. Passages of Greek literature divided into four classifications of topic | 110

Table 13. Some views of the Stoics, their antecedents, and of Paul on the origins of the cosmos | 132

Table 14. Some views of the Epicureans and of Paul on the origins of the cosmos | 134

List of Tables

Table 15. Views of the Stoics and of Paul on the relationship of the divine to the cosmos | 144

Table 16. Views of the Epicureans and of Paul on the relationship of the divine to the cosmos | 146

Preface

IT HAS BEEN A great privilege to spend several years immersed in the study of Paul's message in Acts 17. This study has provided the opportunity to soak in the richness of two areas close to my heart: exegesis of the New Testament text and matters related to cross-cultural communication. I am grateful to the Faculty of Theology at the Potchefstroom campus of North-West University for facilitating this research under the supervision of Dr. Francois Viljoen. Dr. Viljoen has supervised my work with thoughtful care, always gently motivating me to deepen my research. The department was more than gracious during my stay in Potchefstroom. The warm and collegial atmosphere of the Faculty was a great encouragement and a time I will always remember fondly.

Dr. Aída Besançon Spencer and her husband, Dr. William David Spencer, created the Africanus Guild doctoral support program, without which this thesis would not exist. Thanks go to Bill, for getting me into it in the first place, and to Aída for getting me through it. Aída has mentored me in countless ways for many years and is, in many respects, much more than a supervisor. She has been extraordinary in her ability to provide guidance for research and writing. Besides giving insightful comments on the various iterations of each chapter and sharing her wisdom and advice in our meetings, Aída has facilitated opportunities to teach at the Boston campus of Gordon-Conwell Theological Seminary, to publish, to participate in a conference presentation, and to assist with the editing of the *Africanus Journal*. We have also labored together in the work of the ministry at Pilgrim Church in Beverly, Massachusetts.

Preface

Dr. Catherine Kroeger took me on as an independent study student for courses in Greek history, literature, and philosophy before the start of this research. The discussions in her office provided a valuable foundation for the study of the Greco-Roman backgrounds in this thesis. Dr. Kroeger continued to teach at Gordon-Conwell until several days before her passing. I am fortunate to have had the opportunity to study with her before her sudden departure. I am also indebted to Dr. Sean McDonough for his feedback on chapter four and to Dr. Eckhard Schnabel for his input on bibliographic resources. Mary Riso, Jean Risley, and Kris Johnson have carefully proofread the manuscript, for which I am most grateful. Thanks also go to Dr. Tom Petter and Dr. Donna Petter for building foundations for study in my previous training at the School of Biblical Studies and for their encouragement over the years. I also wish to thank the excellent library staff at Gordon–Conwell Theological Seminary for their assistance in locating materials. Jim Darlack, Bob McFadden, and Meridith Kline gave valuable help and guidance with both print and electronic resources.

While doctoral research may appear to be a solitary venture, in reality, it is not. I am deeply grateful to all who have supported me, whether through finances, prayer, or encouragement. North-West University generously provided a doctoral bursary as well as a research scholarship. The Africanus Guild also provided tuition assistance. Heartfelt thanks go to the many who have journeyed with me through their friendship and support. Pilgrim Church has prayed for me regularly, as have friends around the world. Special acknowledgements are due to my father and mother for instilling in me a love for learning and for their support over the years.

CHAPTER 1

Introduction

CONTEXTUALIZATION IS A SUBJECT of great debate among those who labor in a global context. Many difficult questions arise that do not have easy answers. When it comes to engaging contemporary culture in cross-cultural communication, how far is too far? How far is not far enough? The Areopagus speech of Acts makes a helpful study of how Paul (as recorded by Luke) both engaged and confronted the contemporary culture of his day in order to present his message.

Although many (including Gärtner, 1955:66–72; Keener, 2014:2564–2680; Schnabel, 2012:715–748; Winter, 2005:38–59; Witherington, 1998:511–535) have discussed the question of how the speaker of the Areopagus address may have been interacting with the contemporary culture, there is no major work that focuses on the role of God as Creator in Paul's communication. This work aims to make a contribution by addressing this gap.

Two monographs have made a great impact in the academic world and are frequently referred to in commentaries and articles. Martin Dibelius, in his 1939 essay, "Paul on the Areopagus" (Dibelius, 1956:26–77), made a case for the speech being rooted squarely in Greek thought, in such a way as to depart from both Old and New Testament theology. Dibelius acknowledged that the creation motif in Acts 17:24 originates from the Old Testament (1956:41), but then develops his argument that the speech is Hellenistic, and not Christian, in language and content (1956:57). He asks the question of whether "the apostle Paul could have made this speech" (1956:58). At the heart of Dibelius's argument is an alleged incongruity between the theology of Paul in Romans and the theology of the speaker of the Areopagus speech (1956:58–64). In his view, "Luke strayed too far from the Paul who was the theologian of the paradoxes of grace and faith" (1956:77). Dibelius concluded that the speech in Athens was not historical, but symbolic in nature (1956:77).

Some years later, Bertil Gärtner responded with a major work, *The Areopagus Speech and Natural Revelation* (1955). Gärtner argued in favor of the Old Testament and Jewish foundations of the Areopagus speech, while also affirming the Hellenistic environment into which it was spoken. His research includes an investigation of the role of natural revelation in Acts 17 and Romans 1–2 (1955:73). Gärtner (1955:82–83) asks the question, "Is the background to the Pauline ideas to be sought in Old Testament, in Jewish, or in Stoic texts?" Gärtner demonstrates that the Old Testament employed creation as an argument against idolatry (1955:88–89, 101). Both Romans 1–2 and Acts 17 are shown to carry an anti-idolatry context, consolidating his point that Paul's theology finds its roots in the Old Testament and Jewish thought. Further, the Stoic view of god is irreconcilable with the personal God of the Judeo-Christian tradition (1955:170–171). Against the claims of Dibelius, Gärtner concludes that the theology of Acts 17 is not contrary to that of Romans 1–2 (1955:249) and that the Areopagus speech "links up with a Jewish pattern" (1955:251).

More recent studies focus on various aspects of the speech, but still, little is said regarding the proclamation of God as Creator in verse 24. The rhetorical aspects of the speech are explored in some detail by several authors (Given, 1995:357–369; Sandnes, 1993:13–25; Zweck, 1989:94–103).[1] The nature of God has been discussed as it relates to the Stoic and Epicurean schools (see especially Gärtner, 1955:81; Schnabel, 2005:179–180; Winter, 2005:48–53).[2] Many have made note of the rejection of idolatry being an

---

1. Sandnes argues that Paul's approach in Athens is based on the rhetorical technique of *insinuatio*—a subtle approach intended to elicit questions of his audience (1993:15, 17, 25). Both Sandnes (1993:20–24) and Given (1995:365) discuss similarities between Paul and Socrates in Acts 17. Given's primary aim is to analyze the rhetorical features of the speech in a literary-critical approach (1995:357). He applies an "actantial model" (1995:360–361) with the findings that "the Word, proclamation of Jesus and the resurrection, is the paradigmatic object throughout Acts" as well as in the Areopagus speech (1995:371). Zweck builds a case for the *exordium* of the Athens's speech (Acts 17:22–23) containing a *propositio* (the assertion that he will proclaim what is worshipped as unknown), a rhetorical technique detailed by Aristotle and Quintilian (1989:94–96).

2. Both Schnabel (2005:179–180) and Winter (2005:48–53) note similarities in the Stoic and Epicurean understandings of god in comparison to Paul's speech. Stoics believed in immortal gods (Schnabel, 2005:179) and would not have been provoked by

important theme (Barrett, 1974:74–75; Gärtner, 1955:203–228; Keener, 2014:2575–2578; Litwak, 2004:208–210; Pardigon, 2008:192–313; Peterson, 2009:487–492; Polhill, 1992:376; Schnabel, 2005:181–183; 2012:722–723).³ Gärtner (1955:203–204) devoted several pages of his monograph to the critique of idolatry found in Greek literature. Recent scholarship has given some attention to Roman authors of the period who may have also been known in Athens. Juhana Torkki (2004:56–68) discusses Cicero's *De Natura Deorum* with respect to the philosophical backgrounds of the Areopagus speech.⁴ Bruce Winter (2005:49–52) discusses both Cicero and Seneca with regard to the nature of God.⁵ Gärtner (1955:171–174) has briefly discussed the concept of Paul's proclamation of God as maker of the world in light of contemporary (ancient) views of the cosmos,⁶ as have F.F.

---

the reference to God by Paul (Schnabel, 2005:179; Winter, 2005:49). The Epicureans disavowed superstition and did not believe that gods dwell in temples built by humans (Schnabel, 2005:180; Winter, 2005:53). Both Winter and Schnabel make mention of numerous points of cultural confrontation in the speech, including the criticism of idols, temples, and sacrifices (Schnabel, 2005:181; Winter 2005:46).

3. Keener (2015:2575–2577) recites a litany of idols and temples that Paul would have encountered in Athens: the temple of Demeter, a gymnasium dedicated to Hermes, an edifice for the worhip of Dionysus, various shrines and statues of Ares, Aphrodite, Heracles, Apollo, Athena, Artemis, and Zeus, to name a few—not to mention the ubiquitous presence of the obscene Hermes' pillars. Peterson (2009:487) asserts that the debates referred to prior to the speech were in reply to the idolatry that he encountered in that city (also Schnabel 2012:722). Polhill makes brief reference to the Old Testament critique of idolatry (1993:376). Litwak notes the "echoes" of Scripture throughout the speech and makes particular reference to Isaiah 40–48 (Litwak, 2004: 202–206). Pardigon, in his dissertation, also undertakes the study of Isaiah 40 in connection with Acts 17 (2004:204–208). Schnabel identifies Isaiah as an Old Testament precedent for Paul's critique of idolatry (2012:732). The similarity of the Areopagus speech with anti-idolatry texts in the Old Testament (Septuagint) will be investigated further in chapter three of this study.

4. Torkki discusses the themes of piety and superstition in the Epicurean and Stoic philosophical schools, as presented in Cicero's dialogical work. Torrki concludes that matters of worship were "often discussed by philosophers" (2004:99).

5. Winter makes a case for Paul's argument in the Athens's speech finding common ground with Stoics, who believed in the existence of gods as well as providence. He notes key differences between Paul's speech and Stoic doctrines in the areas of polytheism and pantheism (2005:50). Winter also argues that the Stoics did not believe in a personal god (2005:52). Winter concludes that Paul's speech in Acts 17 should be used as a model apologetic in its example of finding common ground as well as confronting misconceptions (2005:58–59).

6. Gärtner notes that while Paul proclaims the Creator of Genesis 1:1, his use of κόσμος is "interesting" (1955:171). He continues on to explain that the concept of "cosmos" was different for the Greeks than for the Old Testament and New Testament writers

Bruce (1990:382) and C.K. Barrett (1998:840), in their commentaries on Acts, but little in-depth work has been done on this important topic.

The central question for this work is as follows: How does Paul, as a Jew, contextualize the message of the gospel for his audience of Stoic and Epicurean philosophers in Athens on the topic of God as Creator in Acts 17:24? In order to answer this question, the problem will be broken down into four subsequent questions. The research will address the following problems:

1. What have scholars suggested regarding the understanding of God as Creator in Acts 17:24?
2. How does an understanding of the literary setting and context help elucidate Acts 17:24?
3. How does an understanding of the semantic context help elucidate Acts 17:24?
4. What were the Stoic and Epicurean understandings of God as Creator and Lord, and how does Paul's view compare and contrast with them?

The main aim of this study is to investigate Paul's methods of contextualization (according to Luke) on the topic of God as Creator in Acts 17:24. In order to reach the aim, the following objectives will need to be met:

- To analyze and evaluate the understanding of God as Creator in Acts 17:24 by various scholars;
- To study the literary setting and context of Acts 17:24;
- To study the semantic context of Acts 17:24;
- To study the creation of the world as it relates to the deity or deities in Greek literature, especially in Stoic and Epicurean writings before the second century A.D., and to compare and contrast Paul's presentation of God as Creator with these views.

The central theoretical argument of this study is that the proclamation of the identity of God as the Creator of the world both engaged and confronted the contemporary worldview of Paul's audience in Acts 17:24.

This study will use the perspective of the Reformed tradition. In keeping with this tradition, emphasis will be placed on the Bible as a primary source document. This research will presuppose an authoritative and

---

(1955:171). Paul intentionally sets parameters for the term that would have enlightened his hearers of his intent (1955:174).

Introduction

historically reliable biblical text. The investigation will proceed with the understanding that Luke recorded events and speeches in the book of Acts in a responsible manner.[7] At the same time, I will also include secondary sources that are not written exclusively from within a Reformed framework in order to bring a wider understanding of the relevant literature.

The focus of this research is on an examination of the primary source documents themselves, whether biblical, extra-biblical, or philosophical. The following methods will be employed. Throughout the chapters, an analysis and evaluation of what recent scholars have written regarding God as Creator in Acts 17:24 will be conducted through a literature review of various monographs, articles, and commentaries. In chapter two, the literary setting and context of Acts 17:24 will be approached in accordance with the historical–grammatical exegetical method presented in Gordon Fee's *New Testament Exegesis* (2002:5–95). The literary setting will address matters regarding Luke as author and Theophilus as the original reader. The literary context of Acts 17:24 will be studied in light of Paul's entire speech in Acts 17:16–34. In chapter three, the semantic context of Acts 17:24 will be approached in accordance with the word study method presented in Moisés Silva's *Biblical Words and their Meanings* (1994). Studies of key words and phrases in Acts 17:24 will be examined through an investigation of passages and contexts in the book of Acts, in the rest of the New Testament, in the Old Testament, and in other Jewish literature that uses Greek. In chapter four, the creation of the world as it relates to the deity or deities will be studied in specific works of Greco-Roman literature, particularly in Stoic and Epicurean writings before the second century A.D. Paul's presentation of God as Creator will be compared and contrasted with Stoic and Epicurean views. In chapter five, the results and conclusions of this investigation will be presented in a final synthesis.

For the purpose of this study, contextualization will be understood as the presentation of the speaker's message in a manner that relates specifically to the culture of the audience. How did Paul, as a Jew, use concepts familiar to Greeks in order to introduce the unfamiliar content of the gospel? This study will focus on the first century example of how Paul built a bridge of communication with his hearers in the Areopagus of Athens, and how his hearers might have understood his message. Special attention will be given to how Paul's approach may have both engaged and confronted contemporary culture in Athens.

---

7. This view will be discussed in greater detail in the second chapter.

Chapter 2

Literary Setting and Context of Acts 17:24

2.0 INTRODUCTION

THE AIM OF THIS chapter is to place Acts 17:24 in its literary setting and context within the Areopagus address as well as within the greater Luke-Acts corpus.[1] This discussion of context contributes to the main research aim by establishing a foundation from which we will investigate Paul's methods of contextualization on the topic of God as Creator in subsequent chapters. The discussion of literary setting will include matters related to the author and the original reader. An examination of Luke, as the author, and Theophilus, as the original reader, will provide a framework from which we approach Paul's identification of the unknown God as the Creator of the world in Acts 17:24 throughout the study. A discussion of the literary context of the Areopagus speech, as it sits within the theme of the gospel advancing to the Gentile world, follows. Next, we survey the entire passage of Acts 17:16–34, giving special attention to style and grammar. Finally, the Areopagus speech will be compared and contrasted with speeches given in Lystra and Pisidian Antioch.

---

1. Translations of ancient texts throughout this study are the author's, unless otherwise noted.

2.1 LITERARY SETTING

This section will address matters related to the author and original reader of the Areopagus speech of Acts 17:16–34. Luke–Acts, as a whole, will provide the basis for the discussion of the literary setting. The prologue of Luke's gospel will provide key evidence regarding both author and reader. All things considered, the evidence sheds light on Acts as written by a Gentile, for a Gentile.

2.1.1 Luke as author

We will examine evidence from Scripture, early manuscripts, and writings of church fathers that points to Luke as a missionary, a doctor, a historian, and the author of Luke–Acts. An analysis of the grammar and style of Luke's prologue provides a starting place for this discussion. The study will continue with a discussion of the reliability of the Areopagus speech.

2.1.1.1 *Evidence for Luke as author*

Admitting that scholarship has long regarded Luke–Acts as a unity and that those who have deviated from this view have been both few in number and unsuccessful in proving their claims, Patricia Walters challenges the traditional understanding of a single author for Luke–Acts in her monograph, *The Assumed Authorial Unity of Luke and Acts: A Reassessment of the Evidence*. Walters (2009:24) undertakes a detailed stylometry study of literary junctures (seams and summaries) in the text. She concludes that the style of Acts differs significantly from that of Luke and, therefore, the two books were written by different authors (2009:189). Her premise is that an author will write only within the parameters of a single style. However, Aída Spencer's comparative study of passages in Romans, Philippians, and 2 Corinthians (Spencer, 1998), using a stylistics method, demonstrates the capacity for a single author to write in differing styles. Mounce also explains that Shakespeare, Dante, and C.S. Lewis all write with great variations in their respective works. Such variations do not prove a difference in authorship (Mounce, 2000:cxiv). In light of these findings, Walters's presupposition seems tenuous.

Acts 1:1 links the book of Acts to the Gospel of Luke as a continuation, "In the first book, Theophilus, I wrote about all that Jesus did and taught from the beginning." This statement picks up from Luke's introduction, "I too decided . . . to write an orderly account for you, most excellent Theophilus" (Luke 1:3). The beginning of Acts not only indicates the two-part nature of the work, but it also asserts a single author by use of the pronoun "I" in both passages. The author of Acts is, then, the same person as the author of Luke (Bock, 2007:15–19; Marshall, 1993:182).

Although the Luke–Acts narrative does not mention the author by name, the author explicates his purposes in the first few verses of the Gospel of Luke. The author thoroughly researched his material before putting the events into an orderly account (Luke 1:3). This shows concern for accuracy. Although not an eyewitness himself, the author relies on accounts handed down from eyewitnesses (Luke 1:2).

The use of first person plural pronouns in specific passages in the book of Acts implies that, at times, the author was a companion of Paul.[2] The author indicates when he was with Paul by means of a pronoun switch—from "they" and "them," to "we" and "us"—at certain points of the narrative. The first of these passages to use the first person plural pronoun, Acts 16:11–17, details the journey of Paul and the author from Troas to Philippi and events occurring there. Paul leaves Philippi, and the pronouns switch back to third person—implying that the author has remained there. Several years later, the author leaves Philippi, joins Paul again at Troas (Acts 20:5), and travels with him as far as Jerusalem (Acts 21:17). The account of Paul's journey from Caesarea to Rome in Acts 27 and 28 also employs the first person plural pronoun "we." These passages seem to indicate that Luke was an eyewitness to events that occurred during the times he accompanied Paul (Bock, 2007:13–15; Bruce, 1990:3–5).[3]

I. Howard Marshall notes further internal evidence pointing to a single author of the Luke–Acts corpus. The book of Acts picks up the narrative of Jesus's ascension with a recapitulation of the event recorded in Luke. Marshall states that this is done in such a way as to prepare the reader for a sequel (1993:175–177).

Evidence from church fathers and early manuscripts supports Luke as author. Several church fathers name Luke as the author of this gospel. Eusebius attributes the authorship of the Luke–Acts narrative to Luke (*Hist. eccl.*

---

2. For further discussion of Luke as a companion of Paul and as a physician, see Keener (2012:402–415).

3. Some scholars have suggested that the use of "we" is a literary device found in fictional works. Others have suggested that "we" refers to a person other than Luke. See Porter (1994:546–573) for a summary and discussion of the scholarly debate.

3.4). Irenaeus (*Hist. eccl.* 5.8) and Origen (*Hist. eccl.* 6.26), likewise, credit the third gospel to Luke. Many early manuscripts of the third gospel bear the inscription κατὰ Λουκᾶν. Some of the earliest manuscripts with such an inscription include p^{75} from the second to third century,[4] A and W from the fifth century, D and Ξ from the sixth century, Ψ from the eighth to ninth century, as well as Θ and 33 from the ninth century. On this basis, we will proceed with the understanding that Luke is the writer of the third gospel and of Acts (see Bock, 2007:15–19; Bruce, 1990:52–59; Marshall, 1980:44–45).

Luke is a man of remarkable commitment; he is not only committed to the gospel, but he is also deeply committed to his coworker, Paul. Three New Testament passages mention Luke by name. Colossians 4:14 refers to Luke as the "beloved physician." Luke sends his greetings in this passage, implying that he is with the author, Paul,[5] in Rome—where the letter is most likely written. Luke is a Gentile (Col 4:11–14). In Philemon 24, Paul lists Luke among his "fellow workers." Paul writes in 2 Timothy 4:11,[6] "Luke alone is with me." Again in Rome, during a second Roman imprisonment, Luke remains faithfully by Paul's side. Paul is facing certain death at the time he writes 2 Timothy; the times are so terrifying that his other companions desert him (2 Tim 4:6–18). Luke, alone, is willing to risk his own safety in order to stand with Paul during this time of peril. Of Luke, Eusebius writes:

> Luke, an Antiochene by birth and a physician by profession, was long a companion of Paul and was closely associated also with the other apostles. In two divinely inspired books, the Gospel and the Acts of the Apostles, he has left us examples of the soul healing that he learned from them. The former, he states, he wrote on the basis of information he received from those who from the first were

---

4. The inscription is found at the end of the text of Luke in p^{75}.

5. Although many scholars accept the authenticity of Colossians, there are some who do not. See Guthrie (1990) p. 572–577 for further discussion of views for and against Paul as author.

6. Not all scholars agree that Paul is the author of 2 Timothy. Three main objections revolve around linguistic, historical, and theological issues. The first objection is that the vocabulary and style of the Pastoral Epistles are too varied from that of Paul's other epistles to assure authorship by Paul (Barrett, 1963:5–7; Conzelmann & Dibelius, 1972:3–4; Hanson, 1982:2–3). A second objection is that Acts lacks an historical framework within which to read the Pastoral Epistles (Hanson, 1982:5; Barrett, 1963:7). A third objection is that the Pastoral Epistles contain a theological character not found in epistles attributed to Paul (Hanson, 1963:3). Scholars who refute such objections and argue in favor of Paul as the author include Gordon Fee (1988:1–25), George Knight (1992:13–52), and William Mounce (2000:lxxxiii–cxxix). See also Marshall (2004:57–79), Spencer (2013:2–12), and Towner (2006:10–26) for discussion of scholarship with regards to author.

> eyewitnesses and ministers of the Word. The latter he composed not from the evidence of hearing but of his own eyes. They say that Paul was actually in the habit of referring to Luke's Gospel whenever he used the phrase "According to my gospel." (*Hist.eccl.* 3.4)

Luke is a devoted coworker and brother to Paul, as well as a missionary, a physician, and a historian.[7]

If Luke was born in Antioch, as Eusebius suggests,[8] he came from a prominent city. After Alexander's conquest of the Persian Empire, Syria found itself "in the center of the Hellenistic world, strategically placed between the three great centers of power: Macedonia, Egypt and Babylonia" (Judge, 2009:210). Syrian Antioch was located at a geographical intersection. It was also located at a cultural intersection. Although Greeks and Macedonians initially settled Antioch at its founding in 300 B.C., there is evidence indicating the presence of a Jewish community (Judge, 2001:211; Schnabel, 2004: 1048). Antioch was both Hellenistic and cosmopolitan. It was the meeting point for cultures from the east and the west and also boasted a bustling commerce (Wineland, 2006:180). It may have been the third largest city in the Roman Empire, following Rome and Alexandria (McDonald, 2000:34). If from Antioch, Luke's roots were in an eminent city with strong Hellenistic underpinnings.

Luke includes frequent references to Antioch, the possible city of his birth, in Acts. According to Luke, Paul spends a year in Antioch with Barnabas, teaching and serving the church before being sent out on his first missionary journey (Acts 11:25–26, 13:1–2). Antioch, then, is the location of Paul's home church. Paul returns to the church in Antioch at the conclusion of his first missionary journey (Acts 14:26–28), after the Jerusalem council (Acts 15:35), and after his second missionary journey (Acts 18:22–23). Antioch was not only a political hub, but also a sending hub for early missionary activity (Judge, 2009:213; Slee, 2003:1–3).[9]

F.F. Bruce (1990:67) establishes Luke's literary capabilities: "Luke has a much ampler vocabulary than other NT writers." In his classic grammar, A.T. Robertson also notes that Luke's vocabulary exhibits a broad knowledge of Greek culture. Luke uses at least 750 words not found in the rest

---

7. For discussion of Luke as a physician, see recent scholarship by Craig Keener (2012:410–420) and Eckhard Schnabel (2012:25).

8. Also Jerome, see *Vir. ill.*, vii.

9. It is possible, though not conclusive (since the text of Acts shows that Luke joins Paul in Troas), that Paul may have met Luke in Antioch.

of the New Testament (Robertson, 1943:121). He includes medical terms throughout his narrative, as well as nautical phraseology in Acts 27 and 28 (Robertson, 1934:121–122).[10] Luke also demonstrates an excellent command of style and grammar. Luke was familiar with the Septuagint (Bock, 2007:13; Robertson, 1934:120–122). Daniel Wallace (2000:20) classifies the Greek of Luke–Acts into the category of literary Koine: "a more polished Koine . . . the language of scholars and littérateurs, of academics and historians." Luke's writing style attests to a fine education in literature and composition, as well as knowledge of the medical arts and sea travel.

2.1.1.2 Luke as a reliable author

This section outlines the scholarly debate over how accurate Luke's rendering of the Areopagus speech may have been and argues in favor of Luke as a reliable historian. Matters specifically related to the Areopagus speech will be addressed first. Matters related to authorial intent and methodology will be investigated next, through an analysis of Luke's own statement in Luke 1:1–4.

2.1.1.2.1 RELIABILITY OF THE AREOPAGUS SPEECH

The topic of the accuracy of Luke as an historian,[11] in general, and the historical reliability of the Areopagus speech, in particular, has received no shortage of scholarly prose for more than one hundred years. Indeed, Bauman & Klauber trace the discussion of the historical reliability of Luke–Acts back to W.M.L. deWette, a nineteenth century scholar (1995:41). The purpose of this section is not to conduct a full literature review, or to address all arguments on the historical Paul, since this would be enough for a thesis of its own. The goal here is to give brief mention of the topic and to

---

10. Cadbury (1920:1–42) argued that the presence of medical terminology in Luke–Acts is no greater than that which is found in other first century Greek authors, and, therefore, does not prove that Luke the physician was the author. While the presence of medical language may not, by itself, prove authorship, it may "support this conclusion" (Bruce, 1990:7).

11. Keener's research (2012:91) points to scholarly consensus with regard to Luke as an historian. Dissenting views include Pervo (1987), who proposes that Acts is historical novel written largely to entertain the reader, and Haenchen. Haenchen (1971:103) claims that Luke lacks "an adequate historical foundation." For an overview of source analysis, see Conzelmann (1987:xxxvi–xl). For a critique of Pervo and those who deem Acts as a work of literary fiction, see Keener (2012:62–89).

offer support for the possibility that Luke could have accurately recorded Paul's Areopagus speech.

The scholarship of Martin Dibelius (published in German in 1951, translated to English in 1956) has been long regarded by some as the definitive work of higher criticism on the Areopagus speech. Building upon the work of Norden and others, Dibelius brought traditional scholarship into question by separating Paul into two: Paul of the Epistles, and Paul of Acts. The theology of the Areopagus speech is different from Paul's theology in his Epistles, so he argues. Therefore, he postulates that the Areopagus speech is not authentically Pauline (Dibelius, 1956:62). After many pages of making a distinction between the Paul of Acts and the real Paul, Dibelius concludes:

> Luke strayed too far from the Paul who was the theologian of the paradoxes of grace and faith; nevertheless, he gave for the future the signal for the Christian message to be spread abroad by means of hellenistic culture . . . The Areopagus speech became a symbol of Christian theology in the environment of Greek culture. (Dibelius, 1956:77).

Soon after the publication of Dibelius's work in German, Bertil Gärtner responded with his monograph, *The Areopagus Speech and Natural Revelation*, in which he argues in favor of the Pauline character of the speech (1955:250).

Scholarship remains divided on the topic of the historical reliability of Acts. Notable scholars who follow Dibelius's line of thought include Conzelmann (1987) and Haenchen (1971). Among those who argue in favor of reliability are F.F. Bruce (1976, 1990), Colin Hemer (1977, 1989a, 1989b), I.H. Marshall (1980, 1988), and D. Bock (2007).

A few considerations in favor of an accurate rendering of the Areopagus speech include the following:

1. Luke establishes his concern for accuracy in his writing in the prologue of his gospel. Concern for accuracy was expressed by historical writers of the Hellenistic period. The historian, Polybius (second century B.C.), criticized a certain Timaeus for inventing speeches rather than recording the actual words:

> The special province of history is, first, to ascertain what the actual words used were; and secondly, to learn why it was that a particular policy or argument failed or succeeded . . . The historian therefore who omits the words actually used, as

well as all statement of the determining circumstances, and gives us instead conjectures and mere fancy compositions, destroys the special use of history. In this respect Timaeus is an eminent offender, for we all know that his books are full of such writing. (*Histories* 12.25)

Continuing his negative evaluation of the writing of Timaeus, Polybius asserts the necessity of carefully investigating a topic among reliable eyewitnesses as well as researching documents:

> Study of documents involves no danger or fatigue, if one only takes care to lodge in a city rich in such records, or to have a library in one's neighbourhood. You may then investigate any question while reclining on your couch, and compare the mistakes of former historians without any fatigue to yourself. But personal investigation demands great exertion and expense; though it is exceedingly advantageous, and in fact is the very corner-stone of history. (*Histories* 12.27)

Lucian (second century A.D.) also stressed accuracy in historical writing and the importance of eyewitness investigation. In his work, *How to Write History*, Lucian describes the careful historian: "As to the facts themselves, he should not assemble them at random, but only after much laborious and painstaking investigation. He should for preference be an eyewitness, but, if not, listen to those who tell the more impartial story" (VI. 47).

2. It is not impossible that a written form of the speech did, in fact, exist. Eckhard Schnabel details the procedure for an orator giving a declamation in the eastern Mediterranean world. An orator would usually be given one day in which to prepare a speech. The declamation would be written down and then memorized by the speaker: "In the early imperial period, such declamations were often copied and circulated in the city. There is evidence for this practice related to Athens" (2005:176).

3. There is abundant evidence for writing in the ancient world (Millard, 2001:17–229). Clerks used abbreviated forms of writing for recording council proceedings and debates in legal courts as far back as the Classical period. Evidence for shorthand in Greece exists from the second century B.C. onward (Millard, 2001:175–176). Furthermore, there is evidence that ancient philosophers took notes. Diogenes Laertius mentioned that Xenophon took notes on Socrates's teachings (*Lives*

II.48). He also mentioned that the Stoic philosopher Cleanthes took notes on Zeno's lectures (*Lives* VII.174). Flavius Arrian took copious notes on lectures by his teacher, Epictetus, also a Stoic philosopher (Oldfather, 1998:xii). It is possible that someone in the Areopagus could have recorded the speech at the time it was delivered.

4. It is generally accepted that ancient letter writers kept copies of their letters. These copies may have been retained in parchment codex form (Richards, 1998:155–166). Paul, likely, also retained parchment copies of his letters. He places great value on his parchments when he requests Timothy to bring them to him in Rome: "When you come, bring the cloak that I left with Carpus at Troas, also the books, and above all the parchments" (2 Tim 4:13, NRSV). If Paul kept a notebook of his letters, it is possible that he could have also kept a copy of his speech in Athens.

5. Memorization was emphasized far more in the ancient world than it is now. In *Memory and Manuscript*, Gerhardsson details the rigorous demands of rote memorization of oral texts in the religious education of Jews (1998:93–112). Memorization of Torah passages was considered the most elementary stage of learning: "Knowing the basic text material in the oral Torah by heart is an elementary accomplishment, presupposed of every teacher and pupil at the more advanced stage" (1998:101). Rabbis would call on their teaching assistants, known as *tannaim*, to recite verbatim—from memory—any text needed for a class (1998:94). This emphasis on memorization found its counterpart in the Greek world with Homeric rhapsodists (1998:95). Paul's speech may have been memorized. In addition, the Spirit could have assisted in memory recall (John 14:26).

6. Luke spent a considerable amount of time with Paul. Although he was not with him in Athens, he was with him on other occasions. Paul may have known about Luke's writing projects and could have been consulted for feedback regarding accuracy.

If Luke, the companion of Paul, is the author of Acts, it is not impossible that he could have recorded words of the actual speech of Paul in Athens. In summary, both Polybius and Lucian outline standards of best practices for historians. The expectation was accurate written history that was based on sound research. According to Polybius, speeches should record the exact words spoken. Luke seems to be an historian of this order.[12] It is possible that a written record of the speech may have existed and that Luke could have had access to it, as well as to the author, in person. It is likewise possible that Luke could have had a personal interview with someone who had been present for Paul's speech in Athens and had memorized it accurately, such as Dionysius or Damaris (Acts 17:34). Finally, the Holy Spirit could have reminded Paul or an eyewitness of the words spoken at the Areopagus.

2.1.1.2.2 GRAMMATICAL AND STYLISTIC ANALYSIS OF LUKE'S PROLOGUE

A central line of argument for those who propose that Luke constructed the words of the speeches in a manner faithful to each event in Acts (rather than replicating the exact words) hinges on comments made by Thucydides to the effect that he constructed speeches in his history of the Peloponnesian war that were suitable for each occasion, since he could not replicate the exact words spoken (*Pel. War* 1.22.1; see also Bock, 2007:20–22 for a summary of scholarship). Conrad Gempf's study of speeches among ancient Greek writers leads him to the conclusion that the speeches in Acts should be thought of in terms of being faithful to the event rather than being transcripts or summaries (1993a:303). Gempf compares the historiography of Acts to the statements of other Greek writers about the nature of their respective works, but does not discuss Luke's own statement in Luke 1:1–4 (Gempf, 1993a:259–303). In my opinion, Luke's writing should be read in light of the matrix he himself presents in the prologue to his gospel. For this reason, the prologue will be studied in this section with a careful analysis of grammar and style. The aim is to discover Luke's method and motivation by elucidating his own statement of intent in Luke 1:1–4.

If "Luke, the beloved physician" of Colossians 4:14 is the same Luke as the author of Luke-Acts, we may surmise that the author was accustomed to giving rigorous attention to detail. The abilities required of a physician—careful observation and examination skills—might have transferred to Luke's approach to research methodology. For a doctor, even a single error in examination or treatment may yield disastrous results. It seems that Luke researched the contents of his gospel with the same meticulous care required of a medical practitioner. Luke's research took him right back

---

12. See also Moles (2011:461–482), who argues for Luke's historiography as superior to that of classical historians.

God as Creator in Acts 17:24

to the source of the narrative accounts. He consulted eyewitness sources before compiling his narrative (Luke 1:2-3), so that he might portray the events and teachings associated with Jesus's life with accuracy.

How may Theophilus know that what he is about to read is reliable? An analysis of the grammar and style of the prologue, with particular focus on the last two clauses (1:3b-4), illuminates Luke's method and intent. The prologue establishes Luke's rationale and purpose for writing, and sets the stage for the rest of the book (Green, 1997:33-36; Stein, 1992:66-68). The prologue is comprised of one lengthy, intricate sentence in Greek. Luke 1:1-4, one sentence, has one main clause: "it seemed good to me also, after having investigated from the beginning everything carefully, in order, to write to you, Most Excellent Theophilus" (v. 3). Two subordinate adverbial clauses precede this clause (vv. 1-2), and one subordinate adverbial clause follows it (v. 4). What is Luke's rationale? The opening adverbial clause shows cause by giving grounds for him to write an account. He is not the first to do so, "Since many have set their hand to arrange in proper order an account concerning the events which have been fulfilled among us" (v. 1). The second subordinate clause flows from the first, by means of comparison. This further clarifies the nature of the accounts that have been written, "just as those who from the beginning, having become eyewitnesses and servants of the word handed down to us" (v. 2). The words αὐτόπται and ὑπηρέται form a pleonasm. They have similar meanings and cadence. Further, these two nouns are among a category of masculine nouns that take first declension endings. Thus, the aspect of repetition in this phrase is carried out in three dimensions: meaning, sound, and visual form. This emphasis serves to draw attention to the author's central point: the content of his narrative finds its roots among eyewitnesses.

The main clause follows (v. 3). Since Luke is not an eyewitness himself, how may the reader be assured of the reliability of his account? Luke conducted careful investigations among eyewitnesses in order to produce his gospel. The dative participle παρηκολουθηκότι is in the perfect tense. This tense carries with it a sense of past time with results extending into the present (Wallace, 2000:246-247). The research of the past influences the writing of the present. Stanley Porter proposes, in his explanation of verbal aspect, that the perfect tense may also convey a "frontground" meaning, by bringing emphasis right before the reader (Porter, 1999:23-24). Luke states that he bases his account on verified historical fact. He makes this statement in a way that honors Theophilus. Luke is not handing Theophilus a work of shoddy scholarship, but a reliable document based on eyewitness evidence.

An examination of word order further displays Luke's intention in writing. A.T. Robertson notes that the propensity of the Greek language to enjoy a "freedom from artificial rules" is seen especially in matters related to word order. A word may be removed from its expected position and placed in an unusual one—typically, either in the beginning or ending of a sentence—for the purpose of emphasis (Dover, 2010:32; Porter, 1999:296; Robertson, 1934:417). There are two conspicuous instances of unexpected word order in the prologue. The first is found in the second adverbial clause (v. 2). Luke pulls the aorist verb παρέδοσαν out of the usual word order and places it in front of, rather than after, its lengthy subject, οἱ ἀπ' ἀρχῆς αὐτόπται καὶ ὑπηρέται γενόμενοι τοῦ λόγου. This facilitates the placement of παρέδοσαν immediately after καθώς. Thus, Luke highlights both the deliberate handing down of the accounts and the unchanged nature of those accounts. Events were narrated just as handed down (Alexander, 1993:118–119; Bock, 1994:31–32; Green, 1997:40). Theophilus may be assured of the reliability of the entrusted accounts. The second major instance is in the final adverbial clause (v. 4). Luke pulls the direct object, τὴν ἀσφάλειαν, out of the expected word order (which would be after the verb ἐπιγνῷς) and transplants it to the end of the sentence. The driving force behind all of Luke's research and writing is that Theophilus would know the secure truth.

A second matter pertinent to word order is the Greek manner of creating a unified concept. In such a construction, an author introduces a unified concept by separating the article and the noun it modifies. The contents in between the article and noun may be central to the unified concept (Robertson, 1934:418). Two of these unified concepts are present in the prologue. The first appears in the first adverbial clause, περὶ τῶν πεπληροφορημένων ἐν ἡμῖν πραγμάτων. Thus, Luke emphasizes that the events actually happened in two ways: by using a perfect participle, and also through word order. What Luke writes about is true. Loveday Alexander also notes the high style of this clause, with its alliteration and "sandwiching of noun and article" (1993:113). The second unified concept appears in the second adverbial clause, οἱ ἀπ' ἀρχῆς αὐτόπται καὶ ὑπηρέται γενόμενοι (v. 2). The article at the beginning of the clause modifies the substantive participle placed at the end of the clause—with five words in between. Alliteration may again be noted. Luke's stylistic emphasis underlines the importance and nature of the eyewitnesses.

Thus, Luke uses three literary means to produce emphasis: style, word order, and the use of the perfect tense. All three of these means serve to intensify his statement regarding the credibility of his sources. Credibility and reliability are key foundations for Luke–Acts. The strong emphasis brings Luke's purpose into sharp focus: to give solid evidence, so that Theophilus may be fully assured of the truth.

2.1.2 Theophilus as the original reader of Luke–Acts

In his monograph, *The Significance of Theophilus as Luke's Reader*, Roman Garrison notes that the original reader of the Luke–Acts narrative has been overlooked by scholars: "Many scholars have disregarded the significance of Theophilus as the intended reader of those books (treating him as irrelevant) and instead have given attention to a generalized Gentile audience that came to read Luke–Acts" (Garrison, 2004:22). Garrison orients his thesis around the significance of Theophilus in relation to the inevitable choices that Luke would have had to make regarding what material to include, or not to include, in his writings–rather than on the identity of Theophilus. This section seeks to present primary source material that will help us to answer the foundational question, "Who is Theophilus?"

Is Theophilus a real person? Johnson (1991:28) allows for the possibility that Theophilus could be a symbolic reference to any reader, since the name means "lover of God." On the contrary, many scholars maintain that Theophilus is, indeed, a real person (including Bock, 1994:52; Bruce, 1990:98; Garland, 2011:55–56; Garrison, 2004:97; Green, 1997:xxxix). Alexander (1993:188) notes that the existence of fictional prefaces in some works of Hellenistic literature does not prove that Luke 1:1–4 is also a fictional preface. Our study of the preface shows that Luke intends to present a carefully researched historical document, not a work of fiction. To understand Theophilus as a general reference to any reader is to ignore the description of a specific person in a specific context (also Garrison, 2004:26). For the purposes of this research, "original reader" should be understood as the man, Theophilus, who was the personal recipient of the dedication in the prologue to Luke (Hengel, 2012:536). In this section, we will examine lexical and literary contexts that point to Theophilus not only as a real person, but as a person of prominence.

Toward gaining an understanding of the original reader, we will examine key terms in Luke's prologue through the analysis and comparison of contexts in various primary sources. This lexical analysis provides the basis for elucidation of how Theophilus, as the original reader, may have understood the Areopagus speech, at a later point in this study. Luke addresses his gospel to Theophilus (Luke 1:3), as he does the book of Acts (Acts 1:1). In his gospel, Luke addresses Theophilus with the formal title κράτιστε, "most excellent" (Luke 1:3). Lexical data leads us to probable information regarding our original reader. Luke explicitly states his purpose for writing his gospel in 1:4, ἵνα ἐπιγνῷς περὶ ὧν κατηχήθης λόγων τὴν ἀσφάλειαν, "that you may know the certain truth concerning of the message which you were taught." The term κατηχέω will also be discussed in the lexical analysis section. Next, the broader literary context of Acts will be considered. We will conclude that Theophilus is likely a man of position, and that he had previously received some introductory teaching about Jesus.

2.1.2.1 Lexical Analysis

What kind of person might Theophilus be? Luke addresses his reader, κράτιστε Θεόφιλε, in verse 3 of the prologue. The term κράτιστος is employed in three other places in the New Testament, solely in writings by Luke. In Acts 23:26 and 24:3, Felix, a governor, is addressed as κράτιστε. Festus, successor to Felix (Acts 24:27), is likewise addressed as κράτιστε in Acts 26:25. In every instance in Acts, the term is used in connection with an explicit identification of the person's official status as a Roman governor (also Bock, 1994:63).

As we broaden our reading to occurrences outside the New Testament, we find two primary categories of meaning for κράτιστος. The first category contains texts using κράτιστος as a superlative adjective from κρατύς that may be translated "best." The superlative identifies an elite part (Liddell & Scott, 1996:991). Examples include "the best of the sheep and the cattle" (1 Sam 15:15, LXX) and "forty of the best of his foot soldiers" (*Ant.* 17.282).[13] This use of the adjective is found in the Septuagint, but not in the New Testament (Moulton & Milligan, 1997:358).

The second domain of meaning of κράτιστος is "most excellent." In this domain, it is a superlative adjective from ἀγαθός (Liddell–Scott, 1996:991). This superlative adjective frequently sits in close proximity to a proper name. This domain comports with the verses surveyed in Luke–Acts. It may be

---

13. See also 2 Macc 3:2, 4:12; 3 Macc 1:2; *Ant.* 18.36, 19.129; *War* 4.170; Philo, *Leg.* 1.66; *Cher.* 1.4; *Post.*1.118; *Gig.* 1.15; *Ebr.* 1.70.

used in an honorary address to a person of high political standing (Friberg, 2000:§16573; Louw–Nida, 1989: §87.55; Moulton & Milligan, 1997:358; Thayer, 1997:§3075). Worthy of note is Josephus's use of κράτιστος in the dedications of two of his books. He dedicates *Antiquities* to Epaphroditus, "But to you, O Epaphroditus, you most excellent of men! do I dedicate all this treatise of our Antiquities" (*Life* 1.430). Josephus addresses Epaphroditus again in the prologue of *Against Apion*, "I suppose, that by my books of the 'Antiquity of the Jews,' most excellent Epaphroditus . . ." (*Ag. Ap.* 1.1). Epaphroditus may have been a procurator of Trajan (see note by Whiston, 1978:773). Scholars have also suggested that although it is not possible to identify Epaphroditus with certainty, he may have been a former instructor for the son of Marcus Mettius Modestus, an Egyptian prefect, or a former secretary to the emperor Nero—with Steve Mason and John Barclay both preferring the latter option (Mason, 2001:173; Barclay, 2007:3–4). In similar fashion, Josephus refers to Vitellius as "most excellent" in *Antiquities* 20.12. Earlier in his *Antiquities*, Josephus refers to Vitellius as governor of Syria (*Ant.* 15.405). These passages establish that κράτιστος may be used in a formal address of a person of political position.

Josephus also refers to members of King Agrippa's royal family with κράτιστος (*Ant.* 18.273; 20.13). The high position of John Hyrcanus is described in *Jewish War* 1.68 with a participle form related to κράτιστος (τὰ κρατιστεύοντα). These first century examples provide evidence that forms of κράτιστος may be used to refer to persons in political leadership.

Another text that uses κράτιστος to show respect to a person of prominence is found in the *Apostolic Fathers*. The *Epistle to Diognetus* uses the vocative form in its dedication to Diognetus in a very similar way to Luke's, κράτιστε Διόγνητε (1.1). Diognetus may have been associated with the royal courts of Hadrian or Marcus Aurelius. The evidence, however, is inconclusive (Holmes, 1989:293).

We have seen that κράτιστος is employed in Acts in formal address of a Roman governor. Likewise, κράτιστος is employed in Josephus's writings to address persons of position in the Roman government. In our example from the dedication of *The Epistle to Diognetus*, it is possible that the term is employed to address a person associated with the Roman government. So then, is Theophilus also a Roman official? This is a possible scenario. Semantic evidence shows that persons addressed with κράτιστος may be persons of high government rank. (See also Bruce, 1990:98; Cadbury, 1922:506; Fitzmyer, 1981:300; Peterson, 2009:102.) This lexical study leads

Literary Setting and Context of Acts 17:24

us to postulate that Theophilus may have been a man of social standing: he could have been a government official with some measure of authority.

What might have been the nature of the message that Theophilus had been taught? Luke uses the verb κατηχέω in three other places in his narrative: Acts 18:25, Acts 21:21, and Acts 21:25. The meaning of κατηχέω is "to teach" in Acts 18:25 (Thayer, 1997:§2881). Apollos had received some general information about Jesus. He knew only of the baptism of John. Therefore, "when Priscilla and Aquila heard him, they took him aside and explained the Way of God to him more accurately" (Acts 18:26, NRSV). It seems that the teaching Apollos received about Jesus may have been of an introductory nature. In Acts 21:21–24, Luke uses κατηχέω with a meaning of "to inform by word of mouth" (Thayer, 1997:§2881). Here, κατηχέω refers to an informal oral report that communicated incomplete and inaccurate information. Alexander (1993:139) argues that in this case, the situation of inaccurate information belongs to the context and not to the word itself.

Alexander also explains that κατηχέω usually refers to instruction given in a school setting, and may involve any of a number of academic disciplines. These may include rhetoric, philosophy, or the medical arts (Alexander, 1993:139). Louw–Nida (§33.225) defines κατηχέω as "to teach in a systematic or detailed manner."

In Christian writings outside of Luke, κατηχέω means teaching regarding the faith. It can refer to oral teaching given in a church setting (1 Cor 14:19; Gal 6:6), or instruction from the Scriptures (Rom 2:18). Writing in the late first century A.D., Clement uses κατηχέω to describe introductory Christian teachings, "For if we have commandments that we should also practice this, to draw men away from idols and to instruct them" (2 *Clem.* 17.1). These contexts fit within the framework offered by Alexander and Louw–Nida. In the writings of Paul and Clement, κατηχέω refers to religious teachings given in an evangelistic or church setting.

This evidence points to the likelihood that Theophilus also had received some kind of instruction about Jesus. That instruction was most likely introductory.

What does Theophilus have to gain by a reading of Luke's gospel? Another subordinate adverbial clause follows the main clause. This final clause shows Luke's purpose, "that you may know the certain truth (ἀσφάλειαν) concerning the message which you were taught" (v. 4). The direct object, ἀσφάλειαν, has to do with assurance and certainty. This word is frequently employed to indicate security, as in with a locked or guarded door (Louw &

Nida, 1989: §994). More specifically, in Luke 1:4 ἀσφάλεια has to do with the "stability of an idea or statement" in the sense of certainty and truth, and "to be clear about the accounts." It can also be used as a "legal term for a written guarantee" (Bauer, 2000: §1229). In his article, Rick Strelan proposes that ἀσφάλεια denotes "the sureness of the words and the soundness of their argument" in Luke 1:4 (Strelan, 2007:163). The related adjective, ἀσφαλής, appears in three particular passages in Acts with the context of the validation (or lack of validation) of the facts pertaining to events that took place. Consider the following:

> Some in the crowd shouted one thing, some another; and as he could not learn the facts (ἀσφαλές) because of the uproar, he ordered him to be brought into the barracks. (Acts 21:34 NRSV)

> But on the next day, desiring to know the real reason (ἀσφαλές) why he was being accused by the Jews, he unbound him and commanded the chief priests and all the council to meet, and he brought Paul down and set him before them. (Acts 22:30 ESV)[14]

> But I have nothing definite (ἀσφαλές) to write to our sovereign about him. Therefore I have brought him before all of you, and especially before you, King Agrippa, so that, after we have examined him, I may have something to write. (Acts 25:26 NRSV)

In all three passages, ἀσφαλής has to do with determining the real facts, or the real story, pertaining to Paul's charge and arrest. The context is one of needing to find out what really happened in the midst of unclear or uncertain accounts. In Acts 25:26, Festus declares that a judicial examination is necessary before having something definite (ἀσφαλής) to write about Paul to King Agrippa. This concept of needing an examination in order to determine the certain truth is a similar idea to what we find in Luke's prologue. Luke conducted careful investigations (Lk 1:3) in order to produce a document that would verify the events and teachings of Jesus with certainty (Lk 1:4). What Theophilus has to gain by a reading of the narrative is a secure validation of the message, about which he had previously received partial information.

Could it be that Theophilus, himself, requested validation from Luke of the teaching he had received? The situation of Theophilus may be compared to that of Apollos, in Acts 18:24–28. As Priscilla and Aquila took Apollos aside and "explained the Way of God to him more accurately" (Acts

---

14. The ESV is cited for Acts 22:30 since the NRS omits a translation for ἀσφαλές in this verse.

18:26, NRSV), so Luke writes his first book for Theophilus that he might know the certain truth regarding Jesus and his teachings. This purpose may extend to the second book as well: that Theophilus might know the truth concerning the spread of Christianity.

2.1.2.2 Further Evidence: Broader Literary Context

Thus far, it has been determined through lexical analysis that Theophilus may have been a person of social and political standing in the Roman government (also Bruce, 1990:98; Cadbury, 1922:506; Fitzmyer, 1981:300; Peterson, 2009:102). Alexander (1993:188) disagrees. In her research, she compares the prologue of Luke with prologues from scientific manuals, in which the person receiving the dedication is not necessarily a person of superior rank. Luke–Acts, though, is not a scientific manual (Bock agrees, 2007:52). John Moles, also disagreeing with Alexander, maintains that Luke follows the tradition of classical historians such as Thucydides and Herodotus (Moles, 2011:463).

The context of Acts should be weighed carefully. A look at the broader context of Acts may add further support to the possibility of Theophilus as a person of prominence. Let us consider the challenge an historian is faced with when choosing which material to include. The historian must be selective with the material in accordance with limitations of space and purpose of writing (Schnabel, 2012:29). Let us also consider how Luke frequently includes information about various leaders throughout his narrative of the expanding church in Acts. The following are a few examples: the proconsul in Paphos, "an intelligent man, who summoned Barnabas and Saul and wanted to hear the word of God" (Acts 13:7, NRSV), Lydia, a businesswoman in Philippi (16:14), Greeks with high standing in Beroea (17:12), and Dionysius the Areopagite (17:34).[15] Further examples include Acts 19:35–41 (a local official ends a riot), 21:31–40 (a tribune saves Paul's life), 22:25–29 (a centurion stops the illegal flogging of Paul), 25:25–27 (Luke shows Festus as reasonable in his assessment of Paul's case), 26:31–32 (Agrippa affirms Paul's innocence), and 27:42–43 (a centurion saves Paul's life). Many of these leaders believe the gospel. Others uphold the Pax Romana, or protect unjustly accused Christians from harm. Why such an emphasis on leaders in the early days of the church? Why such an emphasis

---

15. Of further note, Dionysius the Areopagite became the first bishop of Athens, according to Eusebius (*Hist. eccl.* 3.4).

on Romans who do the right thing? Could it be possible that Luke holds these leaders up as examples and for a point of identification for Theophilus as the reader?

If Theophilus was a person of high social standing, it is likely that he might have also been a person of financial means. It could have been possible for him to fund Luke's research (deSilva, 2000:125; Garland, 2011:56; Peterson, 2009:102; Polhill, 1992:79). In an age of patron-client relationships, this may have been a likely scenario (Alexander, 1993:190–191). Perhaps Theophilus had requested validation of the teaching that he had initially heard. Luke may have written the narrative with the understanding that Theophilus would publish his work, thereby reaching a broad audience (Peterson, 2009:102). This, however, cannot be determined with certainty. Alexander suggests that it is more likely that Theophilus acted as a patron in terms of support for Luke's research than it is that he funded the dissemination of that research (1993:190–200).

Theophilus would have been, by every indication, a Roman Greek rather than a Jew. It would have been unlikely for a Jew to hold political office (see also Bock, 2007:52). Luke's emphasis on the inclusive nature of the kingdom of God in his gospel, as well as the major theme of the breaking in of the Gentiles in Acts (to be discussed in 2.2.1), would further support the likelihood that Theophilus was a Gentile. Christianity is for Greeks, as well as Jews. There is place for Theophilus in the kingdom of God.

David Garland suggests that the name, "Theophilus," may have been an alias. If he was a prominent government official, Theophilus may have desired to keep his true identity concealed (Garland, 2011:56).

Bock (1994:15) suggests that Theophilus may have been a Godfearer before coming to faith in Christ. He lists passages from Acts that refer to Godfearers (including 10:2, 22, 35; 13:16, 26, 43, 50; 17:4, 17; 18:7) as a possible explanation for their inclusion in the narrative. Bock notes the "extensive use of the OT in the two volumes," as further evidence of this possibility.

2.1.2.3 *Summary of Theophilus as reader*

This lexical survey has provided some key information regarding the possible identity of Theophilus as reader of the Luke–Acts narrative. Theophilus was, likely, a person of social and government rank. He was, likely, a Gentile with a background in Roman and Greek culture. If Theophilus were a God-fearer, as Bock suggests (1994:15), he would have also had background with Jewish culture. The generous use of Old Testament texts in the book of Acts suggests that Theophilus, God-fearer or not, would have had some familiarity with Jewish culture. Theophilus had already received instruction about Jesus, likely of an introductory nature, at some point. This shows that he had interest in Christianity, but needed more teaching and factual verification. Theophilus may be assured that faith in Jesus rests on verified historical fact, unlike the fictitious nature of the mythology surrounding Greco-Roman religions. Because of this verification, Theophilus may have full confidence in the truth of the message and proclaim it with boldness, in accordance with Acts 1:8. If a Roman official, he would have had a wide sphere of influence upon people from all walks of life. He also would have had a unique opportunity to explain the message of Jesus to others in like positions. From this, it would seem that Luke had high hopes for his audience of one.

2.2 LITERARY CONTEXT

In this section, we seek to place Acts 17:24 in its literary context. First, we examine the placement of the Areopagus speech within the larger theme of the inclusion of the Gentiles in Acts. Next, we study the literary context of Acts 17:24 within the setting of the Areopagus speech. The speech will then be examined as a whole, with a grammatical and stylistic analysis. This section will conclude with a discussion of the Areopagus speech as it compares and contrasts with Paul's speeches in Lystra (Acts 14:15–17) and Pisidian Antioch (Acts 13:16–41).

2.2.1 Theme of the inclusive nature of Christianity in Acts

The book of Acts narrates the irrepressible expansion of the early church (Blomberg, 2006:17–18; Bock, 2007:6–8; Bovon, 2006:348; Larkin, 1995:30–33; Rosner, 1998:215–234). From the ascension of Christ in chapter one, to the narrative of Paul's house arrest in Rome nearly thirty years later in chapter twenty-eight, Luke chronicles the growth of Christianity. The story begins with the anticipation of the Holy Spirit and Jesus's promise that "you will receive power when the Holy Spirit has come upon you; and you will be my witnesses both in Jerusalem and in all Judea and Samaria, and to the end of the earth" (Acts 1:8). The message blazes from one region to the next after the outpouring of the Holy Spirit on the day of Pentecost. Peter, who buckled with fear at Jesus's arrest, now preaches with remarkable boldness in the second chapter of Acts—after being doused with the power of the Spirit. About three thousand people are added to the church at that time (Acts 2:41). The message spreads geographically. Acts 1:8 serves as a broad outline for the book:

A. Expansion of the church in Jerusalem (chs. 1–7)

B. Expansion of the church in Judea and Samaria (chs. 8–12)

C. Expansion of the church to the end of the earth (chs. 13–28)

With this geographical expansion, an influx of Gentiles comes into the church. Luke writes Acts to Theophilus so that he will also be a witness through the power of the Holy Spirit.

Although the book begins with proclamation of the message to the Jews, the focus shifts to the theme of Gentile inclusion. Wilson notes, "No other narrative in Acts is given quite such epic treatment as the Cornelius episode." This may be for the effect of impressing on the reader the importance of the event (1973:177). Unwittingly, Peter carries the message to the Gentiles. The events in chapter ten involving Cornelius and Peter are supernatural. Both men have visions. Cornelius has a vision in which an angel tells him to send men to Joppa to find Peter (10:3–7). The next day, as Cornelius's men are just about to approach the house where Peter is staying, Peter sees a puzzling vision. He sees a display of all kinds of animals prohibited for consumption by Old Testament law—a vision that is repeated three times (10:10–16). A voice follows the vision. Peter is told to "kill and eat," and not to call profane what the Lord has made clean (10:13–15). The Spirit tells him to go with the men who are searching for him (10:18), and he goes to stay with Cornelius— a God-fearing Gentile (10:2, 19–29). The Holy Spirit orchestrates the meeting (Bock, 2012:85).

What happens after this further demonstrates the work of God in bringing Gentiles into the same blessing as those Jews who believe the message. While Peter preaches the gospel to Cornelius's group of relatives and close friends, "the Holy Spirit fell upon all who heard the word. The circumcised believers who had come with Peter were astounded that the gift of the Holy Spirit had been poured out even on the Gentiles, for they heard them speaking in tongues and extolling God" (Acts 10:44–45, NRSV). The Holy Spirit is poured out on Gentile believers—in the same way as on the day of Pentecost in Acts 2. The Acts narrative shows that Gentile inclusion in the early church is nothing less than a work of the Holy Spirit.

The so-called second Pentecost of Acts 10 marks the beginning of a paradigm shift for the early church (Schnabel, 2004:715; Van Engen, 2004:135–136; Pentecost, 2010:105). Christianity is not only for Jews, but also for Gentiles—who were generally looked down upon by Jews. The second Pentecost also marks the beginning of a debate. How is it that Jews now associate with Gentiles? Jewish believers criticize Peter for eating with Gentiles (11:2–3). It is with his testimony, however, that Peter silences his critics (11:4–18). The Holy Spirit makes no distinction between Jew and Gentile.

By chapter 13, Peter fades into the background as the narrative switches to follow Paul as the main character—the one chosen to bring the gospel to the Gentiles (Acts 9:15). It is the Spirit who calls and sends Paul and Barnabas on their first missionary journey (Acts 13:2, 4). Gentiles respond favorably when Paul and Silas preach in Antioch of Pisidia and in Iconium (chs. 13–14). Later, a teaching arises from "certain persons" (Acts 15:1) that a Gentile could not be saved unless he is circumcised and keeps the Law of Moses. Luke describes the resulting argument with litotes—his stylistic trademark—"no small disagreement and debate" (Acts 15:2).

To end the controversy, Paul and Barnabas bring the matter before the authorities in Jerusalem in Acts 15. Although the church welcomes Paul and Barnabas, they cannot escape the dissenting view: some are teaching that Gentiles must be circumcised if they wanted to be saved. Some believers from the sect of the Pharisees were also teaching likewise in Jerusalem (Acts 15:5). This brings us to the landmark Jerusalem Council.

Gentiles continue to embrace Christianity, but Jews often reject it. This contrast becomes increasingly pronounced as the narrative unfolds. Not only do Jews reject it, they also stir up trouble for believers in city after city. The tension escalates until it reaches a boiling point. Paul's life is in danger: he is falsely accused of bringing a Gentile into the temple (Acts 21:27–30). After receiving a tip from Paul's nephew, the tribune shrewdly orders two hundred armed soldiers to escort Paul to Caesarea (Acts 23:23). Paul's life is endangered by Jews, but saved by a Gentile.

The overarching themes of the witness of the church and the inclusion of the Gentiles are crucial to understanding Acts 17:16–32. Repeatedly, the Jews antagonize Paul and his coworkers for their association with Gentiles. Paul's ministry among the Gentiles so inflames the Jews that it precipitates his arrest (Acts 21:28–29; 22:21–22). The flow of the narrative, however, shows that Gentile inclusion is from the very mind and heart of God. Paul carries out the calling that he received supernaturally upon his conversion: "He is an instrument whom I have chosen to bring my name before Gentiles and kings and before the people of Israel" (Acts 9:15, NRSV).

How might Theophilus, as a Gentile, have understood this overarching theme of Gentile inclusion? The Holy Spirit has done a new thing in bringing both Jews and Gentiles together in Christ. Gentiles are no longer outsiders; the door of faith has swung wide open. The message of Gentile inclusion is an invitation for those who were previously outside to come in—under the new covenant. There is a place for Theophilus in the kingdom of God.

2.2.2 Grammatical and stylistic analysis of Acts 17:16–34

Paul finds himself alone in Athens after fleeing a mob of angry Jews coming from Thessalonica. Silas and Timothy remain in Beroea. Undeterred by the absence of his teammates, Paul continues to evangelize. His ministry begins with the proclamation of the gospel to Jews and Godfearers in the synagogue, as well as with the general public in the marketplace (Acts 17:17). In keeping with the theme of the Gentiles breaking into the kingdom of God, it is the Gentiles who express keen interest in hearing the good news. A survey of the grammar and style of the passage shows the controversy of Paul's message, the initiative of the Greek philosophers to give him a platform to speak, the ingenuity of the message, and the reception—both positive and negative. This section provides an overview of the passage, part of which will be examined in more depth for this study.

Table 1. Structure of the Areopagus speech

Section 1	Section 2	Section 3
Setting (vv. 16–21) a. Paul begins to engage Athenians (vv. 16–17) b. Divided reaction (v. 18) c. Paul brought to Areopagus (vv. 19–21)	*Speech (vv. 22–31)* a. Address (vv. 22–23) b. Nature of Creator God (vv. 24–29) c. Call for repentance (vv. 30–31)	*Response (vv. 32–34)* a. Divided reaction (v. 32) b. Paul departs (v. 33) c. Belief (v. 34)

The text of Acts 17:16–34 may be broken into three main sections. The first section gives the setting: Paul is waiting for Silas and Timothy in Athens, and uses his time to proclaim the gospel in both the synagogue and the marketplace. While there, Paul meets some Stoic and Epicurean philosophers who take him to the Areopagus to hear more of his message (vv. 16–21). The text of the Areopagus speech follows (vv. 22–31). The speech, itself, is composed of three main units: the address to the audience (vv. 22–23), the nature of the Creator God (vv. 24–29), and a call for repentance (vv. 30–31) (also Bock, 2007:558; Bruce, 1990:375–387; Schnabel, 2008:170–171; and Zweck, 1989:96–97). The final section reads like a postscript, describing the response of the people (vv. 32–34). Verses 18 and 32 form an inclusio: a divided reaction to Paul and his message frames both sides of the speech. In verse 18, some insult Paul, while others are intrigued. The crowd is divided similarly in verse 32, with some scoffing at the idea of the resurrection of the dead, but others wanting to hear from Paul again. Ultimately, in verse 34, the result is belief, for a few.

What things lead up to Paul's speech at the Areopagus? Verses 16–21 provide the background and setting for Paul's message, which commences in verse 22. The first section of the passage begins in verse 16 with an initial statement of the account. An adverbial clause showing the time element and location, "And while Paul was waiting for them in Athens," is followed by a main clause that establishes Paul's internal reaction to the abundant evidence of idolatry in the city, "his spirit was greatly distressed within himself when he saw (that) the city was full of idols." The continuous aspect of the imperfect main verb (Porter, 1999:21), παρωξύνετο, draws attention to the intensity of Paul's emotional response. Verse 17 follows with an illative statement. What does Paul do as a result of his distress over idolatry? He engages the local people. The main verb, διελέγετο, is an imperfect, as is παρωξύνετο in the previous verse. The continuous nature of Paul's discussion with the Athenians corresponds to the continuous nature of his inner distress over idolatry. The main clause, "So he kept on debating in the synagogue with the Jews and the Godfearers," shows the result of his distress: dialogue.

At first, Paul debates both in the synagogue and in the marketplace. Beginning in verse 18, however, the Epicurean and Stoic philosophers take the prominent place in the text. There is no further explicit mention of Jews or Godfearers. An adversative statement marks this contrast: "But also some of the Epicurean and Stoic philosophers were conversing with him." Although verse 17 has Paul as the implied subject of the verb, διελέγετο, and τοῖς Ἰουδαίοις καὶ τοῖς σεβομένοις in the dative, in verse 18 there is a reversal. The subject of the main verb συνέβαλλον is τινες, "some." Genitive forms modify this subject: τῶν Ἐπικουρείων καὶ Στοϊκῶν φιλοσόφων. The philosophers take initiative to engage Paul in conversation. This is in character with the initiative that the philosophers display in verse 19, when they take him to the Areopagus.

Despite their initial interest, the philosophers are divided in their reaction to Paul's message. A second main clause in verse 18, "and some were saying," is followed by two noun clauses. The group is polarized. Some think Paul is a scavenger of information; others think he is importing a foreign religion. The first group asks, Τί ἂν θέλοι ὁ σπερμολόγος οὗτος λέγειν. The use of ἂν plus the optative verb is a fourth class condition, indicating a major degree of doubt (Wallace, 2000:314). Further accentuating this perception of extreme doubt is the use of the optative form, θέλοι (Wallace, 1996:484), which emphasizes their disbelief of Paul's message. The word σπερμολόγος occurs only once in the New Testament and not at all in the Septuagint or Josephus. In a literal sense, σπερμολόγος is be used to describe birds that come to eat seeds planted in fields (Strabo, *Georg.* 15.1.41). It can also be used to describe persons of low class who speak as though they have intelligence (Philo, *Legat.* 1.203; Demosthenes, *Cor.* 127.2). In Acts 17:18, some of the philosophers are comparing Paul with low class people who scavenge scraps of food from the market—as birds scavenge seed—but with reference to information (also BDAG, 2000 §6764). It appears that they were looking down on Paul as an outsider and not as a member of their guild: one who picked up scraps of information on his own, rather than within the philosophical schools in Athens (Ramsay, 2001:190). Ramsay identifies σπερμολόγος as a "term in social slang, it connotes absolute vulgarity and inability to rise above the most contemptible standard of life and conduct. It is often connected with slave life" (2001:189–190). Σπερμολόγος is a term of derision. Thus, Τί ἂν θέλοι ὁ σπερμολόγος οὗτος λέγειν may be understood as "what could this scavenger of information possibly be trying to say?" The second noun clause, "He seems to be a proclaimer of foreign gods," shows a milder response by using the indicative form δοκεῖ. The final clause of verse 18 is adverbial. It gives the reason for their response, "because he was preaching the good news about Jesus and the resurrection."

Verse 19 is illative, showing result. The main clause, ἐπιλαβόμενοί τε αὐτοῦ ἐπὶ τὸν Ἄρειον Πάγον ἤγαγον λέγοντες, "So after they took (him), they brought him to the Areopagus, saying," has the philosophers, once again, as the subject of the main verb. They engage Paul, physically bringing him to a public forum. A quotation of what the Athenians were saying

Literary Setting and Context of Acts 17:24

follows. The noun clause, Δυνάμεθα γνῶναι, "May we know," is followed by its own object or noun clause: τίς ἡ καινὴ αὕτη ἡ ὑπὸ σοῦ λαλουμένη διδαχή; "what this new teaching is that you are proclaiming?" This question is causal. In verse 20, a noun clause explains the reason for the request: "For you are bringing foreign things to our ears; therefore we would like to know what these things mean." The explanatory comment in verse 21 elucidates the grounds for their curiosity through hyperbole: "Now all (the) Athenians and the foreigners staying there had time for nothing but to say or hear the latest thing."

The second section of our passage is the Areopagus address (vv. 22–31). In a city overflowing with idols, Paul begins his speech with a necessary statement of clarification. Which God is he talking about? Verse 22 begins with a main clause: "Then Paul, after he stood in the middle of the Areopagus, said." The following noun clause marks the beginning of Paul's Areopagus speech. It is an initial statement: "Fellow Athenians, I perceive that in everything you are very devout." Wallace suggests that the comparative adjective, δεισιδαιμονεστέρους, has an intensifying, rather than comparative, sense (1996:300; also Hemer, 1989:245). Paul appeals to the Athenians' deep sense of devotion, albeit misdirected to idolatry. Hence, an explanatory statement is included in verse 23a: "For while going through (the city) and observing your objects of worship carefully I also found an altar in which had been inscribed, 'To an unknown god.'" The springboard topic for Paul's speech is expressed in the main clause, "I also found an altar in which had been inscribed, 'To an unknown god.'" Paul is about to make the unknown god known in Athens. The expectation is set.

Verses 24–27 are all one sentence in Greek, which serves as an explanatory statement. Paul begins by identifying the nature of the unknown god: the Creator, "The God who made the world and all the things in it, this one, being Lord of heaven and earth" (v. 24a). The substantival use of the demonstrative pronoun, οὗτος, links the identity of the Maker of the world with his nature to rule over heaven and earth as Lord. The word order emphasizes the objects over which this God is Lord. The demonstrative pronoun, οὗτος, is followed by two genitive forms before the participle—and before the predicate nominative they modify: οὗτος οὐρανοῦ καὶ γῆς ὑπάρχων κύριος. The genitive forms are advanced to an unexpected position in the clause. A literal translation of the words in the order they appear in Greek would be "this one–of heaven and earth–being Lord." This fronting of the genitive forms focuses the attention on "of heaven and

31

earth" and also adds to the contrast it makes with the following clause. The Lord of heaven and earth, unlike the multitude of idols in Athens, "does not dwell in temples made by human hands nor is he served by human hands as needing anything, he himself giving to all life and breath and all things" (vv. 24b–25). There is a recurrence of a fourth class condition employing the conditional particle with an optative verb, in the conditional adverbial clause in verse 27, εἰ ἄρα γε ψηλαφήσειαν αὐτὸν καὶ εὕροιεν. This time it is Paul who speaks with optative verbs. He mirrors the philosopher's linguistic style (v. 18) to show high-level doubt.

Verse 28 is an explanatory statement. A main clause, "for in him we live and move and exist" is followed by a subordinate adverbial clause, "as also some of your poets said," and a subordinate noun clause, "for we also are his offspring." Paul quotes one of their poets in this noun clause. Aratus (c. 315–240 B.C), originally from Soli in Cilicia, came to Athens around 291 B.C. and associated himself with Zeno, founder of the Stoic school of philosophy (see comments by Mair in Aratus, 1969:188–189; also Volk, 2010:197). Aratus's *Phaenomena* is notable for the phrase, τοῦ γὰρ καὶ γένος εἰμεν, "For we are also his offspring" (l. 5), which appears to be what Paul is quoting in verse 28b. Cleanthes (c. 331–232 B.C.), originally from Assos, also relocated to Athens. There, he succeeded Zeno (founder of the Stoic school) and served as president of the Stoa for more than thirty years (Inwood, 2003:8). A similar phrase is also found in Cleanthes's *Hymn*, ἐκ σοῦ γὰρ γένος ἐσμεν, "For we are your offspring" (l. 4). Is Paul quoting Aratus or Cleanthes? Although both Aratus and Cleanthes express a similar thought, the Greek of Aratus matches that of Acts 17:28, Τοῦ γὰρ καὶ γένος ἐσμέν, more closely (see Bruce, 1990:385; Williams, 1990:308; Witherington, 1998:530). Polhill (1992:376) suggests that Aratus may have been quoting Cleanthes. Thom (2005:65) states that it is impossible to determine literary dependence since it is unknown whether Cleanthes or Aratus wrote first and suggests that they may have used a common source.

We may also observe that Paul said he was quoting "some" of their own poets, not "one" of their poets. In this regard, it seems that Paul may have been referring to an idea expressed by both Aratus and Cleanthes in a more general sense. The concept of being offspring of a god was in circulation even before the days of Aratus and Cleanthes. Consider the following from Plato:

> Therefore the goddess [Athena], being a lover of war and a lover of wisdom, chose the place that was likely to bear men to herself. She established this first. Therefore you lived under laws of such

a kind, and laws yet better and exceeding all men in every excellence, becoming just as those who are the offspring and pupils of gods. (*Timaeus* 24D)

Both Aratus and Cleanthes echo words from Plato's Timaeus, a work that predates the writings of both. Although the Greek of Acts 17:28 bears greater similarity in form to Aratus's work than that of Cleanthes, we see that Paul appeals to an idea postulated by several Greek philosophers as he prepares to dismantle the logic behind idolatry.

Paul explains further in verse 29 with an illative statement. A main clause follows a participial phrase. Paul extends their belief system to its logical end: "Since being offspring of God, we ought not to think the deity is like gold or silver or stone." Can an idol of gold, silver, or stone generate offspring? The thought is absurd. Idolatry does not make sense and is inconsistent with the teaching of some of their own poets. In this way, Paul implodes the thought system undergirding idolatry.

Verses 30 and 31 are one sentence and conclude Paul's speech. A main clause, "now he commands all people everywhere to repent," shows the evangelistic impetus of Paul's message. The reason is given in verse 31. An adverbial clause, "because he fixed a day," introduces an explanation for the command to repent in the previous verse. Two subordinate adjectival clauses establish the coming time in which the world will be judged: "in which he intends to judge the world in righteousness by a man whom he appointed." The coming judgment is the reason for repentance. Finally, the sentence ends with two participial phrases in which Paul declares the resurrection: "having shown proof to all, having raised him from the dead." After invalidating idolatry in verses 28 and 29, Paul brings his speech to a close with validation of the true God. The resurrection validates the truth of the gospel.

The last section of our text (vv. 32–34) describes the reaction of Paul's audience at the Areopagus. Verse 32 is an adversative statement. The teaching of the resurrection is the subject of contention. Two subordinate noun clauses follow a participial phrase. The use of the alternative personal pronoun with μὲν . . . δὲ (οἱ μὲν ἐχλεύαζον, οἱ δὲ εἶπαν) shows that just as the hearers of Paul are divided in verse 18, so again the hearers are divided in their response. "Some were scoffing" coordinates with the response of those who "were saying" (v. 18) that Paul is a "scavenger of information." "'We will hear from you concerning this also again'" (v. 32) coordinates with the request, "'May we know what this new teaching is that you are proclaiming?'" (v. 19). Verse 33 has a main clause with an illative purpose. "So, Paul went out from their midst" seems anticlimactic. Yet, the adversative statement of verse 34 offers a hopeful twist to the end of the narrative, "but some people, having joined him, believed, among them also Dionysius the Areopagite and a woman named Damaris, and others with them." Despite the divided response of the crowd in Athens, Paul's speech produces results.[16]

To summarize, Acts 17:24, the focal verse of this study, completes the introduction of the subject of Paul's speech in Athens. He speaks as an invited orator at the Areopagus, after discussions in the marketplace elicited mixed reactions among the Stoic and Epicurean philosophers. Paul asserts that he will proclaim the unknown god in verse 23, anchoring his teaching to a familiar concept in Athens. Verse 24 establishes the connection between the unknown god and the God who made the world. This is the bridge that Paul constructs in order to proclaim the nature of God, the futility of idolatry, the coming judgment, repentance, and the resurrection. The "this-is-that" identification of the God who made the world and everything in it with the unknown god provides the foundation for Paul to proclaim the gospel in Athens. Paul gives new information about the unknown god, who was already acknowledged in Athens through the presence of an altar. What the philosophers considered a new teaching actually had old roots in the culture. The material that follows verse 24 in the speech is an expansion of Paul's stated topic. The mixed response of the crowd demonstrates that his speech was effective to ignite belief and also to divide the crowd—illustrating the polarizing nature of the gospel.

2.2.3 The Areopagus speech in comparison with speeches in Lystra and Pisidian Antioch

Few scholarly works have been published in recent years that undertake the comparison of the evangelistic speeches in Pisidian Antioch, Lystra, and Athens. Atef Gendy presents a basic comparison of these three speeches in his article, "Style, Content and Culture: Distinctive Characteristics in the Missionary Speeches in Acts" (2011:247–265). Gendy presents background information about each audience before summarizing the general content of each speech and analyzing "communicational bridges" (2011:261). His comparison demonstrates Paul's flexibility when speaking to different audiences (2011:261), but does not focus on the inclusion or absence

---

16. Cf. Lüdemann (2005:231) and Dunn (2009:692) who argue that Paul's endeavors in Athens were not a success.

of mention of God as Creator in each. Hesselgrave & Rommen mention briefly that Paul develops a pattern for evangelism of Gentiles based on the results of the encounter in Lystra, but do not offer any comment explicating the centrality of creation as a beginning point for the speeches in Lystra and Athens. The speech at Pisidian Antioch is not mentioned at all (Hesselgrave & Roman, 1989:9–10). This study endeavors to compare the speeches given in Lystra, Athens, and Pisidian Antioch with special attention given to the foundations for each address.

A survey of Paul's speeches in Pisidian Antioch, Lystra, and Athens provides contextual clues for the identification of God as Creator in Acts 17:24. How does Paul's reference to the God who made the world in the Areopagus speech compare with other speeches in Acts? Does he use a similar or different approach with other audiences? In this section, we compare Paul's speeches to Gentile audiences in Athens and Lystra and, then, contrast with his speech to a Jewish audience in Pisidian Antioch. Particular attention will be given to the inclusion or absence of mention of God as Creator in each speech. General comments will lead into specific discussion regarding the presentation of God as Creator in Acts 17:24, with the goal of beginning to gain an understanding as to why Paul may have chosen to build his Areopagus speech on this foundation.

Of Paul's speeches in the book of Acts, the speech at Athens resembles most closely his speech in Lystra (Acts 14:15–17), although the Lystra speech is considerably shorter in length. The following chart lists similar themes in the Lystra and Athens speeches.

Table 2. Comparison of speeches in Lystra and Athens

Lystra (14:8–17)	Athens (17:16–31)
Gentile audience (vv. 11–13)	Gentile audience (vv. 16, 18–19)
Call to repentance (v. 15)	Call to repentance (vv. 30–31)
Idols are useless (v. 15a)	God is not like idols (v. 29)
God identified as Creator (v. 15b)	God identified as Creator (v. 24)
Ignorance overlooked in the past (v. 16)	Ignorance overlooked in the past (v. 30)
General revelation as a witness (v. 17)	General revelation as a witness (v. 25)

The settings of the Athens and Lystra speeches are both among Gentiles, although those of a different sort. Béchard characterizes the population in Lystra as "rustic" and "naïve" (2001:86). By contrast, he describes the philosophers in Athens as "urban sophisticates" (2001:101). The argument that the Lystrian people were "rustic" due to their speaking of the Lycaonian dialect, however, is not conclusive. Eckhard Schnabel points out that it was common for the people of Asia Minor, particularly those in the cities, to speak both a local dialect as well as Greek (Schnabel, 2012:605). Nonetheless, it is possible that the audience in Athens may have included more highly educated persons than in Lystra since Athens was known for its institutions of higher learning— "a small university town more concerned with ideas than commerce" (McRay, 1991:299–300).

The episode at Lystra begins with a miraculous healing of a man who could not walk, having been handicapped from birth (14:8–10). The crowd's reaction is tragic, yet nearly comical (also Gempf, 1995:58–60). They deify Barnabas and Paul, calling them Zeus and Hermes, and prepare to host a sacrifice (14:11–13). This faux pas precipitates the speech in 14:15–17. Paul makes an immediate appeal for his audience to turn away from idolatry: "we bring you good news, that you should turn from these worthless things to the living God" (14:15a, NRSV). This may be compared to Paul's statements against idolatry in Athens, "we ought not to think the deity is like gold or silver or stone, an image made by the skill and imagination of a person" (17:29). The appeal to turn from idols in the Lystra speech is followed by a statement identifying God as the Creator, "who made the heaven and the earth and the sea and all that is in them" (14:15b, NRSV). This identification of God is strikingly similar to the text of 17:24, "The God, the one who made the world and all the things in it, this one, being Lord of heaven and earth." The counter-idolatry context is also similar to the speech in Athens. The next point in the Lystra speech has to do with God overlooking Gentile ignorance for a time, "In past generations he allowed all the nations to follow their own ways" (14:16, NRSV). This compares with Paul's words in Athens, "Therefore, indeed, while God overlooked the times of ignorance" (17:30). Paul's final point in his Lystra speech references general revelation, "yet he has not left himself without a witness in doing good—giving you rains from heaven and fruitful seasons, and filling you with food" (14:17, NRSV). Paul's words in 17:25 also reflect general revelation, "he himself giving to all life and breath and all things."

Thus, Paul addresses two different Gentile audiences in a similar fashion. Both speeches aim to dissuade the hearers from idolatry. Both speeches establish whom the true and living God is—the one who made heaven and earth, who also provides for his creation. This is "der Gott des Alten und Neuen Testaments und kein Anderer" (Schweizer, 1988:236). These two main points comprise the entire content of the Lystra speech, with no mention of Christ at all. The speech in Athens continues with fuller arguments that explicate the nature of God. These arguments are dressed in language that bears resemblance to Greek literature throughout (Creamer, 2011:54–55). In utilizing such a technique, Paul does not make a concession to Greek philosophy. Instead, he recasts philosophical language into a new context (also Gärtner, 1955:72). The Areopagus address also includes an unnamed reference to Jesus at the end: "he intends to judge the world in righteousness by a man whom he appointed, having shown proof to all, having raised him from the dead" (17:31). There is no equivalent statement in the Lystra speech. It seems that Paul's speech in Lystra is cut short by the commotion of the misunderstanding crowd (Polhill, 1992:316; Witherington, 1998:426).

Paul's approach with Gentiles in Lystra and Athens stands in contrast to his approach with Jews in Pisidian Antioch (13:16–41). The speech in Pisidian Antioch is the fullest example in Acts of Paul's approach with Jews and Godfearers in an evangelistic setting. His usual manner with Jews is to argue in the synagogue and to try to convince them of Christ (Acts 17:2–3, 10; 18:4; 19:8). While in Antioch of Pisidia, Paul speaks to Jews and those who fear God (13:16b). The foundation for this speech is Old Testament history (Bock, 2007:448). Beginning with the formation of Israel as a nation (v. 17a), Paul builds his case for Jesus as the Messiah from the line of David. He mentions key points of Israel's history from Exodus (v. 17), Numbers (v. 18), Joshua (v. 19), 1 Samuel (vv. 20–21), and 2 Samuel/1 Kings/1 Chronicles (v. 22). Paul includes direct quotes of the Old Testament as further evidence as the speech develops. Verse 22 includes quotations from Psalm 89:20 and 1 Samuel 13:14 in reference to David. He then proceeds to interpret prophetic statements of the Old Testament in light of the advent of Christ for the remainder of his speech. Paul identifies Jesus, who is of the line of David, as the promised Savior: "Of this man's posterity God has brought to Israel a Savior, Jesus, as he promised" (v. 23, NRSV) (also Bock, 2007:453). In verse 33, Paul quotes Psalm 2:7, a royal psalm (Bock, 2007:456), as evidence for Jesus as God's son. Steve Moyise remarks that this psalm may be applied to Jesus as "Messianic king" (Moyise, 2012:23). Moyise also states that this quotation most likely refers to the baptism of Jesus as recorded in Luke 3:22 (Moyise, 2012:23). While the wording of 2.7 certainly is similar to Luke 3:22, the immediate context of Acts 13 suggests a reference to resurrection, rather than baptism (also Marshall, 1980: 226; Bock, 2007:456). In verse 34, Paul quotes Isaiah 55:3 (LXX) as further evidence that connects Jesus with the Davidic covenant of 2 Samuel 7:16 (Beale & Carson, 2007:586). Beale notes that "whenever David is mentioned in connection with Christ in the NT, there are usually discernible prophetic, messianic overtones" (Beale, 2012:143). In verse 35, Paul quotes Psalm 16:10 (LXX)[17] as Old Testament evidence for the resurrection. Witherington notes the similarity of this speech to Peter's speech in 2:31–32, in that it shares a common Old Testament citation. He remarks that Psalm 16:10 may have been part of a testimonia list, "a list of scriptures regularly used to attest to various parts of the kerygma by various early Christian preachers" (Witherington, 1998:413). The speech continues with an interpretation of Psalm 16:10: Paul argues that it cannot refer to David, since David died and, hence, experienced corruption. All the arguments in the speech lead to a summit in verses 38–39: the proclamation that through Jesus there is forgiveness of sins. Paul's speech concludes with a stern warning against unbelief, which includes a quotation of Habakkuk 1:5. This quotation from Habakkuk reminds the audience of how God worked through history in a manner that bewildered not only the ancient Israelites, but also the prophet himself. Indeed, God raised up the ungodly Babylonians to execute judgment on the Israelites by taking Jerusalem in 586 B.C. (also Beale & Carson, 2007:587). In this way, Paul reminds his audience not only that God works in ways beyond their understanding, but also that God is the judge (Bruce, 1988:263). In summary, the Old Testament provides the complete framework for Paul's explanation of Jesus throughout his speech in Pisidian Antioch.

Both the Lystra and Athens speeches are built on concepts familiar to each audience, yet the means of bridge building is different than in Paul's speech in Pisidian Antioch. It is striking that Paul appeals to the God of creation as the foundational topic for further explanation in both Acts 14:15 and 17:24, yet there is no identification of God as Creator in the Antioch speech. Paul points to the Creator and natural theology in familiar Greek terms while speaking to Gentiles in both Lystra and Athens, rather than referring to Scripture and Old Testament history, as he does when speaking to Jews in Antioch. Paul brings his Jewish audience back as far as the exodus of the Israelites from Egypt, as the foundation for his speech in Pisidian Antioch (also Witherington, 1998:409). He brings his Gentile audiences back as far as the creation of the world, as the foundation for his speeches in Lystra and Athens. What might be a reason for this difference?

---

17. Ps 15:10 in LXX.

Paul debunks idolatry in both Lystra and Athens. Creation—an Old Testament concept—is used as foundational evidence against idolatry in both locations. F.F. Bruce, referencing Deuteronomy 6:4, suggests that the presentation of the gospel to pagans must begin with the proclamation of God as one (1990:323). It may be understood that Paul's monotheistic audience in the synagogue in Pisidian Antioch would have already considered idolatry unacceptable. Hence, there was no need to establish the identity of the one God as the God who created the world. The references to the God who created the world in Lystra and Athens clearly establish which God is being preached—a necessary first step in communicating with audiences that lived amidst a plethora of deities.

This brief study shows that the foundations of both the Areopagus speech and the Lystra speech are each squarely established in the Old Testament teaching of God as Creator, even though there is no direct quotation of Scripture in either speech. The repetition of creation as a foundational building block for each sermon shows consistency of practice in evangelism by Paul. The first matter to be settled in each case is that of idolatry. In a culture with a multitude of gods, it is necessary to define the God who was about to be discussed. Each speech begins with the Old Testament concept of creation, expressed in terms familiar to each audience, as a means of debunking idolatry.

In summary, Paul takes a different approach in his speeches to Gentiles in Athens and Lystra, than he does with Jews in Antioch. Whereas his aim with his Jewish audience in Antioch is to prove from the Old Testament that Jesus is the fulfillment of predictions of the Messiah, his aim with Gentile audiences in Athens and Lystra is first to persuade them toward monotheism by starting with God as the Maker of the world, and then by expanding on that idea in familiar terms. Indeed, there is no quotation of Old Testament Scripture at all in his oratory at the Areopagus. Nonetheless, Paul presents an Old Testament concept, creation, as foundational evidence in his arguments against idolatry in both Lystra and Athens. Paul makes his case against idolatry and in favor of the true God in such a way that conversions to the true God ensue. Paul, thus, demonstrates a flexible, persuasive style for each type of audience.

2.2.4 Summary of Literary Context

Paul's Areopagus speech rides on the crest of the wave of Gentiles coming to faith in the book of Acts. Not only do Greek philosophers come to faith as a result of hearing the message, but they are also the ones who request to hear the message. Paul designs his speech with awareness of the culture of his audience, speaking the realities of the gospel in familiar terms. Within the spiritual morass, Paul identifies the altar to the unknown god. The statement that follows, "Therefore, that which you worship without knowing, this I proclaim to you" (Acts 17:23), would have sparked the attention of his audience—setting up a high expectation for those who regarded the discussion of new ideas as a national pastime. Is their speaker about to unveil a great mystery by making the unknown known? What is the nature of this unknown god? Getting right to the point, Paul then states the connection between their unknown god and the Creator God of the Judeo-Christian faith. The assertion of God as Creator precedes an anti-idolatry polemic that includes a presentation of the gospel in Athens. The declaration of God as Creator, within an anti-idolatry context, is also, strikingly, the platform on which Paul builds his speech in Lystra. Paul identifies God as Creator as a starting point for his arguments against idolatry and for the good news of Christ and the resurrection.

2.3 CONCLUSION

In this chapter, I have sought to identify the literary setting and context of Acts 17:24. An exploration of matters related to authorship showed that Luke was from a Gentile background. He was a highly-educated man: a physician. I have argued in favor of Luke as a reliable historian. As a reliable historian, it was not impossible that Luke could have recorded words spoken in Athens since there could have been written documents available. This record of the Areopagus speech would have found a first reading with Theophilus, possibly a man of status. A study of κράτιστος showed a strong possibility that Theophilus was a Roman official. A further implication of this study of κράτιστος is that Theophilus may have been a Gentile. An analysis of the broader literary context located the Areopagus speech squarely within the larger theme of the Gentiles coming to faith in Acts. An analysis of the grammar and literary style of the Areopagus speech located the identification of God as Creator in Acts 17:24 as the starting point from which Paul proclaims the true God, amidst a culture of idolatry. This starting point is remarkably similar to the starting point of Paul's speech in Lystra. In both cities, Paul built his case against idolatry—in speeches to Gentiles—with the foundational building block of God as Creator. By contrast, there was no mention of God as Creator in Paul's speech in Pisidian Antioch. Instead, Paul built his case for Jesus as the Messiah, in his speech to Jews and Godfearers, with the foundational building block of the history of Israel beginning with the exodus. Paul's aim with Jews and Godfearers in Pisidian Antioch was to present Jesus as the fulfillment of Old Testament predictions of the Messiah. In Lystra and Athens, Paul's aim was to present the nature of God as revealed by creation itself.

Luke, a man of Greek background, records this speech for Theophilus, also a man of Greek background. What was cross-cultural for Paul would not have been for Theophilus. This speech is an example to Theophilus of how one man, Paul, became a witness in the Gentile world, fulfilling not only his calling, but also the purposes of the Holy Spirit, that followers of Christ "be my witnesses . . . to the end of the earth" (Acts 1:8).

In the next chapter, we will explore the Jewish understanding of a Creator God as expressed in biblical literature as well as in extra-biblical Jewish sources.

CHAPTER 3

Semantic Study of "The God Who Made the Heaven and Earth" in Biblical and Extra-Biblical Jewish Literature

3.0 INTRODUCTION

THE PREVIOUS CHAPTER, THE study of the literary context of Acts 17:24, showed that the identification of God as Creator forms the starting point for Luke's account of Paul's case against idolatry and in favor of the existence of one true God, who both made and maintains the world. In this chapter, I will endeavor to demonstrate how the technique of using creation as a basis for an anti-idolatry polemic, in Acts 17:24, reflects ancient Jewish practice. To this end, we will first study the phrase in Acts 17:24. We will then survey semantically similar phrases from the New Testament, the Septuagint, the Apocrypha, and other works of Jewish literature written in Greek no later than the first century A.D. This survey will examine the literary context of each phrase, in order that we may better understand the theological setting, patterns of interrelationship throughout Scripture, and the overall meaning. Following the survey, Acts 17:24a will be compared more closely to passages that bear the most similar literary contexts: Isaiah 45:18, Jeremiah 10:11–12, and Jonah 1:9. This comparison will further bring into focus the meaning of Acts 17:24a, as well as illuminate Paul's technique. This chapter contributes to the main research aim by elucidating the way the Athens's speech uses words and establishes theological parameters that import a meaning for Acts 17:24 that is rooted in Jewish thought. We will conclude that Paul used creation theology as an anti-idolatry polemic in his speech, following the tradition of Old Testament prophets who argued against idolatry and in favor of the God of Israel in cross-cultural settings.

3.1 SEMANTIC STUDY OF KEY PHRASES RELATED TO ACTS 17:24

The purpose of this section is to study phrases similar to Acts 17:24, with the goal of gaining an understanding of Paul's purposes (as presented by Luke) in building his speech on the foundation of God as Creator. This study surveys the meaning of similar phrases throughout passages selected from the New Testament, the Septuagint, the Apocrypha, and other Jewish writings using Greek (written no later than the first century A.D.).

3.1.1 Summary of scholarship

New Testament scholars cannot but acknowledge that the presentation of God as Creator is an Old Testament concept that begins with the book of Genesis. In the mid-twentieth century, German scholar Martin Dibelius argued that the speech in Acts 17:22–31 was the precursor to the approach taken by the second century Christian apologists (Dibelius, 1951:63). Dibelius develops his research around the premise that the speech has its roots in Greek philosophy rather than New Testament theology: "The speech is as alien to the New Testament (apart from Acts 14:15–17), as it is familiar to hellenistic, particularly Stoic, philosophy" (Dibelius, 1951:63). While denying that the speech is concordant to the rest of the New Testament (and to Paul's theology), Dibelius readily asserts, "the affirmation of God as Creator belongs to the Old Testament" (Dibelius, 1951:41). Bertil Gärtner responded to Dibelius's claims a few years later in his monograph, *The Areopagus Speech and Natural Revelation*. In his examination of the Areopagus speech, Gärtner argues in favor of "the Pauline character of the speech" (Gärtner, 1955:250 [contra Dibelius, 1951:62–63]). He goes further to state that the style of preaching in Acts 17:22–31 may be associated with a Jewish pattern of preaching, particularly what he terms "Jewish Diaspora propaganda" and which he suggests as a subject for further research (Gärtner, 1955:252).

God as Creator in Acts 17:24

Many have acknowledged echoes of the Old Testament in Acts 17:24a. Others have made general acknowledgements of similarities between the Areopagus speech and critiques of idolatry in the Old Testament as well as with Jewish-Hellenistic monotheistic literature without giving details. Scholars often include a brief comment or footnote in their commentaries regarding the echoes of Old Testament passages such as Genesis 1:1 and Isaiah 42:5 in Acts 17:24 (Barrett, 1998:839; Beale & Carson, 2007:594; Bock, 2007:565; Bruce, 1990:156, 382; Haenchen, 1971:522; Marshall, 1980:286; Polhill, 1992:373; Witherington, 1998:525). Eckhard Schnabel notes briefly the similarities of the Areopagus speech with Jewish-Hellenistic monotheistic sermons (Schnabel, 2005:177; see also Gempf, 1993b:52–53). Schnabel also notes briefly that the critique of idols finds its roots in the Old Testament (Schnabel, 2005:182). Steve Walton makes a brief assertion (without further explication) before continuing his discussion of another topic, the Temple in Acts: "Much of the Athens speech is standard Jewish polemic against pagan idolatry, using ideas (but not usually language) from the Old Testament critique of idols," (Walton, 2004:143). In this chapter we will see that in the case of Acts 17:24a, the speech does use language from the Old Testament critique of idols.

Gärtner's line of further research remains to be investigated. There has not been a systematic examination of the passages in the Old Testament and other Jewish literature that relate closely to the reference to God as Creator in Acts 17:24a. The recent thesis on Acts 17:16–34 by Juhana Torkki focuses on the Hellenistic aspects of the speech and includes no discussion of its Old Testament roots (Torkki, 2004:13–216). Doctoral theses by Conrad Gempf and Lars Dahle also overlook this aspect of Acts 17:24 (Dahle, 2001:1–390; Gempf, 1988:1–416). The study in this chapter aims to illuminate the matter of the intertextuality of Acts 17:24a with Jewish literature through the first century A.D.

3.1.2 Methodology

Passages for comparison to Acts 17:24a are selected on the basis of similar semantic context. This section outlines three categories of semantic correlation and six classifications of literary type.

Three categories may be established that reflect degrees of semantic correlation in comparison passages. Words for comparison are underlined: ὁ <u>θεὸς</u> ὁ <u>ποιήσας</u> τὸν <u>κόσμον</u> καὶ πάντα τὰ ἐν αὐτῷ, οὗτος <u>οὐρανοῦ</u> καὶ <u>γῆς</u>

Semantic Study of "The God Who Made the Heaven and Earth"

ὑπάρχων κύριος ("The God who made the world and all the things in it, this one, being Lord of heaven and earth") (Acts 17:24a).

The criteria for each category are as follows:

Category A: θεός or κύριος + ποιέω + 2 (or more) of οὐρανός, γῆ, κόσμος

Category B: θεός or κύριος + ποιέω + 1 of οὐρανός, γῆ, κόσμος

Category C: θεός or κύριος + 1 of οὐρανός, γῆ

Explanation: in each category, θεός or κύριος may be stated or implied. A synonym may be substituted for ποιέω. The words in common for each category may share either the same lemma or the same exact form as found in Acts 17:24. Category C omits κόσμος in the criteria since the word does not occur in any passages falling within these parameters.

The passages are categorized according to semantic correalates in the following tables:

Table 3.
Semantic Category A (θεός or κύριος + ποιέω + 2 (or more) of οὐρανός, γῆ, κόσμος)

In the NT	In the Septuagint	In the Apocrypha	In other Jewish writings
Acts 4:24 Acts 14:15 Acts 17:24a Rev 14:6–7	Gen 1:1 Gen 14:19 Gen 14:22 Ps 113:23 [115:15 MT] Ps 133:3 [134:3] Neh 9:6 Isa 37:16 Isa 42:5 Isa 45:18 Jer 10:11–12 Jonah 1:9* 2 Chr 2:11 [2:12] Dan 4:37 [4:1] * τὴν ξηράν is used as a synonym for γῆ in Jonah 1:9	Bel 1:5 Pr Man 2	*Ag. Ap.* 2.121 *Ag. Ap.* 2.192 *Sib. Or.* 3.33–35 *T. Job* 2.4

God as Creator in Acts 17:24

Table 4. Semantic Category B (θεός or κύριος + ποιέω + 1 of οὐρανός, γῆ, κόσμος)

In Acts	In the Septuagint	In the Apocrypha	In other Jewish writings
	1 Chr 16:26 Isa 44:24		*Creation* LXI.172 *Embassy* XVI.115

Table 5. Semantic Category C (θεός or κύριος + 1 of οὐρανός, γῆ)

In Acts	In the Septuagint	In the Apocrypha	In other Jewish writings
	Gen 24:3 Josh 2:11 2 Chr 6:14 Ezra 1:2 Dan 2:28, 37, 44, 3:17, 4:17, 27, 31, 33a, 34 (2x), 37 (4:1 [3x])		

Each of the passages in the previous categories will also be classified according to literary type. "Literary type" may be understood as the framework of genre for the immediate context of each passage. Literary type 1, core material, refers to the primary event of creation that is refracted through the lens of subsequent passages throughout the study. Literary type 2, liturgical, encompasses passages that refer to God as Creator of heaven and earth in a setting of worship. Literary type 3, in an oath, includes references to God as Creator in a solemn agreement or promise. Literary type 4, in a prophetic oracle, includes references that occur within a specific poetic message given by a prophet. Literary type 5, in cross-cultural communication, includes references that occur between Jews and Gentiles in direct speech. Literary type 6, in philosophical/historical treatises, includes references in works that discuss the nature of the world or provide a narrative of a specific event.

Table 6. Six classifications of literary type

1. Core material	2. Liturgical	3. In an oath	4. In a prophetic oracle	5. In cross-cultural communication	6. In philosophical/ historical treatises
Gen 1:1	*a. In a blessing* Gen 14:19 Ps 113:23 (115:15) Ps 133:3 (134:3) *b. In worship* 1 Chr 16:26 *c. In a prayer* 2 Chr 6:14 Neh 9:6 Isa 37:16 Acts 4:24 Pr Man 2	Gen 14:22 Gen 24:3 Ag. Ap. 2.121	Isa 42:5 Isa 44:24 Isa 45:18 Jer 10:11–12 Sib. Or. 3:33–35	*a. In statements to Gentiles* Acts 14:15 Rev 14:6–7 Jonah 1:9 Dan 2:28, 37, 44, 3:17, 4:17, 27 Ag. Ap. 2.192 Bel 1.5 T. Job 2.4 *b. In statements by Gentiles* Josh 2:11 Dan 4:31, 33a, 34 (2x), 37 (4:1 [3x]) Ezra 1:2 2 Chr 2:11 (2:12)	*Creation* LXI.172 *Embassy* XVI.115

God as Creator in Acts 17:24

Passages will be examined systematically according to body of literature throughout the first part of this chapter. Passages in the New Testament will be discussed first. Passages from the Septuagint, the Apocrypha, and other Jewish writings will follow.

3.1.3 "The God who Made the Heaven and the Earth" in the New Testament

In this section, we will first examine the meanings of key words in Acts 17:24a. A discussion of the meaning and context of Acts 14:15 and Revelation 14:6–7 will show similarities with respect to contexts of cross-cultural evangelism. Acts 4:24 shows similar nomenclature in a completely different context: reference to God in a prayer.

3.1.3.1 *Cross-cultural communication*

3.1.3.1.1 ACTS 17:24A

The city of Athens was overflowing with idols (McRay, 1991:301)—a situation that causes considerable distress for Paul, and becomes an impetus for his proclamation. As discussed in chapter two, Luke records that Paul identifies God as Creator as the foundational statement for his speech that elucidates the nature of the true God against the backdrop of idolatry in the city of Athens.

Key words are utilized in this foundational statement that establish the subject of Paul's declamation. We begin the semantic study of "the God who made the heaven and the earth" with an examination of each of the key words as they may be understood within the initial context of the Areopagus speech.

θεός

The subject of Paul's speech is θεός, God. In the Greco-Roman world, θεὸς may be used as a general name for a deity or transcendent being (BDAG, 2000 §3538; Kittel vol. 3, 1965:65; Thayer, 1997 §2452). As he speaks to Greek philosophers in the Areopagus, Paul takes immediate care to present defining parameters regarding the God he proclaims. He explicates the nature of the God he presents first by making reference to one of the religious objects he observes in the city, an altar with an inscription "to an unknown god." He equates the θεός of his presentation with the unknown deity of their material culture in verse 23. θεός, then, was already acknowledged by the Athenians, although "unknown." The first thing Paul makes clear about the nature of θεός is that he is the God who made the world (v. 24a). Not only is θεός the God who made the world, but θεός is also Lord over his creation (ὑπάρχων κύριος). Paul immediately sets God apart from the idols made by artisans. The God Paul preaches does not live in shrines (v. 24b), as idols do. God is not served by human hands, in contrast to the idols of the city (v. 25a). Also unlike idols, God is the one who gives life to people (v. 25b). This Creator of the world and Creator of people also determines matters of time and place with respect to human life (v. 26). The θεός that Paul preaches may be sought and found by people, since he is an omnipresent God (v. 27–28a). He may also be understood as the divine parent, since we are "offspring of God" (v. 29a). Since it is impossible for a statue to give life, it is impossible that θεός bears any resemblance to the artistic representation of idols in Athens (v. 29b). This God is not indifferent to the ways of people, but demands repentance of all (v. 30). The God Paul preaches will judge the world on a fixed day (v. 31a). This God has also made his intentions known by raising the appointed One from the dead (v. 31b).

In summary, θεός, in Acts 17:24a is the Creator of the universe as well as the Creator of humankind. He is transcendent, yet present in all creation. He is not anything like the idols the Athenians were familiar with. This θεός created the world, presides over the world, and will judge the world.

ποιέω

The verb ποιέω may be defined as "to do, to make, or to manufacture" (BDAG, 2000 §6015; Friberg, 2000 §22345; Louw–Nida, 1989 §5230). It may be used in specific connection with the creative activity of God (BDAG, 2000 §6015; Friberg, 2000 §22345). In Acts 17:24a, ποιέω refers to the supernatural work of God to create the world that can be seen by all and everything in it. The substantival participle, ὁ ποιήσας, serves to identify God in terms of what he made. This God also made (ἐποίησέν) every nation of people to live on the planet by his divine power (17:26). Ποιέω, in this speech, refers to God's work to both design and bring the universe, including every race of people, into material existence.

God as Creator in Acts 17:24

In verse 24, ποιέω stands in juxtaposition to χειροποιήτοις, "made by human hands." The use of this adjective creates a sharp contrast that causes the art of Athens to pale in comparison to the miraculous abilities of God.

κόσμος

The κόσμος denotes the world or the entire order of the universe (BDAG, 2000 §4371; Kittel, 1965:869; Louw–Nida, 1989 §3822; Thayers, 1997 §3061). The κόσμος in Acts 17:24 is the sum total of creation. It includes the broadest reaches of the universe and all existing matter within (καὶ πάντα τὰ ἐν αὐτῷ). There is nothing in existence that was not created by God. The magnitude of the cosmos is restated in the phrase "of heaven and earth." This phrase may be defined similarly, as the "totality of all creation" (BDAG, 2000 §4371). Luke records Paul as using κόσμος and οὐρανοῦ καὶ γῆς synonymously (Kittel, 1965:884).

Considering this, the usual translation, "world," may not be comprehensive enough for Acts 17:24. "Universe" may show more breadth. Louw–Nida suggests the following as a possible translation for Acts 17:24: "God who made the universe and everything in it" (Louw–Nida, 1989 §3822).

οὐρανός καὶ γῆ

Heaven and earth is the realm of the Lord's dominion as expressed in Acts 17:24a. He is Lord of everything he created. οὐρανός refers to all creation above. This includes the sky, the stars, planets, galaxies, and the entire universe—all that can be differentiated from the earth (BDAG, 2000 §5437; Louw–Nida, 1989 §4710; Thayers, 1997 §3889). The term γῆ encapsulates all creation below, namely, the earth. This is the place that God created to be the dwelling for humans, as seen in Acts 17:26 (BDAG, 2000 §1642; Friberg, 2000 §5431; Louw–Nida, 1989 §1361).

The word combination οὐρανός καὶ γῆ shows equivalence to the universe and is reflective of ancient Hebrew semantics, which had no other word for universe—a concept yet to be discovered (Thayers, 1997 §3889). As discussed above, οὐρανός καὶ γῆ parallels κόσμος in meaning.

Semantic Study of "The God Who Made the Heaven and Earth"

κύριος

When used in a religious context, κύριος may be defined as the God who has authority over humanity, the God who rules the universe (BDAG, 2000 §4471; Louw–Nida, 1989 §3903; Thayers, 1997 §3138). In the Septuagint, κύριος is used to translate the divine Tetragrammaton, יְהוָה. (YHWH, i.e., Gen 2:8). It also is used to translate אָדוֹן ("God," i.e., Ps 114:7 [in the Masoretic text; Ps 113:7 in the Septuagint] and אֲדֹנִי "my Lord," i.e., Gen 15:2). "Lord" is the term employed to refer to the God of Israel (Holladay, 2000 §112; Kittel, 1963:1058; Spicq, 1994:347).

In the immediate context of Acts 17:24a, κύριος is a predicate nominative, an appositive, corresponding with the subject, οὗτος. The use of ὑπάρχων here may carry a more emphatic meaning than its synonym, εἰμί. BDAG allows for the possibility that in this passage, ὑπάρχω may be understood to convey the meaning "be inherently (so)" or "be really" (BDAG, 2000 §7525). In other words, the God who made the world *actually is* the Lord of heaven and earth. This use of ὑπάρχων heightens the connection between κύριος and θεός by revealing that the identity of the Maker of the world is one and the same as the Lord of heaven and earth.

The genitive forms οὐρανοῦ and γῆς indicate the magnitude of the dominion of κύριος. He is the One with jurisdiction over heaven and earth. κύριος may be defined as the Lord over all.

God, thus, is defined with two words in this passage: θεός and κύριος. Acts 17:24a begins with θεός and ends with κύριος. Together, the words form an inclusio. Thus, κύριος is a theologically equivalent term to θεός. All of the attributes of God as described above for θεός may also apply to κύριος. In the immediate context, then, both θεός and κύριος are used to refer to the God who both made and rules over the world—not to be confused with idols.

3.1.3.1.2 Acts 14:15

In Lystra, Paul proclaims the identity and nature of God to Gentiles against a backdrop of idolatry, in a similar manner as he does in Athens. The atmosphere, however, is different: Paul preaches to a people in pandemonium, who mistake Barnabas for Zeus and Paul for Hermes,[1] after a lame man

---

1. Conrad Gempf notes that other literary evidence for the association of Zeus with Hermes in this region includes Ovid's *Metamorphosis* VIII.624–724, in which Zeus and

God as Creator in Acts 17:24

walked for the first time in his life (Acts 14:8–14). The speech contrasts idols—"useless things"—to the "living God" in his opening statement (14:15a). The identification of the living God as the "living God who made the heaven and the earth and the sea and all that is in them" (θεὸν ζῶντα, ὃς ἐποίησεν τὸν οὐρανὸν καὶ τὴν γῆν καὶ τὴν θάλασσαν καὶ πάντα τὰ ἐν αὐτοῖς) (14:15b) is similar to his identification of God to philosophers on the Areopagus in Acts 17:24a, except for the additions of "living" (ζῶντα) and "and the sea" (καὶ τὴν θάλασσαν), and the absence of κόσμος. The polysyndeton (repetition of καὶ) of Acts 14:15 has the rhetorical effect of "extensiveness and abundance" (Spencer, 1998:204). Although Acts 17:24a lacks polysyndeton, the effect of extensiveness is achieved through bringing κόσμος in close proximity to its parallel concept, heaven and earth. In both speeches, God is Creator of all.

Rather than a discussion of where God lives (Acts 17:24b), as was a relevant point of discussion for philosophers (Creamer, 2011:50), the message in Lystra ensues with a statement of God allowing the nations to follow their own ways in times past (v. 16, cf. 17:30) and, then, discussion of the providence of God (14:17). The message in Acts 14 appears to be cut short by the response of the crowd (14:18; Polhill, 1992:316–317).

The similarities of audience and content of each speech in Lystra and Athens establish a pattern for cross-cultural communication in speeches to Gentiles in Acts: God is identified as Creator of all, in contrast to idols, as a foundation for the rest of the message in each location. The vastness of his creation is likewise emphasized in both Lystra and Athens. See 2.2.3 for further points of comparison between the two speeches.

3.1.3.1.3 Revelation 14:7

G.K. Beale points to scholarly consensus for a likely date of A.D. 95 for Revelation, which places the Apocalypse squarely within the framework of Domitian's reign. He does not, however, completely dismiss evidence in favor of a pre-A.D. 70 date, which would place the book within the

---

Hermes (with their Roman names Jupiter and Mercury) visit this region, seeking a place to rest (Gempf, 1995:62). Zeus may have had his temple outside the city to establish that he was the protector of Lystra (Bruce, 1990:322). Later archeological evidence (third century A.D.) includes inscriptions associating Zeus with Hermes in the Lystra valley (Free, 1992:271; Gempf, 1995:62; Holden & Geisler, 2013:362).

Semantic Study of "The God Who Made the Heaven and Earth"

framework of Nero's rule and subsequent persecution (Beale, 1999:4).[2] Although Acts was most likely written before Revelation (Bock, 2007:25–27; Schnabel, 2012:28), the material in Revelation 14:6–7 is still helpful to this study as it underlines further the concept of God as Creator in first-century Jewish thought.

Acts is not the only book in the New Testament that employs an identification of God as Creator in a presentation to Gentiles. In Revelation, an apocalyptic broadcast of God as Maker occurs in the setting of the proclamation of the gospel by an angel. The proclamation occurs in a vision:

> And I saw another angel flying in midheaven, with an eternal gospel to proclaim to those who reside on the earth, to every nation and tribe and language and people, saying in a loud voice, "Fear God and give him glory, for the hour of his judgment has come; and worship the one who made the heaven and the earth (τῷ ποιήσαντι τὸν οὐρανὸν καὶ τὴν γῆν), and sea (θάλασσαν) and springs of water." (Rev 14:6–7)

This apocalyptic scene follows the vision of the Lamb standing with the one hundred forty-four thousand in 14:1–5. The angel of 14:6–7 is the first of three to appear in sequence in chapter fourteen. The admonition to "Fear God and give him glory" is directed to the inhabitants of the earth from "every nation and tribe and language and people." This idea is repeated from Revelation 7:9, in which the great multitude that stands before the throne is composed of people "from all tribes and peoples and languages." The eternal gospel is for all peoples. The angel in Revelation 14:6–7 cites the impending judgment as reason to fear God.

The purpose of referring to God as Creator in Revelation 14:6–7 is evangelistic, as it is in Acts 14:15 and Acts 17:24a. Robert Mounce (1998:271) and G.K. Beale (1999:753) both note the parallel of Revelation 14:6–7 with Acts 14:15 but make no mention of Acts 17:24. Grant Osborne does include a citation of Acts 17:24–27 in his discussion of the passage as he notes the prevalence of creation theology in the book of Revelation as it relates to evangelistic proclamation to Gentiles in the early days of the church (Osborne, 2002:537). In his *Theology of the Book of Revelation*, Richard Bauckham explains that the doctrine of God as Creator was characteristic of both Judaism and early Christianity. He goes on to state, "Jewish monotheism in New Testament times was defined by the doctrine

---

2. Cf. Witulski (2007), who argues in his monograph for a date during the reign of Hadrian in the second century A.D.

God as Creator in Acts 17:24

of creation and by the practice of worship. The one Creator of all things is God and he alone may be worshipped" (Bauckham, 1993:47–48). We will continue to see supporting evidence for this statement as our study unfolds.

3.1.3.2 *Liturgical: Acts 4:24*

The identification of God as Creator forms the preface of the prayer in Acts 4:24: "Lord, you are the one who made the heaven and the earth (Δέσποτα, σὺ ὁ ποιήσας τὸν οὐρανὸν καὶ τὴν γῆν) and the sea and everything in them." The context is not one of Gentile idolatry but one of Jewish persecution. The community prays in response to the ban imposed on Peter and John from proclaiming the name of Jesus. The appeal to God's power in a prayer amidst a dire situation is also seen in Hezekiah's prayer in Isa 37:16 (see 3.1.4.2.4). The preface to God as Creator, then, is a statement about the power of God (Bock, 2007:204). In this prayer, the sovereign Lord who has power to create everything in existence is petitioned in an appeal for boldness in the face of adversity (4:29–30).

The similarity between Paul's statement in his Lystra speech (Acts 14:15b) and the words of the prayer in Acts 4:24 is striking (Witherington, 1998:201). Thirteen words appear in the exact same form and order in both texts: τὸν οὐρανὸν καὶ τὴν γῆν καὶ τὴν θάλασσαν καὶ πάντα τὰ ἐν αὐτοῖς. This connection may suggest that references to God as Creator were common in liturgical use by Jews in the first century A.D. In his commentary on the Greek text of Acts, F.F. Bruce states: "the disciples here follow a well-established liturgical form" (Bruce, 1990:156).

3.1.3.3 *Summary of New Testament passages*

Three of the New Testament passages discussed in this section demonstrate the use of the identification of God as Maker of the heaven and the earth in cross-cultural dialogue. The two instances in Acts (14:15 and 17:24) where Paul is shown to use similar phrases occur in the context of speeches to Gentiles where the nature of the gospel is being explained. The third instance, in Revelation 14:6–7, also demonstrates the identification of God as Maker in a cross-cultural setting of an apocalyptic variety: an angel of heaven proclaims the message of salvation to Gentiles on earth. This establishes a common pattern for proclamation to Gentiles in New Testament texts. The fourth instance, in Acts 4:24, further demonstrates the common phrasing of God as Maker in the time of the New Testament, this time in the context of a prayer.

3.1.4 "The God who made the heaven and the earth" in the Septuagint

References to God as Creator in the Septuagint are abundant. In this section, we survey passages from the Pentateuch, Historical Books, Prophets, and Poetic literature (Psalms). The core material is derived from Genesis 1:1. Passages from each literary type reflect the language and theology of Genesis 1, in a variety of settings. Passages will be grouped according to literary type.[3]

3.1.4.1 Core Material: Genesis 1:1

The essence of this phrase study is the language of the Septuagint reading of the first line of Genesis: "In the beginning God made the heaven and the earth" (ἐν ἀρχῇ ἐποίησεν ὁ θεὸς τὸν οὐρανὸν καὶ τὴν γῆν) (Gen 1:1). The concept of God as Creator is repeated time and again throughout the corpus of the Old and New Testaments, as well as in other Jewish writings. This concept is foundational to the presentation of who God is in Genesis.

In Genesis 1:1, God (θεός) is the initiator, architect, and executor of all creation. The verb ποιέω describes the action of God's work in creation: his design and production of the world. Septuagint scholar Susan Brayford explains that κτίζω is the usual Greek word used to translate ברא from the Masoretic Text. The reason for this variation is, she states, "unclear" (Brayford, 2007:206).

The events of creation all occurred in a specific, past point in time. The opening words, ἐν ἀρχῇ, as well as the aorist form, ἐποίησεν, establish referents for the time in which God created the heaven and the earth. The heaven, οὐρανός, consists of the expanse above the earth (1:8). This expanse, or sky, includes the distant location of the sun and the moon (1:14). It also includes the atmosphere of the earth, as the nearby location of flying creatures and birds (1:20, 26, 28, 30). The earth, γῆ, refers to the entire planet (1:2). The earth is the dwelling place for both people (1:28) and animals (1:22, 25). The earth, γῆ, refers to a singular entity. The heaven,

---

3. Texts cited are from the Old Greek version, as presented in Rahlfs–Hanhart's *Septuaginta, Editio altera* (2006). This edition of the Septuagint primarily draws from Codex Siniaticus, Codex Vaticanus, and Codex Alexandrinus (Rahlfs & Hanhart, 2006:XXXIV).

οὐρανός, refers to the location for flying creatures as well as celestial bodies. Together, οὐρανός and γῆ make up the total extent of God's creation. The "heaven and earth" in the Masoretic Text represents the "organized universe" (Wenham, 1987:15; Waltke, 2001:59). God is the Creator of all.

This initial statement of Genesis 1:1 provides an introductory summary for the passage. The six days of creation are then detailed in the first two chapters of Genesis. Another summary statement is made after the account of the six days of creation that repeats the "heaven and earth" phrase: "And the heaven and the earth were finished, and all their orderly arrangement (καὶ συνετελέσθησαν ὁ οὐρανὸς καὶ ἡ γῆ καὶ πᾶς ὁ κόσμος αὐτῶν)" (Gen 2:1). κόσμος, here, refers to all that heaven and earth encompasses. κόσμος is the word given as translation of צָבָא "host" (Brown, Driver & Briggs, 1997:7982). In Genesis 2:1, κόσμος refers to all the contents of the universe that God created: sun, moon, stars, planets, and galaxies. The summary statement in Genesis 2:1 forms the latter part of an inclusio with Genesis 1:1. Thus, the author establishes the six days of creation as a unit before narrating the seventh day, the history of the sabbath, in 2:2–3.

The motif of God as Creator of heaven and earth makes an immediate reprise in Genesis 2:4: "This is the book of the origin of heaven and earth, when it originated, on the day that God made the heaven and the earth (αὕτη ἡ βίβλος γενέσεως οὐρανοῦ καὶ γῆς ὅτε ἐγένετο ᾗ ἡμέρᾳ ἐποίησεν ὁ θεὸς τὸν οὐρανὸν καὶ τὴν γῆν)." This verse leads into the next section, an amplification of day six, the creation of Adam and Eve. Genesis 2:4 is foundational for the section 2:4–25 in a similar way as Genesis 1:1 is foundational for the section 1:1–2:3 (Wenham, 1987:55).

The vocabulary of Genesis 1:1 is saturated with key words also found in Acts 17:24a, words that are repeated again and again throughout the creation accounts in chapters one and two. These key words include οὐρανός, γῆ, ποιέω, and θεός. In Genesis chapters one and two alone, forms of οὐρανός are found 16 times. Forms of γῆ appear 38 times. Ποιέω appears in various forms 17 times. θεός occurs, remarkably, 47 times within the first two chapters of Genesis. We may note that these four words are also key words in Acts 17:24, and establish a clear link between the two texts. Acts 17:24a does not stand alone in alluding to Genesis 1:1. The common vocabulary between Genesis 1:1 and all texts in this study establishes that the core material originates from Genesis.

Genesis, the book of beginnings, does not begin with the formation of the nation of Israel, as one might normally expect from a history book.

Semantic Study of "The God Who Made the Heaven and Earth"

This material narrating the beginnings of Israel as a nation begins only in chapter twelve, with Abraham as the patriarch of the nation. Instead, Genesis reaches further back in time—all the way back to the creation of the world and the creation of humankind. Before the formation of Israel, God formed the nations. Before the formation of the nations, God formed the heaven and the earth.

What purpose might the author of Genesis have had in beginning the narrative with a teaching about who created the heaven and the earth? The simple answer is that the Israelites who came out of Egypt needed to know who their God is. Their God is the God who made the heaven and the earth. Creation theology is foundational for their understanding.

Kenneth Mathews discusses the matter of "parallelomania" in biblical studies, based on Samuel Sandmel's address to the annual meeting of the Society of Biblical Literature in 1961, in which he gave warnings pertaining to the use and abuse of literary parallels in the interpretation of the text. Mathews argues that the consideration of ancient Near Eastern literature is both justifiable and helpful for the study of Genesis, particularly for discovering the "general ideological climate in which the biblical materials are found" (Mathews, 1996:87). Egyptian creation texts support polytheism, as does the Babylonian creation myth *Enuma Elish* (Mathews, 1996:90–94). The Israelites who were delivered from Egypt needed to be re-educated.

Severian of Gabala, bishop of Syria and preacher in the court of Constantinople in the fifth century A.D., maintained that Moses wrote his account of creation in order to bring correction to Egyptian influences on the Israelites. In his *Homilies on Creation and Fall*, Severian states:

> Why did blessed Moses mention heaven, earth, sea, waters and what came from them but not mention angel and archangels, seraphim and cherubim? Because he was also adapting the lawgiving to his own times, aware as he was that the people he was speaking to had come out of Egypt after learning the error of the Egyptians, sun and moon and stars, rivers and springs and waters. So he omitted the creation of invisible things and confined his treatment to visible things so as to persuade people adoring those things to think of them not as gods but as works of God ... Moses also wanted to drive out of the Jews the Egyptian error, so he made mention of heaven and earth as things that were created. (Glerup, 2010:24–25)

Recent commentators on Genesis also affirm that Genesis 1 is corrective. The text focuses on the sovereignty of God in creation "so as to discount pagan cosmogonies as a valid way of understanding the world's origin" (Hartley, 2000:42). The book of Genesis rejects pagan ideas by establishing monotheism. Egyptians worshiped the sun, moon, and stars but Genesis shows that the sun, moon, and stars are the material product of God's creative power and, hence, are not deities (Wenham, 1987:9). Genesis undermines the ideologies of pagan cosmology through inference rather than by a point-by-point polemic (Mathews, 1996:89). Genesis rejects rival creation myths and hence, also rejects polytheism.

From the exodus to the exile, Israel consistently demonstrated symptoms of spiritual confusion that manifested in idolatry. Despite witnessing the ten plagues, the miraculous deliverance from oppression in Egypt, the pillar of fire, the supernatural appearance of manna and water in the wilderness, the shaking of Mount Sinai and the blast of the trumpet, they still succumbed to idol worship. The golden calf debacle of Exodus 32 demonstrates the propensity of the Israelites to accommodate to the surrounding culture of idolatry even in their early history as a nation. Unfortunately, the nation continued to find idolatry impossible to resist throughout their history. Despite the repeated warnings of the prophets, Israel fails to worship the Lord exclusively as one God. Idolatry is the besetting sin for which the northern kingdom is lost to Assyria (2 Ki 17:5–7). Idolatry is also the besetting sin for which Jerusalem is lost to Babylon in 586 B.C. (Jer 1:15–16).

With the force of idolatry being as strong as it was in the ancient world, the author of Genesis establishes from the outset that the God of Israel is the God who created the world as a teaching to help guard against spiritual confusion. The purpose is instructive. Creation theology in Genesis, then, provides the most basic foundation for the knowledge of God for a people who had stepped out of Egypt, a nation steeped in idolatry.

Acts 17:24a, then, is not only similar to Genesis 1:1 in vocabulary, but also with respect to the context of knowing God in the midst of an idolatrous culture. As the author of Genesis uses creation theology as a foundation for the rest of his instruction, so Luke records Paul as using creation theology as a foundation for the rest of his speech in Athens.

3.1.4.2 Liturgical

In the previous section, God is identified as Creator of the heaven and the earth in the core material of Genesis. The context in that literary type is within introductory teachings about God to Israelites. In this section, we

Semantic Study of "The God Who Made the Heaven and Earth"

will examine liturgical references to God as maker of heaven and earth in blessings, in worship, and in prayer. References to the God of heaven and earth have been made in the context of worship from the time that Abram was blessed by King Melchizedek of Salem (Gen 14:19) through the time of the New Testament.

3.1.4.2.1 Genesis 14:19

The earliest mention of God as Creator of heaven and earth uttered specifically in a blessing in the Hebrew Bible occurs in Genesis 14:19. When King Melchizedek of Salem meets Abram after the defeat of King Chedorloamer and his allied forces, he brings out bread and wine, and blesses Abram: "And he blessed Abram and said, 'Blessed be Abram by the Most High God (τῷ θεῷ τῷ ὑψίστῳ), who created the heaven and the earth' (ὃς ἔκτισεν τὸν οὐρανὸν καὶ τὴν γῆν)." God is identified as the "most high." "Who made heaven and earth" is appositional. The use of the adjective ὕψιστος with reference to God shows that he is of the highest status, as "distinguished from lesser dieties and other objects of cultic devotion" (BDAG, 2000 §7671). In this way, the "God who made heaven and earth" may be known as the Most High God who is described as superior to every idol and every false god, as far back as the book of Genesis.

3.1.4.2.2 Psalm 113:23; Psalm 133:3

The liturgical practice of referring to God as Creator in a blessing also occurs in the psalms. Psalm 113:23 states: "Blessed be you by the Lord who made the heaven and the earth (τῷ κυρίῳ τῷ ποιήσαντι τὸν οὐρανὸν καὶ τὴν γῆν)." This is the second part of a general blessing. In this psalm, the Lord (κύριος) is mindful of his people (v. 20) and will give blessing to those who fear him (vv. 20–22). The Lord (κύριος) is the one who made heaven and earth (v. 23). The heavens (οὐρανός) are the dwelling place of God (θεός) (v. 11). Verse 24 gives further information about the heavens and the earth: "The heaven of the heavens are the Lord's (ὁ οὐρανὸς τοῦ οὐρανοῦ τῷ κυρίῳ) but the earth he gave to the sons of humanity (τὴν δὲ γῆν ἔδωκεν τοῖς υἱοῖς τῶν ἀνθρώπων)." Heaven (οὐρανός), then, is not only a place created by God (Gen 1), but also it is the place where God dwells. Earth (γῆ) is the place given to human beings by God (v. 24).

God as Creator in Acts 17:24

It is significant that the earlier part of this psalm contrasts the God of the heavens with idols: "But our God is in the heaven (ἐν τῷ οὐρανῷ) above, in the heavens (ἐν τοῖς οὐρανοῖς) and on the earth (ἐν τῇ γῇ); whatever he wanted he did. The idols of the Gentiles are silver and gold, works of human hands" (Ps 113:11-12). The description of idols as nothing more than inanimate objects continues in vv. 13-15. The power of God to create and maintain the world stands in stark opposition to the theme of the impotence of idols throughout this psalm. Athanasius quotes Deuteronomy 4:19 with reference to the creation and the Creator:

> "And do not, when you look up with your eyes and see the sun and moon and all the host of heaven, go astray and worship them, which the Lord your God has given to all nations under heaven." But he gave them, not to be their gods but that by their agency the Gentiles should know, as we have said, God the Maker of them all. (Wesselschmidt, 2007:282)

The reference to God as Maker in verse 23 is significant for drawing attention to the power behind the blessing.

The contrast between idols and the Creator God in Psalm 113 is similar in concept to the discussion of the nature of the true God over and against that of idols in his Areopagus speech.

A blessing similar to Psalm 113:23 is found in Psalm 133:3: "May the Lord, who made the heaven and the earth (ὁ ποιήσας τὸν οὐρανὸν καὶ τὴν γῆν), bless you from Zion." The psalmists continue a tradition started by Melchizedek when he blessed Abram.

3.1.4.2.3 1 Chronicles 16:26

1 Chronicles 16 narrates the events that surround the momentous occasion of worship when David brings the ark into the tent that he had set up in Jerusalem. David appoints the Levites as ministers before the ark of the covenant and establishes the priests as ministers of music (1 Chr 16:4-6). David also appoints Asaph to "the singing of praises to the Lord" (v. 7). What follows in 1 Chronicles 16:8-36 is an extended passage of praises from the psalms that were sung on that occasion.

1 Chronicles 16:23-33 quotes most of the text of Psalm 95 (96 [Braun, 1986:193]). This psalm declares that the Lord is to be praised among all nations. He is the Creator and king over all the nations and should "be praised

Semantic Study of "The God Who Made the Heaven and Earth"

by the entire range of his lordship and possessions" (Kraus, 1993:252). This psalm is a missionary psalm (Kaiser, 2012:34).

The opening statement of Psalm 95 (96) is an exhortation to all the earth to sing to the Lord (Ps 95:1; 1 Chr 16:23). Israel is called to be a witness to the Lord in the midst of the Gentiles: "Proclaim his glory among the Gentiles (ἐν τοῖς ἔθνεσιν), his wonders among all the peoples" (Ps 95:3).[4] The reason for worshiping the Lord is given in verses 4 and 5. Verse 4 cites the greatness of the Lord. Verse 5 gives further information. God is great because he made the heaven. This verse contrasts idols with God as Creator: "For all the gods of the Gentiles are demons (ὅτι πάντες οἱ θεοὶ τῶν ἐθνῶν δαιμόνια), but the Lord made the heavens (ὁ δὲ κύριος τοὺς οὐρανοὺς ἐποίησεν)" (Ps 95:5). The Septuagint reading of 1 Chronicles 16:26 has a slightly different rendering: "for all the gods of the Gentiles are idols (ὅτι πάντες οἱ θεοὶ τῶν ἐθνῶν εἴδωλα), but our God made heaven[5] (καὶ ὁ θεὸς ἡμῶν οὐρανὸν ἐποίησεν)."[6]

This passage makes a direct contrast between the gods of the Gentiles and the Creator God. 1 Chronicles 16:24 gives a directive for Israelites to proclaim the glory of the Lord among the Gentiles. The Creator God is the one who should be declared to idol-worshiping Gentiles (1 Chr 16:26). The use of these texts establishes a charge for Gentile mission in the days of David's reign. Paul, in Acts, may be seen as fulfilling the charge from 1 Chronicles 16:24-26 and Psalm 95:3-5 in the approach that he takes among Gentiles in Athens. The foundation of the speaker's argument against idolatry is built on the foundation of God as Creator.

---

4. 1 Chronicles 16:24 appears in the Masoretic text but is omitted in the Septuagint.

5. Cf. *New English Translation of the Septuagint (NETS)* translates 1 Chron 16:26b as "but our God made the sky." NETS makes liberal use of the translation of "sky" for οὐρανός in the books of 1 and 2 Chronicles. Of the 52 occurances of οὐρανός in these two books, the translation uses "sky" 46 times and "heaven" 6 times. Other books also reflect an interchangeablity of "heaven" and "sky" as translation options (e.g., Isa 37:16 and Neh 9:6 use "heaven" but Jer 39:17 and Ps 113:24 use "sky." The reasoning behind the choice of one option over the other in any given context is unclear except, perhaps, that the translators regarded them as interchangeable words. Septuagint commentator Sara Japhet translates οὐρανός as "heaven" in 1 Chron 16:26 (1993:321), as does Brenton (1851). I have chosen to translate οὐρανός as "heaven" in order to remain consistent with the translation of the core material from Genesis 1:1.

6. Other passages from psalms that refer to the Lord as Maker of heaven and earth include Psalms 120:2 (121:2), 123:8 (124:8), and 145:5-6 (146:5-6).

God as Creator in Acts 17:24

3.1.4.2.4 2 CHRONICLES 6:14

References to the Lord of heaven and earth figure prominently in several public prayers by Jews in ancient times. As in Acts 4:24, the reference occurs in the opening address to the Lord for each prayer.

Just as there is mention of the God of heaven in an anti-idolatry context during the worship service of David's dedication of the ark when brought into the tent he had made, Solomon makes mention of the supreme God, in an anti-idolatry context, during the inaugural prayer of the dedication of the temple. Solomon kneels in the presence of the whole assembly, stretches his hands toward heaven, and begins his prayer: "Lord, God of Israel, there is no god like you in heaven and on the earth (οὐκ ἔστιν ὅμοιός σοι θεὸς ἐν οὐρανῷ καὶ ἐπὶ τῆς γῆς), keeping the covenant and mercy toward your servants who walk before you with their whole heart" (2 Chr 6:14).

Solomon includes several further mentions of heaven in his prayer. In verse 18 he exclaims, "If heaven and the heaven of heavens will not be sufficient for you, how will this house, which I have built!" This exclamation makes a foundational theological statement about the location of the presence of God, which further underlines the incomparability of the Lord with idols.

Heaven is the dwelling place of the Lord. It is also the place from where God may hear the prayers of his people (2 Chr 6:21). Solomon punctuates his prayer eight times with repeated variations of the phrase "may you hear from heaven" (vv. 21, 23, 25, 27, 30, 33, 35, 39). Not only does he petition the Lord on behalf of the Israelites, but also for foreigners who might call on his name: "in order that all the peoples of the earth may know your name and fear you, as do your people Israel" (2 Chr 6:33). This God, who is like no other in heaven or on earth, is a global God. Hence, Solomon is mindful of both Israelites and foreigners in his prayer.

Several commentators have downplayed the importance of this prayer for the foreigner in 2 Chronicles 6:32–33. J. Thompson remarks, perhaps with intentional understatement, "there is a fine spirit of tolerance toward the foreigner" (Thompson, 1994:230). Sara Japhet states, "this section has the nature of an afterthought" (Japhet, 1993:597). The thread of Scripture, however, from the Abrahamic covenant to the prophets, details the importance of the call of Israel to be a light to the Gentiles (Kaiser, 2012:xi). Israel was called to more than mere tolerance of the foreigner. Like his father, David, Solomon has concern for mission to the Gentiles. It is significant

Semantic Study of "The God Who Made the Heaven and Earth"

that he includes them in his prayer of dedication. God is to be known by Jews and Gentiles alike.

Although Solomon's prayer does not make mention of idols, the theology of the presence of God emerges in a similar manner as Paul's oratory on the Areopagus. Solomon begins his prayer with a proclamation of who God is (2 Chr 6:14) and continues, a few verses later, with a statement in the negative regarding where God lives (v. 18): the house that he built cannot contain him. Likewise, the Areopagus speech begins with a proclamation of who God is (Acts 17:24a) and continues with a statement in the negative regarding where God lives. The presence of God cannot be contained within a structure made by hands (v. 24b).

3.1.4.2.5 ISAIAH 37:16

Other Old Testament prayers that share an anti-idolatry context include those of Hezekiah and Ezra. Hezekiah petitions the Lord for help during a time of national crisis (Smith, 2007:616). The book of Isaiah recounts how the Assyrians deliver a message instructing Hezekiah not to trust in the Lord to deliver the city against their assault. The stated reason is the inability of the gods of conquered nations to defend them from Assyrian conquest: "Have the gods of the nations delivered them whom my fathers destroyed, Gozan and Haran and Raphes, which are in the country of Thelsad?" (Isa 37:12). After receiving this letter, Hezekiah responds by spreading it before the Lord. He, too, begins his prayer with an appeal to the God who alone "made the heaven and the earth (ἐποίησας τὸν οὐρανὸν καὶ τὴν γῆν)" (Isa 37:16). His prayer has a notable anti-idolatry tone (Smith, 2007:619). He states that the gods of the defeated nations "were no gods, but the works of human hands" (v. 19). Hezekiah concludes his prayer with a request that God would save Jerusalem from the hand of Sennacherib "so that every kingdom of the earth may know that you alone are God" (v. 20), showing a commendable interest in the Gentile mission—despite the escalating tension of a national crisis. The Lord delivers Jerusalem in a supernatural manner by sending the angel of the Lord to strike down one hundred eighty-five thousand Assyrians outside the city (v. 36). Although Sennacherib survives to return to his home in Nineveh, his sons "struck him with swords" while he was worshiping his god, Nasarach (v. 38). Hezekiah's prayer and the historical events that immediately follow serve to highlight the futility of idolatry. Idols deliver neither the conquered nations nor the conquerer in the events of 701 B.C. but the living God hears Hezekiah's prayer and rescues Jerusalem.

3.1.4.2.5 NEHEMIAH 9:6

Ezra builds his prayer of rededication of the people to the Lord on the identification of God as Creator: "You yourself are the Lord alone (σὺ εἶ αὐτὸς κύριος μόνος), you made heaven (σὺ ἐποίησας τὸν οὐρανὸν), the heaven of heaven, and all their existence, the earth (γῆν) and everything that is in it, the seas and everything that is in them, and you give everything life" (Neh 9:6). Like Solomon's prayer, this is spoken at a public assembly during a significant time in the history of Israel. Although the Israelites had been restored to Jerusalem and also had the temple restored to them in this time after returning from exile, they still needed spiritual restoration. So, Ezra prays this prayer of national repentance. The statement that the Lord alone made the heaven also places this passage in a context that contrasts the Lord with other gods.

3.1.4.3 Oath

In the previous section, we surveyed several passages from the Septuagint in which Israelites give a blessing, worship the Lord, or pray a prayer, using language that comports with the vocabulary of Genesis 1–2. In this section, we will continue to overview similar phrases, this time, as they occur as part of an oath.

3.1.4.3.1 GENESIS 14:22

Abram names the God who made the heaven and the earth when he proclaims an oath to the King of Sodom after vanquishing four enemy kings (Gen 14:1–24). He rescues his nephew, Lot, as well as the people and goods of Sodom. The king of Sodom offers the booty of war to Abram (v. 21), an offer that Abram declines. In verses 22 and 23, Abram swears to the king of Sodom: "I will extend my hand to the Most High God (τὸν θεὸν τὸν ὕψιστον), who created the heaven and earth (ὃς ἔκτισεν τὸν οὐρανὸν καὶ τὴν γῆν), I will not take [anything], from a small cord to a sandal strap from all that is yours, so that you may not say 'I made Abram rich.'" Thus, Abram invokes the God who made the heaven and the earth as his divine witness, thereby guaranteeing his word (Brayford, 2007:296–297). The phrase ὃς ἔκτισεν τὸν οὐρανὸν καὶ τὴν γῆν in verse 22 is syntactically identical to the blessing he just received from Melchizedek, high priest of Salem in verse 19 (see section 3.1.4.2.1).

3.1.4.3.2 Genesis 24:3

When the time comes for Abraham to find a suitable wife for his son, Isaac, the matter of marriage within his tribe is of such importance that he requires his servant to invoke the name of the God of heaven and earth in an oath in Genesis 24:3: "and I will make you swear by the Lord, the God of heaven and the God of earth (κύριον τὸν θεὸν τοῦ οὐρανοῦ καὶ τὸν θεὸν τῆς γῆς), that you will not get a wife for my son Isaac from the daughters of the Canaanites, among whom I live, but go into my land, where I was born, and to my tribe, and get a wife for my son Isaac from that place." The semantic context is very similar to the oath he made with the king of Sodom in Genesis 14. The phrase κύριον τὸν θεὸν τοῦ οὐρανοῦ καὶ τὸν θεὸν τῆς γῆς (Gen 24:3) identifies the same God as Genesis 14:22, the God of heaven and earth, as divine witness to the oath. The vocabulary of heaven and earth as witnesses in the legal context of a covenant or treaty is also found in Deuteronomy 30:19 as well as in documents from other ancient Near Eastern civilizations (Wenham, 1994:141). The identification of God as Lord of heaven and earth in the context of an oath is more than a general reference to God. It specifies him as a God of cosmic power, the enforcer of a solemn promise between two parties (Matthews, 2005: 326).

3.1.4.4 *In a Prophetic Oracle*

In this literary type, a reference to God as Creator may be included in either the preface or the body of a prophetic oracle. Isaiah prefaces three oracles in this manner: 42:5, 44:24, and 45:18. Isaiah 45 continues to use the creation motif as a central argument against idolatry in the body of the oracle. Jeremiah 10, likewise, uses the creation motif as a prime argument against idolatry.

God as Creator in Acts 17:24

3.1.4.4.1 Isaiah 42:5

The first oracle in which Isaiah prefaces his message with a reference to God as the maker of heaven and earth begins in Isaiah 42:5: "Thus says the Lord God (οὕτως λέγει κύριος ὁ θεὸς), who made the heaven and fixed it in place (ὁ ποιήσας τὸν οὐρανὸν καὶ πήξας αὐτόν), who made firm the earth and the things in it (ὁ στερεώσας τὴν γῆν καὶ τὰ ἐν αὐτῇ) and gives breath to the people on it and spirit to those who walk on it." It may be that Isaiah identifies God as Creator immediately after the prophetic formula, "Thus says the Lord God," as a means of establishing authority. The same Lord God that created the heaven and the earth now speaks through Isaiah. The hearer should listen attentively to what follows because the God who has the power to create the heaven and the earth also has the power to bring the prophecy to fruition (Smith, 2009:165). The oracle proclaims, "And I will take your hand and strengthen you and give you as a covenant to the people, a light to Gentiles to open blind eyes, to lead out from bonds those who have been bound, and out of the prison house those who sit in darkness" (Isa 42:6-7). Acts 13:47 quotes a version of this text that is more similar to the Masoretic Text than to the Septuagint, as a key argument for the Gentile mission (Beale & Carson, 2007:588). The oracle continues with an assertion that the Lord God has nothing at all to do with idols: "I am the Lord God; this is my name; my glory I will not give to another, nor my excellences to the carved images" (Isa 42:8).

3.1.4.4.2 Isaiah 44:24

Isaiah begins a second oracle with reference to God as Creator in Isaiah 44:24. He stands alone is this act of his creative power: "Thus says the Lord, who redeems you, who forms you from the womb: I am the Lord (κύριος), who accomplishes all things; I alone stretched out the heaven (ἐξέτεινα τὸν οὐρανὸν μόνος), and I made firm the earth (καὶ ἐστερέωσα τὴν γῆν)." The mention of the creative power of God in this passage, as in many of the previous passages in this study, strikes against idolatry. In the words of Gary Smith, "such a statement undermines the mythology of all other religious systems because it claims creative power for Israel's God over everything that exists. There are no exceptions" (Smith, 2009:246-247). This restoration oracle is significant for its assertion that the Lord will speak to Cyrus, a Gentile, to "bring about all my will," and that the temple will be rebuilt in Jerusalem (Isa 44:28; Smith, 2009:252).[7]

3.1.4.4.3 ISAIAH 45:18

The third oracle in which Isaiah refers to the Lord as Creator in the preface begins in Isaiah 45:18. In verse 18, the identification of the God as Creator appears in apposition to the introductory prophetic formula: "Thus says the Lord, who made the heaven (οὕτως λέγει κύριος ὁ ποιήσας τὸν οὐρανόν), this is the God who displayed the earth and made it; he himself set limits to it; he did not make it to be empty but to be inhabited. I am, and there is no other" (Isa 45:18). The assertion that "there is no other" at the end of the verse establishes that the God who created the heaven and the earth is the only real God in the midst of a culture of idols. Isaiah 45:18–25 picks up themes from the previous passage: God is the Creator (45:12); idolatry is useless (45:16); and salvation is from the Lord (45:17). The previous passage concludes in 45:17 with God as the means of salvation for Israel. The reiteration of these themes in 45:18–25 come in the same order: God is Creator (45:18); the futility of idols (45:20–21); and salvation (45:22–23). The difference is that in 45:18–25, God is presented as the savior of all the nations—not just of Israel. The passage, then, has a broad audience: it is intended for all nations. The same God who offers salvation for Israel also offers salvation for Gentiles.

This oracle includes two specific references to Gentiles. The Lord summons the Gentiles to make their case in verse 20: "Gather together; come, take counsel together, you who are being saved from among the nations!" God then calls them to a response in verse 22: "Turn to me, and you will be saved, those from the end of the earth! (οἱ ἀπ' ἐσχάτου τῆς γῆς) I am God (θεός) and there is no other." John Watts takes a divergent view. He maintains that in these verses it is Cyrus—not God—who offers salvation to the nations (Watts, 2005:707). There are no grounds for this view. The immediate context must be considered. The last reference to Cyrus appeared in Isaiah 45:13. The antecedent subject of the surrounding verses in Isaiah 45:18–25 is the Lord—not Cyrus. Watts has extended the prophecy about Cyrus beyond its limit. Gary Smith agrees, and calls Watts's view "baffling" (Smith, 2009:274).

The statement that there is "no other" God appears three times: in the introductory verse, "I am, and there is no other (ἐγώ εἰμι καὶ οὐκ ἔστιν

---

7. See Ezra 1:1–4; 2 Chronicles 36:22–23.

God as Creator in Acts 17:24

ἔτι)" (v. 18); in verse 21, "I am God, and there is no other besides me (ἐγὼ ὁ θεός καὶ οὐκ ἔστιν ἄλλος πλὴν ἐμοῦ)"; and in verse 22, which has "I am God and there is no other (ἐγώ εἰμι ὁ θεός καὶ οὐκ ἔστιν ἄλλος)." Not only does verse 22 issue the third declaration that there is no other God, but it also sums up the message of the entire passage found in Isaiah 45:18-25: God calls Gentiles from the end of the earth to come to him for salvation. Thus, the prophet issues a call for Gentiles to repent. We may conclude that this oracle is evangelistic in nature (Smith, 2009:274, 279). This evangelistic context to Gentiles in Isaiah 45:18 is similar to the evangelistic context to Gentiles in Acts 17:24.

The first of the Ten Commandments identifies God as the one who delivered the people from Egypt as the basis for which the Israelites should know him, before prohibiting the worship of other gods (Exod 20:2-3; Deut 5:6-7). Isaiah roundly condemns idolatry in 45:18-25, but makes no reference to God as the deliverer from Egypt for the Gentile hearer. Instead, the identification of God as Creator of the heavens and the earth forms the basis of his case against idolatry (v. 18).[8] A reference to the exodus would not resound with the hearts of Gentile audiences since it was not part of their history, but the manifestation of God's works of creation are visible to all. Paul's approach in Athens (as well as in Lystra, cf. Antioch—see 2.2.3) demonstrates the same referent of creation for a similar audience: Gentiles.

3.1.4.4.4 JEREMIAH 10:11-12

Jeremiah speaks to the nation of Israel, a nation on the brink of judgment. This judgment is recompense for Israel's moral turpitude, which included many generations of idol worship (Jer 9:11-15 [12-16]). The oracle he proclaims in 10:1-16 is one of many pronouncements of judgment in the book. In this passage, Jeremiah denounces and proclaims judgment on idol worship. The message begins with an injunction for the house of Israel not to learn idol worship from Gentile nations: "Do not learn according to the ways of the Gentiles" (v. 2). The verses that follow describe the process of making idols and issue a command not to revere them: "Do not fear them, for they cannot do evil and there is no good in them" (Jer 10:5).[9]

---

8. See also Romans 1:18-23.

9. Verses 6-8 and 10 from the Masoretic Text are omitted in the Septuagint. Verse 9 from the Masoretic Text is embedded in verse 5 of the Septuagint.

Semantic Study of "The God Who Made the Heaven and Earth"

The first two verses of the second part of the oracle (vv. 11–16) warrant particular attention for this study. This stanza draws the contrast between the true God and idols into sharp focus by condemning the gods that did *not* create heaven and earth:

> Thus you will say to them: Let gods which did not make the heaven and the earth (τὸν οὐρανὸν καὶ τὴν γῆν οὐκ ἐποίησαν) perish from the earth and from below this heaven. It is the Lord who made the earth (κύριος ὁ ποιήσας τὴν γῆν) by his strength, who set upright the inhabited earth by his wisdom, and by his understanding he stretched out the heaven. (Jer 10:11–12)

Thus, the prophet uses the ability to create the heaven and the earth as key differential between the living God and useless idols. Not only does this passage provide a key differential, but it also provides a key identification. The identification of false gods as "gods which did not make the heaven and the earth" (v. 11) is antithetical to the identity of the Lord as the one who "made the earth" (v. 12). Only the Lord has the power to create the heaven and the earth.

Verse 11 appears in Aramaic, rather than Hebrew, in the Masoretic Text. This abrupt change of language for a single verse has led some to question the integrity of the text (Craigie, Kelley, & Drinkard, 1991:160). Garrett Reid argues that Jeremiah 10:11 is a genuine part of the Masoretic Text, against those who surmise that the use of Aramaic indicates an interpolation or gloss. He proposes that structural evidence boosts the authenticity of the text: the verse sits in the apex of a chiastic parallelism (Reid, 2006:229). The translation of Jeremiah 10:11 into Greek and its inclusion in the Septuagint also may attest to its genuineness. But this still does not answer the question, why does it appear in Aramaic in the Masoretic Text? F.B. Huey suggests that it may have been a proverb in circulation in Jeremiah's time, and that he may have retained the Aramaic for emphasis (Huey, 1993:127). If a proverb, then the concept that false gods "did not make the heaven and the earth" would have been a well-known idea among the Israelites. Craigie, Kelley, and Drinkard affirm that the presence of Aramaic in this verse "confirms that the passage was addressed to the exiles, for Aramaic was the language of the land where they were exiled" (Cragie, Kelley, & Drinkard, 1991:160).

The *Targum of Jeremiah* surrounds Jeremiah 10:11 with additional text to suggest that this verse originally may have been part of a letter sent to the exiles by Jeremiah (Craigie, Kelley, & Drinkard, 1991:160; McKane, 1986:225; Reid, 2006:233):

> *This is a copy of the letter which Jeremiah the prophet sent to the remnant of the elders of the Exile who were in Babylon. "If the nations among whom you are should say to you, Worship the idols, O house of Israel: thus you shall answer and thus shall you say to them: 'The idols which you worship are idols in which there is no profit. They cannot bring down rain from heaven, and they cannot make fruits sprout forth from the earth. They and those who worship them shall perish from the earth, and shall be destroyed from under these heavens.'"* (Hayward, 1987:79)

In this Targum, Jeremiah 10:11 comprises the content of what the Israelites were instructed to say to their Babylonian captors. It is an anti-idolatry polemic.

Whether verse 11 was originally part of a letter to the exiles, as the Targum suggests, or a proverb, as Huey suggests, or both, the presence of Aramaic in the Masoretic Text suggests that Jeremiah intended this anti-idolatry message to extend further than his Israelite audience. In the words of Reid, "it is a capsule worldview polemic for the people of God living in a pagan culture" (Reid, 2006:232). A polemic against the idolatry of the nations is given to Israel in the lingua franca of the nations so that they may proclaim it cross-culturally (Reid, 2006:237–238).

3.1.4.5 Cross-cultural communication

In this section, we survey several passages of direct discourse in which God is identified either as Creator or as the Lord/God of heaven in a cross-cultural setting. Rahab and King Huram of Tyre are the earliest historical examples of Gentiles referring to the God of Israel with language similar to Genesis 1:1. Next, Jonah identifies the God he worships as the Lord God of heaven and as the Creator God in his conversation with Gentile sailors. In a similar way, Daniel and his compatriots identify their God as the Lord/God of heaven. This identification of the God of Israel is ultimately heard from several powerful Gentile kings: Nebuchadnezzar, Cyrus, and Darius—whether from their lips or from their pen.

3.1.4.5.1 JOSHUA 2:11

Rahab exhibits great faith in her act of saving the lives of the spies sent by Joshua. This demonstration of faith is followed by a confession of faith, embedded in a request that her life be spared. The knowledge of the works of the Lord preceded the arrival of the spies, and brought both fear and faith to Rahab. Her people had heard that the Lord had made the Red Sea dry in order for the Israelites to come out of Egypt. They had also heard of the victory over the kings of Sidon and Og. The imagery Rahab uses to describe the reaction to the report, "our hearts melted" (v. 11a, MT), shows that she acknowledges the power of the Lord to enable the Israelites to overtake her people, as well. The statement that she makes to the two spies is of particular interest to this study: "for the Lord your God is God in heaven above and on the earth below (ὅτι κύριος ὁ θεὸς ὑμῶν θεὸς ἐν οὐρανῷ ἄνω καὶ ἐπὶ τῆς γῆς κάτω)" (v. 11b). It is striking that Rahab acknowledges the Lord to be the Lord who is in heaven and on earth. The wording reflects the second of the Ten Commandments, which acknowledges the exclusive sovereignty of God (Howard, 1998:103). The knowledge of the Lord had come to Rahab in a pagan land, and she affirms belief in the language of the Pentateuch.[10]

3.1.4.5.2 2 Chronicles 2:11 (12)

Next, we turn to a statement made by a king in the preface of an official letter. In response to Solomon's request that King Huram of Tyre assist him by sending an artisan (2 Chr 2:6 [7]) and timber (2 Chr 2:7 [8]) for the building of the temple, he writes: "Blessed be the Lord God of Israel (εὐλογητὸς κύριος ὁ θεὸς Ισραηλ), who made the heaven and the earth (ὃς ἐποίησεν τὸν οὐρανὸν καὶ τὴν γῆν), who gave to king David a wise son, endowed with knowledge and insight, who will build a house for the Lord and a house for his kingdom" (2 Chr 2:11 [12]). The statement functions as an acknowledgement of the love and sovereignty of the Lord in establishing Solomon as King over Israel. The language of the Lord making him king over them as a result of his love compares to the speech of the Queen of Sheba in 2 Chronicles 9:8 and may be the vocabulary of diplomatic relations (Dillard, 1987:20; Selman, 1994:301). King Huram had supplied David with cedar

---

10. Rehab's confession of faith is genuine (Howard, 1998:104). This genuineness is confirmed by writings in the New Testament. The epistle of James upholds Rahab as an example of a person whose faith expressed itself in works (Jas 2:25). Likewise, Rahab is commended for her faith in Hebrews 11:31. Rahab, the Gentile, is honored as an example of faith right alongside the patriarchs, Moses, the judges, the prophets, and King David. Finally, Matthew's genealogy shows that Rahab becomes the mother of Boaz (Mt 1:5). Rahab is, therefore, the great-great grandmother of David, and hence, included in the bloodline of Christ.

God as Creator in Acts 17:24

for his house (2 Chr 2:3 [4]). King Huram had also enjoyed a long-standing friendship with David (1 Ki 5:15 [1]). It may be that he came to identify the God of Israel as the God "who made heaven and earth" (2 Chr 2:11 [12]) as a result of this friendship. It is significant that non-Jews identified the God of the Israelites as the God "who made heaven and earth" as far back as the reign of Solomon. This evidence demonstrates that the designation of God as Maker of heaven and earth had been in use in cross-cultural dialogue nearly one thousand years before Paul stood in the Areopagus.

3.1.4.5.3 JONAH 1:9

Our next passage occurs in the context of a Jew elucidating the nature of his God to Gentiles. The first chapter of Jonah narrates the journey of a recalcitrant prophet. Rather than traveling east to Nineveh as commanded by the Lord, Jonah travels west, toward Tarshish, in an attempt to flee from the presence of the Lord. The drama that ensues portrays the heathen crew crying out to their gods after the Lord sends a fierce storm that threatens the ship. The contrast between the response of the crew and Jonah's lack of response—he was fast asleep (v. 5)—shows that Jonah was neither active in seeking God during a crisis nor interested in engaging the crew. Answering only the last of four questions he is asked by the crew in verse 8 (Bosma, 2013:68), Jonah identifies himself as a Hebrew and adds voluntary information about his spiritual life: "And he said to them, I am a servant of the Lord (κυρίου); and I worship the Lord God of heaven, who made the sea, and the dry land (καὶ τὸν κύριον θεὸν τοῦ οὐρανοῦ ἐγὼ σέβομαι ὃς ἐποίησεν τὴν θάλασσαν καὶ τὴν ξηράν)" (v. 9). The initial identification of his God as the "Lord" amplifies to "the Lord God of heaven." "Who made the sea, and the dry land" is a relative clause that modifies the initial identification of the Lord as the Lord God of heaven. Therefore, the "Lord God of heaven" is identified—by a Jew, to Gentiles—as being the same God as the God who made the sea and dry land.

In his commentary on Jonah, Douglas Stuart explains the usefulness of the phrase "God of heaven" for cross-cultural communication in the ancient world:

> The epithet "God of heaven"... was a convenient way for the Israelites to describe Yahweh's identity to syncretistic, polytheistic foreigners. The sounds in the name Yahweh meant little to non-Israelites. This was an age in which hundreds of different deities

Semantic Study of "The God Who Made the Heaven and Earth"

> were worshiped in various areas of the fertile crescent and Mediterranean. Later, in the Persian period, the Jews in foreign lands would be well served by this convenient application of an old (Gen 24:3, 7) title. It answered the question "Yahweh—what's he god of?" very nicely and simply, while having the additional merit of implicitly suggesting that Yahweh was at least chief of all the gods. (Stuart, 1987:461)

Jonah spoke in language the non-Jew could understand.

The immediate response of fear shows that the men acknowledged the sovereignty of the Lord God of heaven to preside over turbulent seas. The episode unfolds with the Gentile crew crying out to Jonah's God, the Lord, in verse 14. When they observe the calm after tossing Jonah overboard, "the men feared the Lord with great fear, and they sacrificed a sacrifice to the Lord and vowed vows" (v. 16). The men not only heard about the identity of the Lord (v. 9), but they also witnessed the immediate effect of his power to calm the sea. This demonstration of God's power is a three-dimensional illustration of the nature of God as Lord over his creation, as identified in Jonah's brief apologetic. The result is belief.

Jonah's statement about the God he worships in 1:9 is placed strategically within the passage to show emphasis. His declaration is at the heart of a chiastic pattern. James Limburg counts ninety-four Hebrew words from the beginnings of the scene in 1:4 until the beginning of Jonah's testimony in 1:9 and another ninety-four words from 1:10–15.

Limburg outlines the chiastic pattern as follows (Limburg, 1993:47):

A The Lord hurls storm (1:4)
  B Sailors pray, act (1:5ab)
    C Jonah acts (lies down, sleeps, 1:5c)
      D Captain, sailors question Jonah (1:6–8)
        E Jonah speaks (1:9)
      D' Sailors question Jonah (1:10–11)
    C' Jonah speaks ("hurl me," 1:12)
  B' Sailors act, pray (1:13–14)
A' Sailors hurl Jonah, storm ends (1:15)

  Conclusion (1:16)

The text of 1:16 "stands outside the pattern as a conclusion" (Limburg, 1993:48). Douglas Stuart observes 1:16 as a "post-script of sorts" (Stuart,

1987:464; c.f. Smith & Page, 1995:236). Limburg's word count supports this calculation, but Bosma disagrees, noting that the identification of 1:16 as a post-script places the necessary theme of "fear" outside the parameters of the chiasm (Bosma, 2013:72). In my view, it is not necessary to expand the parameters of a carefully arranged chiastic structure in order to accommodate the presence of a theme. A theme may run through a text far beyond the bounds of immediate literary form.

In his monograph, *Chiasmus in Antiquity*, John Welch elucidates authorial intent for the implementation of chiastic structures: "An emphatic focus on the center can be employed by a skillful composer to elevate the importance of a central concept or to dramatize a radical shift of events at the turning-point" (Welch, 1999:10). If Welch's comments are an accurate assessment, then Jonah's confession in 1:9 is not only central to this portion of the narrative for the purpose of emphasis (also Bosma, 2013:67–72), but it also marks a radical turning point. Previous to Jonah's declaration, the sailors each worshiped their own god (1:5). From this point on, the sailors fear the Lord (1:10, 14, 16). Thus, the author structures the material of 1:4–16 in such way as to highlight Jonah's declaration as pivotal.

In his article, "Jonah 1:9—An Example of Elenctic Testimony," Carl Bosma argues that Jonah's statement of faith serves as an "elenctic": a polemic or apologetic designed to dismantle false beliefs and propel the hearer toward the true God (Bosma, 2013:65–90). After a discussion of the chiastic structure, Bosma offers five arguments in support of 1:9 as an elenctic. First, he notes that Jonah's statement constitutes an unsolicited testimony. Jonah's declaration of ethnicity receives only a two-word answer (in Hebrew), but he adds lengthier supplemental information that strikes emphasis on his religious beliefs (72). Second, he demonstrates that the word order of 1:9 brings emphasis to the Lord. "The Lord," together with the phrase "the God of the heaven" is fronted, as the direct object, before the subject "I" and the verbal form (a participle in the Masoretic Text) (73). The third feature Bosma notes is the use of the phrase "the God of the heavens" to demonstrate that the Lord is the supreme God over all and not a local deity. He infers that Jonah uses this appellation as a "subversive polemical claim that Yahweh, not Baal Shamen, is superior to all other gods" (75). In his fourth argument, Bosma details a discussion of the Lord as the maker of the sea in the light of ancient pagan beliefs that deify the creation rather than the Creator. The motif of "dramatic fear" constitutes the fifth point: the escalation of fear on the part of the sailors culminates in their forsaking

Semantic Study of "The God Who Made the Heaven and Earth"

their own gods to fear the Creator God (79–81). Thus, it is argued, Jonah is an example of missionary apologetic proclamation that may be applied to contemporary evangelistic efforts today, particularly when countering pantheism (90). Overall, Bosma offers compelling arguments in favor of Jonah 1:9 as a refutation of false beliefs associated with idolatry and as a presentation of the Creator as the supreme, and only, true God.

The context of Jonah 1:9 is thus established as the effective proclamation of the Lord to Gentiles who believed in other gods. Paul's speech in Athens, likewise, is a polemical declaration by a Jew to Gentiles against a setting of idolatry. In each dramatic episode, the result of the proclamation of God as Creator results in belief.

3.1.4.5.4 Daniel

Phrases identical or similar to either "God of heaven" or "Lord of heaven" appear thirteen times within Daniel chs. 2–4 in the Old Greek manuscript. Each occurrence involves the pagan Babylonian king, Nebuchadnezzar. Nebuchadnezzar comes to know of God as identified with these terms. He also makes his confessional statement with these same terms.

The prophet Daniel is the first to proclaim the identity of the God he serves to Nebuchadnezzar. When asked to tell and interpret Nebuchadnezzar's troubling dream, Daniel replies that even though the wise men could not do this, "there is a God in heaven (θεὸς ἐν οὐρανῷ) revealing mysteries" (2:28). This statement communicates the uselessness of all paganism to the king with great tact (Lucas, 2002:73; Miller, 1994:89). Daniel credits his God before describing the dream of the great statue and giving the interpretation. Similar phrases emerge two more times in the interpretation of the dream. Daniel informs Nebuchadnezzar that it is the "Lord of heaven (ὁ κύριος τοῦ οὐρανοῦ)" who gave the kingdom to him (2:37). It is also the "God of heaven (ὁ θεὸς τοῦ οὐρανοῦ)" who will set up an everlasting kingdom (2:44). In this way, Nebuchadnezzar learns that the God of heaven is the God who reveals mysteries. He is the God who established Nebuchadnezzar's Babylonian regime, and the God who will establish a never-ending kingdom. The Babylonian king responds to the interpretation of the dream by falling in front of Daniel and making a statement acknowledging the supremacy of Daniel's God (2:46–47). He also gives Daniel a promotion to a high post (2:48). The God of heaven in this passage is identified as the supreme God over all gods. Nebuchadnezzar's statement is most likely a simple acknowledgment of the Most High made by a polytheist rather than a conversion (Collins, 1993:172; Miller, 1994:103).

After building a colossal golden statue (ch. 3), Nebuchadnezzar hears again about the God of heaven, also in connection with a supernatural experience. The context is one of heinous idolatry. When he accosts Shadrach, Meshach, and Abednego for their refusal to bow to the statue, they make an assertion: "For God in the heavens is our Lord (ἔστι γὰρ θεὸς ἐν οὐρανοῖς εἷς κύριος ἡμῶν) whom we fear; he is able to deliver us from the furnace of fire, and out of your hand, King, he will deliver us" (3:17). In response to witnessing the miraculous survival of the three men from the flames, Nebuchadnezzar utters his second acknowledgement of God in the book of Daniel. He blesses their God (3:95 [28]), issues a decree that no one may blaspheme their God "because there is no other god who is able to deliver in this way" (3:96 [29]); and gives Meshach, Shadrach, and Abednego a promotion. Thus, Nebuchadnezzar's understanding of the Jewish faith progresses from an acknowledgment of God in chapter two, to the establishment of Judaism as a legally recognized religion in chapter three (Goldingay, 1989:75). Again, the context is one of God's supremacy over and against the worthlessness of idols. Nebuchadnezzar learns from this episode that the God in heaven is able to deliver by miraculous means—something to which no other god can make a claim.

The next scene in which God reveals himself to Nebuchadnezzar as the God of heaven is through the proclamation of an angel during a dream. The angel proclaims that he will "feed on grass like an ox" for seven years (4:15–16). The purpose is explicit: "until he comes to realize that the Lord of heaven (τὸν κύριον τοῦ οὐρανοῦ) has authority over all things in heaven (ἐν τῷ οὐρανῷ) and all things on the earth (ἐπὶ τῆς γῆς) and does with them whatever he wishes" (4:17). It is Daniel's God, the Lord of heaven, who deals directly with Nebuchadnezzar by issuing such a punishment. Daniel's interpretation of the dream nears an end with the reiteration of the theme of God's supreme authority: "The Lord lives in heaven (κύριος ζῇ ἐν οὐρανῷ), and his authority is over all the earth (ἐπὶ πάσῃ τῇ γῇ)" (4:27). Nebuchadnezzar is in the midst of speaking his own praises when he hears a voice from heaven declaring that his kingdom has departed (v. 31). God's dealings then become intensely personal as he is humiliated by the taking on of animal-like characteristics.

The words Nebuchadnezzar uses in his confession, after coming back to his senses, are significant. The Old Greek version has Nebuchadnezzar

Semantic Study of "The God Who Made the Heaven and Earth"

confessing to God as the "Lord God of heaven (κυρίου τοῦ θεοῦ τοῦ οὐρανοῦ)" (4:33). We may note the similarity of this phrase to statements already discussed about God that Nebuchadnezzar had heard from Daniel and others. Nebuchadnezzar also refers to God as "God of heaven" six times: in 4:31, in 4:34 (twice) and in 4:37 (three times). Not only this, but Nebuchadnezzar makes an acknowledgement of the supremacy of God by speaking words of praise to the Creator: "I thank the Most High, and I praise the one who created the heaven and the earth (τῷ κτίσαντι τὸν οὐρανὸν καὶ τὴν γῆν) and the seas and the rivers and everything that is in them" (Dan 4:37 [4:1]).[11] The God of heaven is the God who created the world, the Most High God. Nebuchadnezzar identifies the Creator God with the theology of Genesis 1–2.

Thus, God's revelation of his nature to Nebuchadnezzar crescendos from being a revealer of mysteries, to being a supernatural deliverer, to being the supreme authority over everything in heaven and on earth. Nebuchadnezzar is informed with the identification of God as "God (θεὸς) of heaven" and "Lord (κύριος) of heaven." His confession of acknowledgement of the Lord echoes these phrases.

The language of Daniel corresponds with two key phrases from Jonah 1:9. Just as Jonah identified God as the "Lord God of heaven" to Gentiles

---

11. There are significant differences between the Old Greek manuscript of the Septuagint (quoted here) and Theodotion's "rival version" (Brotzman, 1999:75) of the second century A.D. Theodotion has a much shorter reading than that of the Old Greek manuscript. Theodotion's content of 4:37 reads as follows: "Now, therefore, I, Nebuchadnezzar, praise and extol and glorify the king of heaven (τὸν βασιλέα τοῦ οὐρανοῦ)." The Old Greek begins a lengthy counterpart to Theodotion at 4:37, which breaks into additional sections (4:37 a, b, and c). The first few lines of 4:37 (Old Greek) read as follows: τῷ ὑψίστῳ ἀνθομολογοῦμαι καὶ αἰνῶ τῷ κτίσαντι τὸν οὐρανὸν καὶ τὴν γῆν καὶ τὰς θαλάσσας καὶ τοὺς ποταμοὺς καὶ πάντα τὰ ἐν αὐτοῖς ἐξομολογοῦμαι καὶ αἰνῶ ὅτι αὐτός ἐστι θεὸς τῶν θεῶν καὶ κύριος τῶν κυρίων καὶ βασιλεὺς τῶν βασιλέων ὅτι αὐτὸς ποιεῖ σημεῖα καὶ τέρατα καὶ ἀλλοιοῖ καιροὺς καὶ χρόνους ἀφαιρῶν βασιλείαν βασιλέων καὶ καθιστῶν ἑτέρους ἀντ' αὐτῶν. The verses that follow (4:37 a, b, and c) comprise 29 lines of additional text not found in Theodotion. The Masoretic Text follows Theodotion, rather than the Old Greek, also with "king of heaven" (לְמֶלֶךְ שְׁמַיָּא). Brotzman explains that Theodotion's version of Daniel eventually replaced the Septuagint in the church, due to its popularity (Brotzman, 1999:75). The first three references discussed in this section (Dan 2:28, 37, 34) find their companion in the Masoretic Text. The remaining ten occurrences (3:17; 4:17, 27, 31, 33, 34*2, 37*3) find no counterpart in the Masoretic Text. For a detailed study of the manuscripts, see T. J. Meadowcroft, *Aramaic Daniel and Greek Daniel* (1995). Textual matters aside, the Septuagint rendering demonstrates that an acknowledgement of the God who created the heavens and the earth was present in Hellenistic Jewish thought.

God as Creator in Acts 17:24

on the high seas, Daniel identifies God to Nebuchadnezzar using variations "Lord of heaven," "God of heaven," and, once, using the same exact wording: "Lord God of heaven." Daniel's friends, an angel, and "a voice from heaven" all use similar language to identify God to Nebuchadnezzar. Ultimately, Nebuchadnezzar makes an acknowledgement to the Most High God with repeated references to the "God of heaven." He also includes a reference to God as Creator in his confession. We may also observe that the end result of Nebuchadnezzar worshiping God (Dan 4:34–37 [4:34–36; 4:1]) corresponds with the end result of the sailors in Jonah offering a sacrifice to the Lord (Jonah 1:16).

The appearance of elements from each key phrase of Jonah 1:9 in the book of Daniel gives rise to the question of whether Daniel considered Jonah a model for evangelism. It appears as if this may be the case. In a similar fashion, Paul identifies God in Athens with elements from each key phrase of Jonah 1:9. Paul, then, presents his explanation of the identity and nature of God by using vocabulary that was common not only to Genesis 1, but also to great prophets of the past.

3.1.4.5.5 Ezra 1:2

The identification of God as the "Lord God of heaven" (or variations) was known to Gentiles in three successive world powers in the Old Testament: Assyria (in Jonah), Babylon (in Daniel), and to Persia (in Ezra). Cyrus is the second pagan king in our study to acknowledge the God of the Israelites in a statement. He begins his written edict with these words: "Thus said Cyrus, king of the Persians: the Lord, the God of heaven (κύριος ὁ θεὸς τοῦ οὐρανοῦ), gave me all the kingdoms of the earth, and he called upon me to build him a house in Jerusalem, which is in Judea" (Ezra 1:2). Cyrus sends out a herald to broadcast his decree "in all his kingdom" (1:1). As a result, the pagan nations of the vast Persian Empire would have become familiar with the identification "the God of heaven" if they were not already so. Even though Cyrus includes an identification of the God of the Israelites in his decree, he shows no sign of conversion. In verse 3, Cyrus identifies the God of whom he speaks as their God ("his God" in the Septuagint) (Williamson, 1985:13). Cyrus was a polytheist (Fensham, 1982:44).

Besides the occurrence in the text of Cyrus's decree in 1:2, the phrase "God of heaven" is repeated several times throughout the text of Ezra. The phrase appears twice in official correspondence to King Darius (5:11 and

5:12), both times citing words of the Jews. The phrase appears twice more in official correspondence from King Darius in his royal decree for the rebuilding of the temple in Jerusalem to continue, and with a full subsidy from the royal revenue, in the next chapter (6:9 and 6:10).[12] This phrase appears to be a common way for both Jews and Persian kings to refer to the God of Israel in the book of Ezra.

In his essay, "Yahweh the God of the Heavens," D. K. Andrews explicates the cross-cultural nature of the designation in the ancient world. Andrews observes that the phrase "the God of the heavens" is found nine times in Aramaic portions of the papyri, written during the fifth century B.C., found at the Jewish colony of Elephantine in Egypt. He also observes that the Aramaic form is found more frequently than the Hebrew formulation in the Old Testament: most of the iterations of the phrase occur in the Aramaic portions of Daniel and Ezra. In Ezra, the phrase surfaces several times in texts that were translations of official documents originating from the Persian courts (Andrews, 1964:45–46). Andrews notes three contextual patterns for the phrase: 1) in references to Yahweh made by Persian officials (and similarly, Nebuchadnezzar), 2) in references to Yahweh made by Jews in the service of the Persian courts when they use official terminology, and 3) in references by Jews to officials of the Persian court or to foreigners (46–47). Andrews notes further that, apart from Genesis 24, the phrase is used in cross-cultural settings rather than "in a purely Jewish context" (48). This appellation is used to convey the power and authority of the supreme God (53).

In summary, texts from the book of Ezra continue the pattern of the identification of God as the "Lord/God of heaven" in cross-cultural settings that begin with Jonah in the days of the Assyrian empire.

3.1.4.6 Summary of Septuagint passages

This survey of relevant Septuagint passages has unearthed a plethora of relevant texts for this study. The relevant texts examined fall into five of the six categories of literary type: core material, liturgical, in an oath, in a prophetic oracle, and in cross-cultural communication. The core material from Genesis 1:1 established the identification of God as Maker as the foundation upon which the rest of the book is built. The liturgical use of the identification of God as Maker in a prayer emerges in key points of Israel's history, including the bringing of the ark into the tent by David (1 Chr

---

12. See also 2 Chronicles 36:23 and Nehemiah 1:5; 2:4, 20.

16:26), the dedication of the temple by Solomon (2 Chr 6:14), Hezekiah's prayer when he was under the eminent threat of Assyrian aggression (Isa 37:11), and the rededication of the people to the Lord in the post-exilic era (Neh 9:6). The appellation of God as Maker in an oath surfaces twice in the book of Genesis (14:22 and 24:3–4). Both references occur during solemn occasions when a binding promise was made. Passages that were examined in the category of prophetic oracle commonly find the identification of God as Maker in prophetic oracles that condemned idolatry, in particular. Creation, in these texts, is used as an anti-idolatry polemic. Finally, we examined numerous instances of God identified as the Maker in cross-cultural dialogue. Such a reference appears first in Rahab's declaration (Josh 2:11), and resurfaces in Jonah 1:9, throughout the book of Daniel (particularly in spoken discourse between Daniel and the Babylonian king, Nebuchadnezzar), and also in the decree of the Persian king, Cyrus (Ezra 1:2). Thus, the semantic reference makes the transition from the use in the royal courts of Babylon, during the zenith of the Babylonian empire, to the use in the royal courts of Persia from the beginning of Cyrus's reign and continuing through Darius's reign, and is found as far away as Egypt. This designation for the God of Israel was far from arcane in the ancient world.

3.1.5 "The God who made the heaven and the earth" in other Jewish literature

If the phrase "God of heaven" was a known designation for God by Jews and Gentiles in the days of the Babylonian and Persian Empires, could it also have been known by Hellenistic Jews communicating to Gentiles in the days of the Greek and Roman Empires? This section will present a brief overview of several passages with relevant texts from the Apocrypha, Pseudepigrapha, Philo, and Josephus. We will continue to see references to God with terminology similar to Acts 17:24 in anti-idolatry contexts, some in literature written right in the first century A.D.

3.1.5.1 *Apocrypha*

In this section, we will discuss two passages from the Apocrypha. The first text, from the Prayer of Manasseh, portrays a prayer of repentance from idolatry by a wicked king. The second text, from *Bel and the dragon*, comes from a colorful addition to the book of Daniel, which narrates Daniel's demonstration of faith in the Lord amidst a culture of idolatry within the royal precincts of Babylon.

3.1.5.1.1 Liturgical: Prayer of Manasseh 2

The Prayer of Manasseh speaks of the repentance of the seventh century king of Judah from idolatry. It was a pseudonymous attempt to recreate the prayer of king Manasseh, corresponding to the narrative in 2 Chronicles 33:11–13. Charlesworth believes that the prayer may have been written sometime in the first or second century B.C., as an expansion of Chronicles (Charlesworth, 2009b:627–629). The earliest extant text of this prayer is found in a citation in an early Christian work, *Didascalia*, in the second or third century A.D. (Dancy, 1972:243; van der Horst & Newman, 2008:147–155).

The text of the second verse follows the initial address of the prayer to the God of the patriarchs (v. 1). The prayer continues with a description of God, "The one who made the heaven and the earth (ὁ ποιήσας τὸν οὐρανὸν καὶ τὴν γῆν) with all their establishment (σὺν παντὶ τῷ κόσμῳ αὐτῶν)" (v. 2). This passage contains κόσμος, a word that we have not yet seen in any other passage included in this study besides Acts 17:24a. Κόσμος is used in Prayer of Manasseh 2 with a meaning of "establishment" (NRSV) or "order" (NETS) rather than "world" or "universe," as it is in Acts 17:24a. Acts 17:24a remains unique, in this sense.

3.1.5.1.2 Cross-cultural communication: Bel and the dragon 1.5

Bel and the dragon features additions to Daniel (Dancy, 1972:235). In this text, the king accosts Daniel for not worshiping the idol, Bel. Daniel responds: "I worship no one except the Lord God (κύριον τὸν θεὸν), who created heaven and earth (τὸν κτίσαντα τὸν οὐρανὸν καὶ τὴν γῆν)" (Bel 1.5). Daniel clearly identifies his God as the Creator to a Gentile in a context of idolatry. The narrative continues as an anti-idolatry polemic, with Daniel debunking the fabrication that Bel physically consumes the offerings given to him. Daniel debunks both idolatry and zoolatry. Daniel destroys the dragon, much to the king's chagrin, and ends up in the lion's den. The entire book exposes the fallacy of false gods (Dancy, 1972:238–239). Thus, the pattern of referring to God with creation and heaven/earth terminology in cross-cultural presentations of the nature of the one God extends to apocryphal literature.[13]

3.1.5.2 Pseudepigrapha

In this section, we explore two passages from the Pseudepigrapha. The first is a poetic text from the third Sibylline oracle and the second is a narrative text from an elaboration on the Old Testament story of Job.

3.1.5.2.1 Prophetic oracle: Sibylline oracle 3.33–35

The third Sibylline oracle was likely written in Egypt during the first to second century B.C. (Buitenwerf, 2003:126; Charlesworth, 2009a:355, 360; Collins, 1972:33). Although the date is difficult to determine with precision, there is consensus that book three of the Sibylline oracles forms the earliest part of the corpus. It is generally regarded as a collection of shorter oracles from a variety of sources (Collins, 1972:21). The text condemns idolatry and directs the reader toward monotheism (Buitenwerf, 2003:41). After establishing the one God as Creator (3.10), the author contrasts God with idols (3.11–14). The author denounces the practices of idolatry and zoolatry:

> You neither revere nor fear God, but wander to no purpose,
> worshiping snakes and sacrificing to cats,
> speechless idols, and stone statues of people;
> and sitting in front of the doors at godless temples
> you do not fear the existing God who guards all things.
> You rejoice in the evil of stones, forgetting the judgment
> of the immortal savior who created heaven and earth (ὃς οὐρανὸν ἔκτισε καὶ γῆν).
>
> (*Sib. Or.* 3.29–35, Charlesworth)

Once again, God is identified as Creator over and against useless idols in a monotheistic Jewish polemic (Charlesworth, 2009a:360). This text also mentions God as judge, as does Paul (Acts 17:31).

---

13. Other references in the Apocrypha include Judith 5:8, 6:19, 11:17; and Tobit 7:17 (16), 10:11, 13.

Semantic Study of "The God Who Made the Heaven and Earth"

3.1.5.2.2 Cross-cultural communication: Testament of Job 2:4

The *Testament of Job* was probably written during the first century B.C. or first century A.D. It may have been written as a Hellenistic Jewish missionary apologetic in Egypt (Charlesworth, 2009a:833–836; contra Gruen, 2009:168, 179, who proposes that is an allegorical rendering of historical events for the community for which it was written). Although it cannot be determined with certainty whether this text pre-dated or post-dated the Areopagus speech, the passage demonstrates the continued pattern of introducing the Creator as the true God in an anti-idolatry context. The narrative is a reinvention of the story of Job (Knibb & van der Horst, 1989:1, 7; DiTomasso, 2012:314). Job is portrayed as a man who lives near an idol temple. He asks, "Is this, then, the God who made heaven and earth (ὁ θεὸς ὁ ποιήσας τὸν οὐρανὸν καὶ τὴν γῆν), the sea, and us ourselves? How, then, will I know?" (2.4). An angel answers him with the information that the power behind the idol is the devil (3.3). Job proceeds to destroy the idol's temple, "brought down to the ground" (5.2). The text of the *Testament of Job* shows that references to the Creator God continued to be a salient feature of anti-idolatry literature well into the Hellenistic period.

3.1.5.3 Philo

Philo's writings date to the early–mid first century A.D. (Williamson, 1989:1). Two passages warrant examination for topics related to creation as a foundational doctrine for Jews: *On the Creation of the World* LXI.172 and *On the Embassy to Gaius* XVI.115.

3.1.5.3.1 Philosophical/historical works: On the Creation of the World LXI.172

In his philosophical treatise, *On the Creation of the World*, Philo summarizes his five lessons of Moses in the final verse (Runia, 2001:392):

> For it follows of necessity that the Creator must always care for that which he has created, just as parents do also care for their children. And he who has learnt this not more by hearing it than by his own understanding, and has impressed on his own soul these marvellous facts which are the subject of so much contention—namely,

> that God (θεὸς) has a being and existence, and that he who so exists is really one, and that he has created the world (πεποίηκε τὸν κόσμον), and that he has created it one as has been stated, having made it like to himself in singleness; and that he exercises a continual care for that which he has created will live a happy and blessed life, stamped with the doctrines of piety and holiness. (*Creation* LXI.172, Jonge)

Philo came from Alexandria, possibly the most intensely Hellenized Jewish community of his day (Williamson, 1989:6). His scholarship demonstrates competency with Greek philosophical texts as well as with the Septuagint (Winston, 1981:2–4). He alerts us to a "subject of so much contention" right in the Hellenistic world of the early to mid first century A.D.—the existence and nature of God as Creator. If this debate extended to philosophers in Athens a few years later, as it presumably would have—given Philo's interaction with Greek culture (Williamson, 1989:5–6)—then it would appear that Paul begins his speech by engaging a current topic of heated debate among philosophers. In this passage, Philo also includes other themes similar to Paul's speech: providence and the uniqueness of God.

The semantic construction of this passage interrupts our usual pattern of seeing a combination of οὐρανός/γῆ as the usual direct object for ποιέω, particularly in passages from the Septuagint reflecting Genesis 1:1. *On the Creation of the World* LXI.172 is the only text (besides Acts 17:24a) that we have seen that injects κόσμος as the direct object of a form of the verb ποιέω. This variation from the pattern exhibits a minor language change introduced by a writer heavily influenced by Greek culture. This minor change is one that Luke shows Paul as also making when speaking to a Greek audience.

3.1.5.3.2 Philosophical/historical works: Embassy XVI.115

A second passage by Philo comes from his *Embassy to Gaius*. This historical account details the plight of the Jews during the time that Gaius Caligula declared himself a god and demanded worship by his subjects (Williamson, 1989:6–18). Philo describes Caligula's attitude toward the Jews:

> For he regarded the Jews with most especial suspicion, as if they were the only persons who cherished wishes opposed to his, and who had been taught in a manner from their very swaddling-clothes by their parents, and teachers, and instructors, and even

> before that by their holy laws, and also by their unwritten maxims and customs, to believe that there was but one God, their Father and the Creator of the world (ποιητὴν τοῦ κόσμου θεόν). (*Embassy* XVI.115, Yonge)

This passage is significant for defining the nature of the primary religious instruction that Jewish children were taught during the first century A.D. Children were instructed that the one God was the Creator of the world from a very young age, a lesson prerequisite to all others. This teaching defines the Creator God as the only God to those who would grow up in polytheistic societies. Philo's mention of "one God" echoes the confession of the Shema in Deuteronomy 6:4 (Smallwood, 1970:2009). This fundamental teaching of monotheism diametrically opposed Caligula's agenda of legislated imperial worship. It also identifies the core reason that Caligula viewed the Jews with suspicion.

Again, Philo uses κόσμος as a substitution for the usual οὐρανός καὶ γῆ, a variation on the theme of Gen. 1:1. As such, κόσμος may be understood as having a similar meaning to οὐρανός καὶ γῆ by the first century A.D. The Areopagus speech uses κόσμος in close proximity to οὐρανός καὶ γῆ in Acts 17:24, also in a way as to suggest an interchangeability of the terms.

3.1.5.4 Josephus

Writing at or near the end of the first century A.D. (Whiston, 1987:773; Barclay, 2007:XXVI–XXVIII), Josephus mentions God as Creator in his polemic against the erroneous writings of the grammarian, Apion, in book two of *Against Apion*. The book has the flavor of a defense speech and bears resemblance to an apologetic with regard to its overall genre (Barclay, 2007:XXX–XXXVI). His intended audience is primarily non-Jewish, although Jews would have also read his work (Barclay, 2007:XLV–LI). In this section, we explore the contexts of two different passages in *Against Apion*. The first text includes words of an oath formula. The second text contains elements of monotheistic Jewish polemic.

3.1.5.4.1 OATH: *AGAINST APION* 2.121

Apion had written many accusations against the Jews. Josephus takes corrective measures to set the historical record straight on numerous topics.

God as Creator in Acts 17:24

One such topic has to do with a false understanding about Jewish–Gentile relations: "Apion also tells a false story, when he mentions an oath of ours, as if we 'swore by God, the maker of the heaven (τὸν θεὸν τὸν ποιήσαντα τὸν οὐρανὸν), and earth (καὶ τὴν γῆν), and sea, to bear no good will to any foreigner, and particularly to none of the Greeks'" (*Ag. Ap.* 2.121, Whiston). Greek oaths were often sworn by gods of the earth (Demeter or Ge), sea (Poseidon), or sky (Zeus or Helios) (Barclay, 2007:231). The citation of God as maker of heaven in earth in an oath shows that the (supposed) speaker appeals to the power of God as witness to the words spoken. It also shows that Abraham's example (Gen 14:22–24; 24:3–4) was paradigmatic for Jews well into the first century A.D. Not only that, but it also demonstrates that the practice was known to those outside of Judaism. This provides us with evidence that those outside the Jewish tradition, indeed, may have known the God of the Jews with the terminology "maker of heaven and earth" during the time of Paul's speech in Athens. This would have been true, at the least, for Apion and his readers.

3.1.5.4.2 Cross-cultural communication: Against Apion 2.192

Josephus refers again to God as Creator in *Against Apion* 2.192. After stating that no image may be made for God (2.191), he explains that God made everything: "We see his works, the light, the heaven (οὐρανὸν), the earth (γῆν), the sun and the moon, the waters, the generations of animals, the production of fruits. These things hath God made (θεὸς ἐποίησεν)." He continues with an appeal: "All men ought to follow this Being, and to worship him in the exercise of virtue" (2.192, Whiston). The passage refutes idolatry and promotes monotheism. It has an evangelistic tone.

This passage from Josephus demonstrates that Paul was not the only Jew to use creation theology in the first century A.D. to prove monotheism. He was in good company.

3.1.5.5 *Summary of passages in other Jewish literature*

The passages examined in this section span across five categories of literary type: liturgical, in an oath, in a prophetic oracle, in cross-cultural communication, and in other philosophical works. The apocryphal Prayer of Manasseh includes the word κόσμος in its prayer as it identifies God as

Maker, as do works by Philo. Philo's works are significant, in part, due to Philo's background as a Hellenistic Jew. His familiarity with Greek philosophical literature, no doubt, informed his choice of words. Philo also informs us of the foundational lesson in theology that Jewish children learned from infancy: that there is one God alone, and that he created the world (*Embassy* XVI.115). The practice of identifying God as Maker in the words of an oath all the way through the first century is attested in Josephus's work, *Against Apion*. The practice was, apparently, prevalent enough that even the Gentile world knew it was the manner in which a Jew might make an oath. The author of the third Sibylline oracle references God as the Creator of the world, over and against a culture that promoted idolatry and zoolatry, in a prophetic oracle. In a similar way, the Daniel of Bel and the dragon opposes both idolatry and the worship of living creatures and identifies himself a worshiper solely of the God who created heaven and earth—this time in cross cultural communication.

3.1.6. Summary

This section has surveyed a range of passages in six classifications of literary type that include mention of the creation motif. The discussion of each of these categories of meaning has unearthed a rich literary environment in which phrases using vocabulary related to Acts 17:24a bear significant theological weight.

We have learned that the identification of God as Creator may be central in various liturgical uses or central in an oath. The identification of God as Creator may be the foundation on which a prophetic oracle is prefaced. We have also seen that both Isaiah and Jeremiah used an identification of God as Creator in prophetic oracles. The knowledge of God as the God of heaven was not limited to the Jewish world. The identification of God as the "Lord/God of heaven" was spoken to Gentiles in evangelistic settings. Gentiles, including several kings, also identified the God of Israel as the "Lord/God of heaven." With the exception of Genesis 1 and passages from Psalms, the identification of God as Creator occurs in passages of direct, person-to-person discourse, whether spoken or written.

The contextual backdrop behind many of the texts we have explored is a deliberate contrast between the Lord and idols. What sets the Lord apart from other gods is that only he can create the heavens and the earth. Genesis begins with the creation narrative as a foundational lesson about God.

Melchizedek incorporates a creation motif into liturgical use, as seen in the blessing he pronounced on Abraham. Abraham invokes the name of the Lord in an oath he makes to the King of Sodom, identifying the God who made heaven and earth as the Most High God, establishing that the Lord is superior to all other gods. Isaiah identifies God as Creator in the preface of several oracles that contain a contrast of the Lord with idolatry in the context. Both Isaiah and Jeremiah build anti-idolatry oracles on the foundation of God as Creator of the heaven and the earth. When asked which god he serves, Jonah replies with the assertion that he serves the "Lord God of heaven, who made the sea, and the dry land" (Jonah 1:9). The pagan Babylonian king, Nebuchadnezzar, gives praise to the "one who created the heaven and the earth" after being humbled by the Lord. Some years later, the pagan king of Persia, Cyrus, acknowledges the God of heaven in his decree to rebuild the temple in Jerusalem, a decree that was made known throughout the kingdom. Over and against other gods, the God of Israel is repeatedly identified as the Maker of heaven and earth by both Jews and Gentiles in the ancient world.

What have we learned about the nature of God, as revealed through phrases referring to God as Creator or Lord/God of heaven and earth? First of all, God is absolutely unique. This uniqueness is established first in the first chapter of Genesis. He is the God who made heaven and earth. No other can make this claim. Melchizedek establishes that this unique God is supreme: "God Most High" (Gen 14:19). David's dedication of the ark includes citation from Psalm 95 (96) that displays the uniqueness of God in contrast with idols. Only the Lord can make the heavens (1 Chr 16:26). Solomon makes a foundational statement regarding the uniqueness of God in his prayer of dedication, "there is no God like you" (2 Chr 6:14). Hezekiah also appeals to the unique and supreme God in his prayer, "you alone . . . made heaven and earth" (Isa 37:16). Likewise, Ezra prays to the God who "alone" created the heavens and the earth (Neh 9:6). Isaiah and Jeremiah both appeal to the uniqueness of God in oracles against idolatry (Isa 45:18–25; Jer 10:11–12).

We have also learned that God is powerful. His act of creation in Genesis 1 is a display of his power. It may be that Isaiah mentions God as Creator in order to persuade his hearer: the God who is powerful enough to create the world is also powerful enough to bring to fruition the words of Isaiah's prophecy (Isa 42:5; 44:24; 45:18). God's power is also seen in references to him as divine witness in oaths (Gen 14: 22–24; 24:3–4; *Ag Ap* 2.121). In each passage, the God of heaven and earth is invoked—the God who has the power to enforce a solemn statement. The God of heaven displays power through the miraculous in the book of Daniel: he is the revealer of mysteries (Dan 2:47) and the deliverer from the furnace (Dan 3:19–95 [19–28]). This powerful God is also sovereign over kings and kingdoms (Dan 4:17). It is within the scope of God's power to give blessing (Gen 14:19; Ps 113:23), to answer prayer (Acts 4:24, Isa 37:16–36), to provide for creation through providence (Acts 14:17; 17:25), and to judge (1 Chr 16:33; Acts 17:31).

Several of the passages we have studied feature the identification of God as Creator in contexts that show impetus for evangelism. The first text we have examined that falls within this classification comes from the quotation of Psalm 95 (96) in 1 Chronicles 16 with its directives to proclaim the Lord among the nations (1 Chr 16:24, 31) and contrast of idols with the Creator God. Solomon's dedication begins with an address to the God who presides over heaven and earth (2 Chr 6:14) and speaks of concern for Gentile mission, "so that all the peoples of the earth may know your name both to fear you, as your people Israel, and to know that your name has been called upon this house" (2 Chr 6:33). Hezekiah's request for deliverance from the Assyrian threat begins with an appeal to the Creator (Isa 37:16) and, remarkably, concludes with a petition that the Gentiles would know that he is the Lord as a result (Isa 37:20).

The mention of God as Creator at the outset of Paul's speech in Athens carries with it an understanding that God is unique and powerful. God is supreme and not to be rivaled by any other god. Paul uses creation theology to set precedence for monotheism amidst a polytheistic society.

3.2 ANALYSIS: COMPARISON WITH ACTS 17:24

The phrase study establishes that the identification of God as the Creator of heaven and earth, in contrast with idols, was an ancient Jewish practice beginning with the Old Testament. Many passages in Scripture allude to the core material in Genesis 1:1 in a variety of contexts that often include a contrast with idolatry.

How might Paul's identification of God as Creator in the Areopagus speech fit in with the categories outlined in the previous section?

God as Creator in Acts 17:24

3.2.1 Core material: Genesis 1:1

Paul's statement that identifies the God of whom he speaks as the Creator of the world alludes to the core material of Genesis 1:1. Acts 17:24a includes four words that are in common with the Greek version of the first verse of Genesis. Words in common are underlined:

Table 7. Comparison of Acts 17:24 with Genesis 1:1

Acts 17:24	Genesis 1:1
ὁ θεὸς ὁ ποιήσας τὸν κόσμον καὶ πάντα τὰ ἐν αὐτῷ, οὗτος οὐρανοῦ καὶ γῆς ὑπάρχων κύριος οὐκ ἐν χειροποιήτοις ναοῖς κατοικεῖ	ἐν ἀρχῇ ἐποίησεν ὁ θεὸς τὸν οὐρανὸν καὶ τὴν γῆν

Paul's statement in Acts 17:24 reflects the language of the Septuagint in Genesis 1:1 as do other passages discussed in this chapter. Paul follows a well-worn path when he identifies the God of whom he speaks with an allusion to Genesis 1:1.

3.2.2 Liturgical/Oath

Paul's speech is not as similar to the second two types, liturgical or oath, as it is to the others in this study. Although the speech is neither part of a prayer, a blessing, worship, or an oath, it does sit squarely in the middle of a setting that demanded a positive identification of God, in contrast to idols. Many of the passages discussed under the liturgical/oath categories are remarkable for their concern for the worship of the true God rather than idols, as was Paul in Athens.

Genesis 14 contains passages that first identify God as maker of heaven and earth as an appositive for the Most High God, first in a blessing (Gen 14:19) and then in an oath (Gen 14:22). These initial contexts establish a meaning for the Lord God of heaven and earth, and similar phrases in this study that is indicative of the supremacy of the true God over idols. This meaning and context is seen repeatedly throughout passages in this study.

Hezekiah's prayer is notable for expressing trust in God to deliver "so that every kingdom of the earth may know that you alone are God" (Isa 37:20). Hezekiah petitions for deliverance from the Assyrians not only for the benefit of his own people. The gods of the other nations failed to save, and were burned by fire (Isa 37:19). Hezekiah's prayer to the God who made the heaven and the earth has a view for evangelism of Gentiles. David's use of Psalm 95 (96) when the ark was brought into the tent shows worship with a view for evangelism of Gentiles (1 Chr 16:24–26). Solomon's prayer at the dedication of the temple also has a view for evangelism of Gentiles (2 Chr 6:32–33).

The oath that Abraham has his servant make in the name of the Lord God of heaven and earth (Gen 24:2–4) has concern for the spiritual heritage of future generations. The potential for idolatry would be very high in a situation of intermarriage with a Canaanite. In this case, Abraham's concern is for his descendants to avoid idolatry. Again, we see the mention of God with the vocabulary of Genesis 1:1 in a setting that presents the Lord as supreme, in contrast to the gods of other nations.

We have also seen the Creator God in an anti-idolatry context in the Prayer of Manasseh. The apocryphal expansion of Chronicles portrays Manasseh as repenting of idolatry after addressing the God who made the heaven and the earth.

3.2.3 Prophetic oracle

Paul's speech in Athens carries a strong anti-idolatry tone, and may be considered an anti-idolatry polemic. Paul makes reference to the material evidence of idolatry in Athens at the beginning of his speech (Acts 17:23), but quickly moves on to identify the God he proclaims, the God who created the world, as the subject of his declamation. As discussed in chapter two, Paul deconstructs the logic behind idolatry in the course of his speech. The God who created and maintains the world is the God who gives life and breath to all (v. 25). What image made of gold or silver or stone can be like him (v. 29)? In this way, Paul uses the identification of the Creator God as a foundational argument in an anti-idolatry apologetic, as do the prophets Isaiah and Jeremiah.

The oracles in Isaiah 45 and Jeremiah 10 have more points in common with Paul's declamation in Athens than the oracles in Isaiah 42 and 44, and in the third *Sibylline oracle*. The overarching theme of the oracles in Isaiah 42 and 44 is one of restoration, rather than the condemnation of idolatry (although the uniqueness of God as Creator is explicitly expressed in both, and a brief mention of idolatry is made in Isa 42:8). The third Sibylline

God as Creator in Acts 17:24

oracle roundly condemns idol worship, yet contains fewer points of direct similarity to Paul's speech in Athens than Isaiah 45 or Jeremiah 10.

The table below lists primary points of structural similarity between Acts 17, Isaiah 45, and Jeremiah 10.

Table 8.
Structural similarities between Acts 17:24–30, Isaiah 45:18–22, and Jeremiah 10:12–16

Acts 17	Isaiah 45	Jeremiah 10
v. 24 God identified as Creator:	v. 18 God identified as Creator:	v. 12 God identified as Creator:
ὁ θεὸς ὁ ποιήσας τὸν κόσμον καὶ πάντα τὰ ἐν αὐτῷ, οὗτος οὐρανοῦ καὶ γῆς ὑπάρχων κύριος	οὕτως λέγει κύριος ὁ ποιήσας τὸν οὐρανόν οὗτος ὁ θεὸς ὁ καταδείξας τὴν γῆν	κύριος ὁ ποιήσας τὴν γῆν
vv. 25–28 Nature of God described	v. 19 Nature of God described	v. 13 Nature of God described
v. 29 Idolatry useless	v. 20 Idolatry useless	vv. 3–5, 11, 14–15 Idolatry useless
v. 29 The Lord not like idols	v. 21 The Lord not like idols	v. 16 The Lord not like idols
v. 30 Call to repent	v. 22 Call to repent	

The comparison of these three speeches shows similar content and sequence. All three passages have an identification of God as Creator, details about the nature of God, a description of the futility of idolatry, and an assertion that the Lord is not like idols. Acts, like Isaiah, also includes a call to repentance. These aspects of literary correspondence show that Paul's speech in Athens follows the tradition of the prophets Isaiah and Jeremiah who spoke against idolatry.

3.2.4 Cross-cultural communication

Acts 17:24 also fits in our study within the final literary classification: in cross-cultural communication. According to Luke's account, Paul, like Jonah, uses an identification of God as Creator in direct speech to Gentiles. As Jonah needed to distinguish his God from the array of pagan gods in the

Semantic Study of "The God Who Made the Heaven and Earth"

ancient Near East, so Paul also needed to distinguish the God he proclaims from the array of pagan gods in Athens.

Table 9. Structural similarities between Acts 17:19–34 and Jonah 1:6–16

Acts 17	Jonah 1
vv. 19–20 Gentiles request information	vv. 6–8 Gentiles request information
v. 24 God identified as Creator: ὁ θεὸς ὁ ποιήσας τὸν κόσμον καὶ πάντα τὰ ἐν αὐτῷ, οὗτος οὐρανοῦ καὶ γῆς ὑπάρχων κύριος	v. 9 God identified as Creator: δοῦλος κυρίου ἐγώ εἰμι καὶ τὸν κύριον θεὸν τοῦ οὐρανοῦ ἐγὼ σέβομαι ὃς ἐποίησεν τὴν θάλασσαν καὶ τὴν ξηράν
v. 34 Gentiles fear the Lord	v. 16 Gentiles fear the Lord

The side-by-side comparison of the two texts shows points of broad similarity between Acts 17 and Jonah 1. Both texts involve an episode that begins with Gentiles requesting information. The answer to the request, in both passages, includes an identification of God as Creator. The comparison of the phrase in each passage shows four words in common. Both passages allude to Genesis 1:1 in a communication to Gentiles. Both passages show that some fear the Lord as a result of the communication.

The two phrases of Acts 17:24a bear similar content to Jonah 1:9, although in reverse order. Paul begins with God as Creator and then follows with the explanation that this God really is "Lord of heaven and earth." Jonah begins with "the Lord God of heaven" and then follows with an explanation: this "Lord God of heaven" is the Creator of the sea and the dry ground. Paul's approach is similar to Jonah's method of identifying God both as Creator and the Lord of heaven to Gentiles as a paradigm for his speech, with minor variations.

Paul, however, is not the first to use a similar approach to Jonah. We have already seen a pattern emerge in texts by prophets Isaiah and Jeremiah. Texts from Daniel also bear great similarity in form and context to Jonah 1:9. As previously discussed (section 3.1.4.5.4), Daniel seems to echo Jonah's approach in identifying God as the Lord/God of heaven in statements to the Babylonian king, Nebuchadnezzar. Nebuchadnezzar eventually echoes such language in his confession. This manner of referring to the God of Israel later becomes common in the royal courts of Persia.

3.2.5 Further discussion of κόσμος

The appearance of κόσμος in Paul's presentation on the Areopagus is something of a surprise. There is a conspicuous difference between Acts 17:24 and other texts citing God as Creator in this study, with the singular exception of Philo's writings. Other texts typically have "the heavens and the earth" as the direct object when a verb or participle form of ποιέω is used. The emergence of κόσμος as the direct object here is unexpected, particularly considering the similarity of language to the Septuagint in the rest of the passage. A similar construction will be found only in Philo.

Κόσμος is used relatively infrequently in the Septuagint. When it is used, it is with meanings other than "world" or "universe." The range of meanings in the Septuagint includes ornaments (Exod 33:5–6; Isa 3:18–20; Jer 2:32, 4:30; Ezek 7:20, 16:11, 23:40), beauty (Prov 17:6, 20:29), and celestial bodies or stars (Gen 2:1; Deut 4:19; Isa 13:10, 24:1, 40:26).

In the Apocrypha, the Prayer of Manasseh does also contain κόσμος as part of the established criteria for this study. In the Prayer of Manasseh, however, κόσμος is not the direct object. Furthermore, the definition of κόσμος in the prayer falls within a different category of meaning. Κόσμος is not translated as "world" or "universe" in the Prayer of Manasseh, but "order" (NRSV), "beauty" (Charlesworth, 2009b:634), or "embellishment" (Charlesworth, 2009b:635). These definitions comport with the meanings attributed to κόσμος in the Septuagint.

In Philo, however, we do find κόσμος used in a similar manner to Acts 17:24a. Κόσμος does appear as the direct object in *On the Creation of the World* LXI.172, and may be translated "world." More than 700 occurrences of κόσμος, in various forms, appear throughout Philo's works. Philo is known for his attempts to fuse the Old Testament with Greek philosophy (Yonge, 1993:xix). This may have prompted his use of a higher concentration of words common to Greek writings, including κόσμος. *Timaeus* 28C, Plato's account of creation, gives a Greek understanding of creation that is quite different from that of the Old Testament (Barrett, 1998:840; Bruce 1990:382). The *Timaeus* features the use of κόσμος in the context of the God who made the world. It appears that κόσμος emerges more typically in works of Greek literature, while γῆ is the word more typically seen in Jewish works, particularly the Septuagint. Paul, therefore, uses a term that "would be familiar to every Greek" (Polhill, 1992:372) but immediately reframes it within the context of the Old Testament worldview (Witherington, 1998:525).

Gärtner observes correctly that Luke uses κόσμος with a lower frequency than that of most other New Testament writers (Gärtner, 1955:174). The use of κόσμος is more strongly associated with Paul's style than Luke's. Paul frequently used κόσμος in his epistles (forty-three times altogether). Luke uses κόσμος just four times in all his writings: three times in his gospel (Luke 9:25, 11:50, and 12:30—each time when quoting words of Jesus) and only once in Acts (17:24). Luke only uses κόσμος when it is a word spoken by others; it is not found in any other context in the Luke–Acts narrative. This evidence may lend further support to the authenticity of Paul's speech (see 2.1.1.2.1).

Why does Paul insert κόσμος where an immediate use of "heaven and earth" would be more congruent to Jewish literature? It seems that Paul— like Philo— adds a new twist to an old technique when he speaks of the one who created the κόσμος. In order to answer this question more fully, we will investigate the Greek understanding of κόσμος in relation to a Creator in the next chapter.

3.3 CONCLUSION

In conclusion, this chapter has shown that the technique of presenting God as Creator as a foundational argument in Acts 17:24 has its roots in Jewish thought. The evidence spans nearly one thousand years and cuts across the regimes of major world powers from Assyria, to Babylon, to Persia, to Greece, and to Rome. Paul's identification of God as Creator in discourse to Gentiles was by no means unique. The Areopagus speech uses words in a similar manner and context as have been employed by numerous Jewish authors from the time of the writing of Genesis through the first century.

The text of Acts 17:24 alludes to core material found in the Septuagint of Genesis 1:1. This study has examined phrases similar to Acts 17:24 (and also, therefore, Gen 1:1) that share a common semantic base. Genesis 1:1 may be considered the primary material to which all other texts in this study allude. Texts containing language similar to Acts 17:24 were categorized into five further categories of meaning: in an oath, in various liturgical contexts, in the preface of an oracle, in direct speech in cross-cultural communication, and in philosophical/historical works.

Our study of phrases related to Acts 17:24 has shown an underlying Old Testament theme that occurs through all categories of meaning: the contrast of the true God with idols. Paul's identification of God as Creator fits squarely within this broader Old Testament theme. More specifically, the use of this rhetorical approach is in accord with the Old Testament oracles denouncing idolatry as well as with the approach of prophets in cross-cultural evangelism. Paul, in Acts 17:24, stands in the tradition of Old Testament prophets Jonah, Daniel, Isaiah, and Jeremiah.

This technique of identifying God as Creator, therefore, is well founded in Jewish thought and practice. This is further illustrated by the common recurrence of the theme of God as Creator in other Jewish literature. This technique, however, seems to be customized for Paul's audience of Greek philosophers. The use of κόσμος as the direct object for ὁ θεὸς ὁ ποιήσας is a significant variation from the usual format. Further investigation is necessary to help us understand what the intention may have been for introducing this new element in the Athens's speech.

In the next chapter, we will explore the Greek understanding of a Creator God as expressed in Greco-Roman philosophers contemporary to Paul, and in an important source for them: Plato's *Timaeus*.

CHAPTER 4

Greek Views of the Creation of the Universe as it Relates to the Deity or Deities in Philosophical Writings Influential in the First Century A.D.

4.0 INTRODUCTION

THIS CHAPTER EXPLORES HOW Paul's identification of God as Maker and Lord may have interacted with contemporary philosophical thought in Athens. Luke records the apostle Paul as identifying the subject of his speech as "The God who made the universe and all the things in it, he who is Lord of heaven and earth" in Acts 17:24a. These phrases encompass two related concepts: first, God is the Creator of the entire universe and, second, he is the Lord over all he has made. This declaration forms the foundation for the rest of the speech (Acts 17:24b–31). There is only one Creator of the totality of creation, including the universe and its planetary spheres as well as humankind (Acts 17:25, 28b). As Creator, God is also the Lord in his immanence (Acts 17:27–28a). The Lord of creation is not anything like idols (Acts 17:24b, 29). As Lord and judge, the Creator exercises jurisdiction over all he has made (Acts 17:30–31). How might Paul's Stoic and Epicurean audience have understood his identification of God as Maker of the universe and Lord of all?

God as Creator in Acts 17:24

Paul's views, as discussed in the previous chapter, emanated from a traditional Jewish understanding of creation. The account of creation was the foundational starting point for the Pentateuch. The account of creation was also a foundational aspect of various Jewish apologetic works written before the first century A.D. This brings us to the subject of what the worldview of the Stoics and Epicureans might have been with respect to the creation of the universe. This topic may be divided into two parts: 1) what was the understanding of the creation of the universe as it relates to the deity or deities in early Stoic and Epicurean writings, and 2) how does Paul's understanding of God as Creator and Lord compare and contrast with Stoic and Epicurean views?

A primary focus will center on determining key facets of Stoic and Epicurean cosmological thought that correspond with Paul's statements in Acts 17:24a about God being the Creator of the cosmos as well as being Lord over all he has made. After an explanation of methodology, we will sketch an introduction to the Athenian setting, including an overview of the philosophical schools in Athens. A brief history of Athens will place us in a city sitting in the shadow of its resplendent past in the Classical era but still fomenting with intellectual inquiry, debate, and dispute in the Hellenistic era. From there, we will continue with discussion of views held by the Stoic and Epicurean schools with respect to God and the cosmos. Paul asserted that God is Creator and Lord. But what did his Stoic and Epicurean hearers believe about these topics? How was the world created? Were, or were not, the deities involved in this process? What is the nature of the cosmos? Does, or does not, God have lordship, superintendence, or jurisdiction over the universe? Are the deities near or far from the world? These questions were topics of keen debate by Stoics and Epicureans alike during the Hellenistic era. We will discuss the doctrine of the origins of the universe in philosophical literature pertinent to the Stoic school, first, and to the Epicurean school, second. We will discover that, more often than not, the Stoic and Epicurean schools were polarized on topics related to cosmology. Stoic and Epicurean views on creation, cosmos, and the gods also will be compared and contrasted with Paul's speech. This chapter contributes to the main research aim by clarifying what the Stoic and Epicurean views were regarding the deity (or deities) and how Paul's word choice in his identification of God might have interfaced with the views of those in his audience.

4.1 SUMMARY OF SCHOLARSHIP

There has been a steady growth of interest in Stoicism among scholars of ancient Greek philosophy in contemporary research. This interest has centered on Stoic doctrine and, consequently, on the Platonic antecedents of Stoic belief. A.G. Long (2013:1), in the introduction to *Plato and the Stoics*, notes that the interest in Stoicism has coincided with a "surge of interest in Plato's *Timaeus*" (also Sedley, 2009:95). This combination results in a rich resource for academics to plunder, particularly with respect to ancient beliefs on the topic of cosmology. David Sedley has written a helpful overview of the ancient Greek debate over divine cause for the existence of the universe, or lack thereof, in his 2009 monograph, *Creationism and its critics in antiquity*. Despite the growing volume of research on these topics—the text of the Areopagus speech in Acts, with its Stoic and Epicurean audience—those who conduct research in ancient Greek philosophical literature have paid little, if any, attention to the speech in Acts 17.

New Testament scholars, however, have not entirely overlooked Stoic and Epicurean beliefs in their treatment of the Areopagus speech. The twentieth century saw great scholarly debate on the subject of the Hellenistic tone to Paul's speech. Dibelius (1956:58) declared that the speech was entirely Hellenistic and that the only Christian element appears at the end. In response, Gärtner's publication, *The Areopagus speech and natural revelation* (1955) identified the roots of the speech in the Old Testament but also examined the Hellenistic vocabulary. Despite a fabulous debate, neither Dibelius nor Gärtner made a systematic investigation of ancient views of cosmology as they relate to the speech in Acts 17:24a.

While there has been an increase in the study of cosmology in the New Testament in recent years (McDonough, 2015), the standard commentaries on Acts lack space to address it. Many scholars make at least a passing reference to the beliefs of the Stoics or the Epicureans in their discussion of the Areopagus speech. Craig Keener, in volume three of his commentary on Acts, gives an extensive and careful treatment to the Areopagus speech but lacks space in which to give details regarding the debate between Stoics and Epicureans on the topic of the origins of the universe. F.F. Bruce (1990:382) cites *Timaeus* 28C as a text for comparison and states that the God Paul declares is not drawn from Plato or from Stoic theology, but from the Old Testament. Similarly, C.K. Barrett (1998:840) notes briefly that the creation account of Plato's *Timaeus* is quite different than that of Genesis.

While there has been some mention of topics pertaining to Stoic and Epicurean beliefs among New Testament scholars, the topic of Stoic and Epicurean cosmology, as it informs Acts 17, has not been discussed at length. Likewise, the impact of Plato's *Timaeus* on ancient philosophical thought has not been discussed at length. This chapter addresses these gaps.

4.2 METHODOLOGY

At the core of this study is an examination of primary source Stoic and Epicurean texts. Consideration of particular philosophical texts is based on the following criteria: 1) the text must be written either during the Hellenistic era or else be an antecedent work based on teachings of Socrates; 2) the text must be written by either Stoic or Epicurean philosophers or else by an author describing the Stoic or Epicurean position; 3) the text must be concerned with the gods, creation, or the cosmos. Not included are pre-Socratic texts.[1] Philosophical texts to be discussed are a representative sample. Texts have been selected by several means. First, texts meeting the criteria above were identified in A.A. Long and David Sedley's sourcebook, *The Hellenistic Philosophers* (1999). These texts were supplemented by readings of the broader context of the extracted passages, as well as by lemma searches on electronic databases Thesaurus Linguae Grecae (TLG) and Perseus. Finally, some texts were selected on the basis of their inclusion in other secondary sources.

Central to our discussion is the need to identify, as accurately as possible, the cosmology of Stoics and Epicureans in the first century A.D. In order to discern philosophical thought during this particular century, it is necessary to look at writings within a somewhat larger radius of time: from the fourth century B.C. to the early second century A.D. The reasons for this are several. First, neither Stoic nor Epicurean writers wrote in isolation but, rather, expounded and built upon the works of their predecessors. The Stoics, especially, interacted with Socratic thought. Socrates taught extensively but published nothing. It was his students, primarily Plato and Xenophon, who preserved his teachings by writing them down (*Lives* II.48; *Lives* III.6; Ferguson, 2003:329). For this reason, we will include passages from Plato and Xenophon that were antecedent to Stoic thought.

---

[1]. For an overview of the cosmologies of pre-Socratic philosophers, see Algra (1999:45–65).

Greek Views of the Creation of the Universe

Second, although many earlier philosophers were prolific writers, there are few extant texts. The works of the early Stoic philosopher Chrysippus, for instance, are no longer in existence. His thought, however, is preserved in the form of quotations by others who expounded his work. Some of the authors included in this study wrote later than the first century A.D. but, due to the nature of their work, are relevant to our examination. The writings of biographer Diogenes Laertius are an example. His *Lives of Eminent Philosophers* traces the history of Greek philosophy, philosopher by philosopher. Scholars of philosophy consider him a relevant source for understanding the Stoicism and Epicureanism of the Hellenistic era. The main reason for this is that Diogenes Laertius quotes original sources no longer available. Although there are no extant texts from Zeno (founder of the Stoic school), Chrysippus (seminal author and third director of the Stoic school), or from Epicurus (founder of the Epicurean school), Diogenes Laertius quotes them frequently and sometimes at length in his *Lives of Eminent Philosophers*. Herbert Long, author of the introduction to the Loeb volume for Diogenes Laertius volume 1, remarks: "Diogenes has acquired an importance out of all proportion to his merits because the loss of many primary sources and of the earlier secondary compilations has accidentally left him the chief continuous source for the history of Greek philosophy" (Diogenes Laertius, 1991:xix; also O'Keefe, 2010:3–4). The writings of Diogenes Laertius are, then, relevant to our search of Stoic background, even though he wrote no sooner than the third century A.D. This brings us to another point: the relevance of texts originating from the founders of both the Stoic and the Epicurean schools to philosophical thought throughout later centuries. For instance, Diogenes Laertius's discussion of Stoicism in the section on Zeno (*Lives* VII.1–160) provides evidence that interaction with primary texts by Zeno continued for many hundreds of years beyond the author's own lifetime. Works by Chrysippus, in particular, as well as others, were included in a body of canonical works for their school, works that were regularly studied and expounded (Gill, 2003:36).

In the section on Epicurus (*Lives* X), Diogenes Laertius mentions that Epicurus was more prolific than his predecessors, having written "about three hundred rolls" that "contain not a single citation from other authors; it is Epicurus himself who speaks throughout" (*Lives* X.26, Loeb). Unfortunately, these three hundred rolls are lost to us today. Diogenes Laertius, however, does cite several of Epicurus's works. Among these, he quotes, verbatim, three letters written by Epicurus. These include the *Letter to*

Herodotus, on the topic of physics (*Lives* X.35-83), the *Letter to Pythocles*, on scientific explanations for weather patterns (*Lives* X.84-116), and the *Letter to Menoeceus*, on life and conduct (*Lives* X.122-135). Diogenes Laertius also replicates a set of forty maxims written by Epicurus (*Lives* X.139-154) as well as his personal will (*Lives* X.16-21). Diogenes Laertius, then, provides us with a rich—though incomplete—resource of Epicurus's teachings and thought.

Because the Stoics interacted with the teachings of Socrates, Socrates's teachings—as presented in works by Classical philosophers Plato and Xenophon—will be included in this study. Both Plato and Xenophon were students of Socrates and citizens of Athens. Stoic authors to be discussed include Zeno, Cleanthes, Chrysippus, Aratus, Seneca, Cornutus, and Epictetus. Epicurean authors include Epicurus and Lucretius. Authors who may not necessarily have personally identified as Stoic or Epicurean, yet wrote about their views, include Cicero and Plutarch.

All of the philosophers cited in this chapter not only had a knowledge of philosophy that originated in Athens, but they also had a connection with Athens, either as permanent residents or as visitors All of the philosophers cited in this chapter had knowledge of philosophy that originated in Athens. Some were citizens of Athens, such as Plato, Epicurus, and Xenophon. Others traveled from homes abroad to Athens for the purpose of the study of philosophy with the masters. Zeno, Cleanthes, and Chrysippus are among those who arrived in Athens as internationals seeking to learn philosophy. Still others were taught philosophy by Athenian masters in locations other than Athens. Cicero, for example, studied philosophy in Rome with instructors who came from Athens. The diagram below illustrates the centrality of Athens to the philosophers discussed in this chapter.

Table 10. Philosophers, work cited, and connection to Athens

Philosopher	Work cited	Philosopher's connection to Athens
Plato	*Timaeus*	Citizen of Athens. Student of Socrates (*Lives* III.5-6).
Xenophon	*Memorabilia*; also cited in Sextus Empiricus's *Against the Physicists*	Citizen of Athens. Student of Socrates (*Lives* II.48).

Greek Views of the Creation of the Universe

Philosopher	Work cited	Philosopher's connection to Athens
Zeno	Cited in Diogenes Laertius's *Lives*	Studied in Athens. Founded the Stoic school in Athens (*Lives* VII.2–6; Sedley, 2003:10–11).
Cleanthes	*Hymn to Zeus*	Second leader of the Stoic school in Athens (*Lives* VII.174; Sedley, 2003:15).
Epicurus	Cited in Diogenes Laertius's *Lives*	Citizen of Athens (*Lives* X.1). Founded the Epicurean school in his garden (Clay, 2010:9–10).
Aratus	*Phaenomena*	Studied under Zeno in Athens (Jones, 2003:332).
Chrysippus	Cited in Diogenes Laertius's *Lives*	Third leader of the Stoic school in Athens (*Lives* VII.179; Sedley, 2003:15–17).
Cicero	*De natura deorum*	Was taught by leaders of the Athenian schools of philosophy while living in Rome. Later, studied philosophy in Athens (Cicero, 1972:x).
Lucretius	*De rerum natura*	May have studied philosophy in Athens (Lucretius, 1982:xvi). Studied Athenian authors (Sedley, 2010:41).
Seneca	*Epistles*	Studied Athenian authors (Erler, 2010:49).
Cornutus	*Epidrome*	Studied Athenian authors (Boys–Stones, 159–161).
Epictetus	*Discourses*	Traveled to Athens at least once (Epictetus, 1998:xi).
Plutarch	*Moralia*	Studied philosophy in Athens (Plutarch, 1998:xi).

It may be helpful, at this point, to introduce each of the philosophers in a bit more detail, particularly with respect to their involvement with philosophy and the city of Athens. Philosophers are listed in chronological order, according to year of birth.

4.2.1 Plato (427–347 B.C.)

Plato was a student of Socrates, founder of the Academy, and author of Classical philosophical works. Plato was born into a family of the Athenian aristocracy. Not only a born citizen of Athens, Plato was also a sixth generation descendant of the sixth century B.C. Athenian statesman, Solon, through his maternal line (*Lives* III.1). Plato became a pupil of Socrates at age twenty (*Lives* III.6). It is possible that if it were not for his early association with Socrates, Plato might have entered the realm of politics. After the death of Socrates, Plato left Athens for a period of about twelve years (Ferguson, 2003:332). Upon his return to the city of his birth, Plato began to teach in what was to become his Academy (Ferguson, 2003:332). Plato taught at his Academy for forty years (Ferguson, 2003:332). Plato's legacy included the established Academy, which remained in operation for hundreds of years after his demise, as well as numerous written works including his famed *Republic*. Although Plato was by no means the first philosopher, he was the first to present a comprehensive, yet unified, philosophy covering a wide range of topics (Kraut, 1999:2).

4.2.2 Xenophon (426–354 B.C.)

Xenophon was a student of Socrates and an author of Classical works. According to Diogenes Laertius, Xenophon was approached by Socrates in the market in Athens. Socrates asked him several questions about where in the market he could purchase certain kinds of food. Socrates then asked Xenophon, "where do men become good and honorable?" Xenophon was perplexed. Socrates replied, "Then follow me." Diogenes Laertius comments: "From that time onward he was a pupil of Socrates. He was the first to take notes of, and to give to the world, the conversation of Socrates, under the title of *Memorabilia*" (*Lives* II.48, Loeb). Like Plato, Xenophon recorded the yet-unpublished teachings of Socrates (Ferguson, 2003:329).

4.2.3 Zeno (333–261 B.C.)

Zeno of Citium was the founder of the Stoic school (Ferguson, 2003:354; Pomeroy, 2008:479). As a young man, Zeno was drawn to philosophy through the reading of books about Socrates that his father brought to him from business trips abroad. While in his early twenties, Zeno relocated to Athens from Cyprus to study philosophy. Zeno became the founder of

Stoicism only after many years of study with Socratic philosophers (Sedley, 2003:9–10). According to Diogenes Laertius, Zeno was held in high regard in Athens, even being entrusted with the keys to the city walls and "their honouring him with a golden crown and a bronze statue" (*Lives* VII.6, Loeb).

4.2.4 Cleanthes (331–232 B.C.)

Cleanthes served as the second director of the Stoic school from 332–263 B.C. (Ferguson, 2003:355). According to Diogenes Laertius, Cleanthes arrived in Athens from Assos with a mind to study but with only four drachmas in his pocket (*Lives* VII.168). Unlike other students who were supported by family funds, Cleanthes needed to work in order to survive. He funded his studies by drawing water and working as a gardener at night *(Lives* VII.170). During the day, he studied philosophy with Zeno (*Lives* VII.168). Cleanthes studied with Zeno for nineteen years (*Lives* VII.176). Cleanthes produced an impressive collection of writings on an array of topics but only his *Hymn to Zeus* remains, along with some fragments (*Lives* VII.175–176).

4.2.5 Epicurus (341–271 B.C.)

Epicurus was a citizen of Athens. He was brought up in Samos but came to Athens at the age of eighteen (*Lives* X.1). Epicurus cultivated an interest in philosophy from the time he was a young teenager: "he turned to philosophy in disgust at the schoolmasters who could not tell him the meaning of 'chaos' in Hesiod" (*Lives* X.2, Loeb). He later founded a school of philosophy in 306 B.C. on his own property, the Garden, where his disciples lived together in community. He led his school with the strictest authoritarianism, forbidding anyone to disagree with his ideas (Rist, 1972: 2–9). Epicurus had numerous friends and students who adhered strongly to his teachings (*Lives* X.9). He also faced the harsh criticisms of opponents (Ferguson, 2003:370). The absence of citations of other philosophers in his three hundred rolls of writings attests to his self-perception as an original thinker. Although Epicurus learned atomism from Nausiphanes, he claimed to be self-taught (Rist, 1972:4–6).[2]

---

2. The doctrine of atomism was the invention of Leucippus and Democritus in the fifth century B.C. (Broadie, 1999:220). According to C. Taylor (1999:181), Epicurus denied that Leucippus ever lived. See G. Betegh (2006:261–284) and P. Morel (2010:65–83) for discussion of Epicurus's doctrine of atomism.

4.2.6 Aratus (c. 315–240 B.C.)

Aratus was a poet, student of Zeno, and a contemporary of Cleanthes (Ferguson, 2003:355). Aratus came to Athens from Soli in Cilicia, where he studied with Zeno and other Stoics. It is likely that Aratus remained in Athens for several years (Kidd, 2004:3–4). He is the author of *Phaenomena*, which is quoted in Acts 17:28b (Ferguson, 2003:355–356).

4.2.7 Chrysippus (c. 282–206 B.C.)

Chrysippus served as the third director of the Stoic school in Athens (c. 230–206 B.C.), following Zeno and Cleanthes (Ferguson, 2003:355; Sedley, 2003:7). Chrysippus came from either Tarsus or Soli to study in Athens, where he was a pupil of Cleanthes and, later, a student at the Academy (*Lives* VII.179, 183). David Sedley (2003:17) remarks that Chrysippus "is universally recognized as the most important thinker in the history of the school." Chrysippus was known to disagree frequently with both Zeno and Cleanthes (*Lives* VII.179, Loeb). Diogenes Laertius credits more than seven hundred separate writings to Chrysippus but also remarks, "He increased their number by arguing repeatedly on the same subject, setting down anything that occurred to him, making many corrections and citing numerous authorities" (*Lives* VII.180, Loeb). Unfortunately, none of Chrysippus's works are extant (Ferguson, 2003:355). They were, however, known to other ancient philosophers—who expounded them. The texts we will examine here are those that are written by authors who quote and interact with Chrysippus's teachings on pantheism. While they may, then, be considered of secondary nature, they are all that remain. Many passages concur in thought and, thus, may be considered a consistent representation of Chrysippus's teachings.

4.2.8 Cicero (106–46 B.C.)

Cicero was a Roman statesman, orator, and philosopher during the first century B.C. (Burge, 2009:89–90; Ferguson, 2003:380; Pomeroy, 2008:418). As a young man, he studied philosophy in Rome under the teaching of the leaders of three main schools of philosophy. The head teachers of the Stoic, Epicurean, and Academic schools of philosophy had relocated from Athens to Rome in the wake of the Mithridatic War, so affording Cicero a remarkable educational opportunity. Later, taking a sabbatical from public duty, Cicero

Greek Views of the Creation of the Universe

traveled to Athens and continued study with leading philosophers of various schools. Upon return to Rome, he would resume his studies of Greek philosophy whenever his schedule permitted. After a lifetime of public service, Cicero set himself to the task of writing. Cicero wrote in Latin, seeking to make Greek philosophy accessible to his readers in Rome. Most of his works were completed between 46–44 B.C (Ferguson, 2003:381; Cicero, 1972:xi).

4.2.9 Lucretius (c. 99–55 B.C.)

Lucretius was an Epicurean poet from the aristocratic class in Rome and a contemporary of Cicero (Lucretius, 1982:xiv; Sedley, 2010:40). Few concrete details are known about his life. In the introductory comments to *De rerum natura*, W. Rouse suggests that, in all likelihood, Lucretius would have been educated in Rome. It is possible that he also may have traveled to Athens to study at the Epicurean school (Lucretius, 1982:xv–xvi). To say that Lucretius was an avid follower of Epicureanism would be understatement. Lucretius elevated the status of Epicurus beyond the realm of ordinary mortals, comparing him to a god (*De rerum natura* 5.8). Lucretius had an unwavering faith in Epicureanism (Lucretius, 1982:xliv). Lucretius dedicates his work to Memmius—an eminent politician who had been exiled to Athens, who may not have held a favorable view of the Epicureans— apparently in an effort to convert him to Epicureanism (Lucretius, 1982:xlviii; Lucretius, 2008:xii).

4.2.10 Seneca (c. A.D. 1–65)

Seneca was a statesman, philosopher, and tutor to Nero. He was born in Spain but reared in Rome (Moran, 2005:343). He came from a family of financial means. He was the brother of Gallio, the proconsul of Corinth mentioned in Acts 18:12 (Ferguson, 2003:364). Seneca served as a senator until he was appointed as a tutor for Nero (*Lives of the Caesars* 6.7). Seneca served in Nero's palace until his tragic demise, when commanded by Nero to commit suicide in A.D. 65 (*Lives of the Caesars* 6.35; Tacitus, *Annals* 15.60–64). Seneca himself was taught by several philosophers and was well read in Stoic philosophy. It is likely that a wide range of classic Stoic texts would have been available to him through Attalus, his third teacher—who was a Stoic (Sellars, 2014:102). Seneca's letters contain numerous quotations of both Epicurus and Lucretius, demonstrating his fluency in

Epicureanism, as well (Erler, 2010:49). Seneca authored numerous books besides his *Epistles*, which will be discussed in this chapter.

4.2.11 Cornutus (c. A.D. 20–)

Cornutus was a Stoic philosopher of the first century A.D. Before being manumitted, Cornutus served as a slave either to Seneca or to one of Seneca's relatives. Cornutus taught philosophy in Rome during the reign of Nero. The work of Cornutus, then, may display representative Stoic thought in the Roman Empire during the time of Paul's visit to Athens (Ferguson, 2003:365; Torres, 2011:42).

4.2.12 Plutarch (c. A.D. 50–120)

Plutarch was a Middle Platonist, also of the mid-first to early second centuries A.D. He was born to a prominent family in central Greece (Ferguson, 2003:389). Plutarch (1998:xi) studied philosophy in Athens before moving to Rome. Among his prolific works are *Parallel lives*, an historical study, and the *Moralia*. The *Moralia* is a work of great length, occupying seventeen volumes in the Loeb series (including fragments and an index). The *Moralia* is composed of seventy-eight essays and letters on various topics, mostly related to philosophy and religion. Also included in the *Moralia* are several polemics against Stoicism and Epicureanism. Plutarch served as a priest at Delphi for the last thirty years of his life (Ferguson, 2003:389).

4.2.13 Epictetus (c. A.D. 50–120)

Epictetus was a Stoic philosopher. He was born as a child of a slave and, for some years, was himself a slave (Ferguson, 2003:366). He studied under the Stoic teacher, Musonius Rufus, while a slave to Nero's secretary in Rome. He was unable to walk, likely a result of severe abuse in his youth by a master. His schooling included the standard works of Homer as well as some texts by Plato and Xenophon (Epictetus, 1998:vii–ix). As a free man, Epictetus became a philosopher and set up a school in the cosmopolitan city of Nicopolis. He gave advice to those of the prominent class in Rome, including the emperor Hadrian (Long, 2004:11). The teachings of Epictetus are an important source for understanding Stoicism in the late first to early

Greek Views of the Creation of the Universe

second century A.D. (Gill, 2003:35). Epictetus, like Socrates, published none of his own teachings. His teachings were recorded by Flavius Arrian, a student of his, who took detailed lecture notes (Epictetus, 1998:xii–xv).

4.2.14 Explanation of approach to the texts

Athens, then, as the birthplace of both Stoic and Epicurean schools of thought, is central to the philosophers to be examined in this study. For us to have a glimpse of how Paul's message might have interfaced with Athenian thought on the topic of God as Creator and Lord of his creation, we need first to attempt to reconstruct (as best as we can, nearly two millennia later) what the Epicurean and Stoic worldview was like in the first century A.D. It is for this reason that we will investigate works by the philosophers above.

For the sake of clarity, passages to be investigated are divided into the three philosophical schools to be discussed: Classical, Stoic, and Epicurean. The Classical authors, as previously mentioned, are included as sources important to the philosophy of the first century A.D. The Stoic and Epicurean schools are included for the reason that Paul's audience on the Areopagus included adherents to both schools. See below for the classification of passages into philosophical school represented.

Table 11. **Passages as divided by branch of philosophy articulated**

1. Classical	2. Stoic	3. Epicurean
Timaeus 28C–29A	*De natura deorum* II.16	*De rerum natura*
Timaeus 69C	*Discourses* I.9.7	5.156–188
Memorabilia I.4.3–7	*Discourses* II.8.19–21	*De rerum natura*
	Against the physicists	5.195–199
	I.99–100	*De rerum natura*
	Lives VII.147	5.416–457
	Lives VII.137–138	*De natura deorum* I.18–23
	Hymn to Zeus 1–3	*De natura deorum* I.53
	Phaenomena 1–7	*Lives* X.123–124
	De natura deorum II.3–4	*Lives* X.139
	Epistles XCV.48–50	*De natura deorum* I.52
	De natura deorum I.39	*De rerum natura*
	Moralia 1052C–D	2.646–651
	Epidrome 2.1–8	

God as Creator in Acts 17:24

Section 4.3.2 will detail Stoic and Epicurean thought on the topic of creation. This topic corresponds with Paul's subject in his words, "The God who made the universe" (Acts 17:24). The sequential placement of sections will reveal that the two schools were polarized on the topic of the origin of the universe. Section 4.3.3 will detail Stoic and Epicurean thought on the topic of the gods in relationship to creation. This subject corresponds with Paul's topic in his words, "he who is Lord of heaven and earth" in the second phrase of Acts 17:24a. Once again, the sequential placement of sections will illustrate the opposing views of each school. See below for the classification of passages as categorized by topic.

Table 12. Passages of Greek literature divided into four classifications of topic

1. Creation by design	2. Creation by chance	3. Gods superintend creation	4. Gods do not superintend creation
Timaeus 28C–29A	*De rerum natura* 5.156–188	*Hymn to Zeus* 1–3	*Lives* X.123–124
Timaeus 69C	*De rerum natura* 5.195–199	*Phaenomena* 1–7	*Lives* X.139
Memorabilia I.4.3–7	*De rerum natura* 5.416–457	*De natura deorum* II.3–4	*De natura deorum* I.52
De natura deorum II.16	*De natura deorum* I.18–23	*Epistles* XCV.48–50	*De rerum natura* 2.646–651
Discourses I.9.7	*De natura deorum* I.53	*De natura deorum* I.39	
Discourses II.8.19–21		*Moralia* 1052C–D	
Against the physicists I.99–100		*Lives* VII.137–138	
Lives VII.147		*Lives* VII.148	
Lives VII.137		*Epidrome* 2.1–8	

An examination of each of these four classifications of topic should lead us to a reasonable assessment of what the Stoic and Epicurean understanding of the gods and the universe was like in the minds of the philosophers who listened to Paul at the Areopagus in Acts 17.

4.3 INTRODUCTION TO THE ATHENIAN PHILOSOPHICAL SETTING

Athens, the setting for Paul's speech at the Areopagus, was a city with a glorious past. It was the birthplace of the world's first democracy (Pomeroy,

Greek Views of the Creation of the Universe

2008:237–242). It was the seat of political domination in the fifth century B.C. Athens towered over other cities in nearly every sphere of the arts, particularly in the Classical Period (Pomeroy, 2008:242). It was the home of the Parthenon, built in honor of Athena (McRay, 2001:24). It was the birthplace of tragic dramatists Sophocles, Aeschylus, and Euripides. The satirist Aristophanes hailed from Athens. The great historian Thucydides also had roots in Athens (Pomeroy, 2008:225).

Not only was Athens at the center of Greek culture, but Greek culture also became central throughout the lands that would later comprise the Roman Empire. Under the influence of his tutor, Aristotle, Alexander the Great developed a deep affinity for Greek culture. Alexander the Great was so enamored with all things Greek that he embarked on a mission to plant Greek culture across the whole empire. As the Greek Empire expanded, so did the reaches of Greek culture. Alexander the Great accomplished this by setting up Greek cities in conquered lands (McRay, 1991:37–39; Pomeroy *et al.*, 2008:462). Despite the shift of political power to Rome in the first century B.C., Greek language and culture continued to reign supreme from border to border of the empire. Hellenistic culture was so pervasive, in fact, that even families of the Roman aristocracy demanded an education for their children in the language and literature of the Greeks by the first century B.C. (Pomeroy *et al.*, 2008:508).

Famous not only for arts and culture, Athens was also an academic hub for Greek philosophy. Socrates espoused his ideas, day after day, in the marketplace of Athens (Plato, *Apology* 17C). Socrates's teachings were recorded by some of his students, among whom are Plato and Xenophon. Athens was the birthplace of Plato's Academy and Aristotle's Lyceum, both founded in the fourth century B.C. Plato, student of Socrates, created his Academy as an institution of higher learning. Aristotle, student of Plato, established the Lyceum (Ferguson, 2003:332, 338).

Athens was also the birthplace of the Stoic and Epicurean schools of philosophy.[3] Zeno founded the Stoic school in around 300 B.C. Originally called "Zenoians," the group soon became known as the "Stoics," so named after the Painted Stoa (open air stone building) in the Agora where they held their meetings (*Lives* VII.5). The draw of philosophy in Athens was powerful to attract internationals to study in the city. The first three leaders of the Stoic school had all relocated from their homelands to Athens,

---

3. Other branches of philosophy included the Skeptic, Academic, Cynic, and Eclectic schools.

where they studied philosophy. Zeno was from Cyprus. Zeno's successor, Cleanthes, came from Assos. Cleanthes's successor, Chrysippus, came from Soli (Sedley, 2003: 8–10). The Stoic and Epicurean schools were the two best-known philosophical schools in Athens (Keener, 2014:2582; Kurz, 2013:269).

The distance between the Stoa, in the Agora, and Plato's Academy was about two miles. In between the Stoa and the Academy, Epicurus started his own school of philosophy. He met with students in his Garden (*Lives* X.10–11). Epicurus's voice was the voice of dissent. He neither cared for Aristotle's arguments nor followed the teachings of Socrates. In his teachings, Epicurus made efforts to free the people from their fear of natural phenomena, such as thunder and lightning, and to free them from their fear of death (Sedley, 2009:134; Warren, 2010:242–248). Epicurus presented scientific and natural explanations for weather patterns in order to release his hearers from an unreasonable fear of the gods (Taub, 2010:105; Warren, 2010:234–242).

By the first century A.D., however, Athens was no longer the international headquarters for philosophy. The Mithridatic War against Rome, in the early part of the first century B.C., left Plato's Academy and Epicurus's Garden damaged, if not destroyed. Consequently, Athenian philosophy became decentralized as the leading teachers dispersed. The lifeblood of the Athenian philosophical schools continued in diaspora settings (Boys-Stones, 2009:141; Erler, 2010:48). Some of the displaced leaders of the Athenian schools found themselves in Rome. Cicero is among those who learned from these masters and, ultimately, folded Greek philosophy into Latin works. Schools of philosophy emerged in cities outside Athens: in Rome, Alexandria, and Rhodes, to name a few (Sellars, 2014:98). Although the heyday of Greek philosophy in Athens was long past,[4] both Epicurean and Stoic schools continued to have a succession of leaders in Athens by the time Paul arrived in the first century A.D. (Hutchinson, 2013:90).

Would Paul have known Greek philosophy? By the time of Strabo (c. 64 B.C.–A.D. 25), and perhaps much earlier, Paul's hometown of Tarsus was known for offering education in all subjects, including philosophy, at a level rivaling even Athens and Alexandria:

> The people at Tarsus have devoted themselves so eagerly, not only to philosophy, but also to the whole round of education in general,

---

4. But Richard Pervo (2009:424) says that Athens was still in its "golden age" even in the first century A.D.

> that they have surpassed Athens, Alexandria, or any other place that can be named where there have been schools and lectures of philosophers. (*Geography* XIV.5.13, Loeb)

Tarsus, then, was an even greater hub for philosophy than Athens by the first century A.D. Strabo continues on to list numerous philosophers who came from Tarsus—many of whom ended up working abroad. Two of Stoicism's greatest scholarchs, Zeno and Chrysippus, had roots in Tarsus (Sedley, 2003:30). Unlike the schools at Athens, however, the schools at Tarsus mainly attracted locals. Philosophy flourished in Tarsus. It is possible that Paul had gained some knowledge of Greek philosophy in his hometown. Furthermore, as a student of Gamaliel in Jerusalem (Acts 22:3) it is likely that he received training not only in Torah, but also in Greek philosophy:

> But is Greek philosophy forbidden? Behold Rab. Judah declared that Samuel said in the name of Rabban Simeon b. Gamaliel ... There were a thousand pupils in my father's house; five hundred studied Torah and five hundred studied Greek wisdom ... they permitted the household of Rabban Gamaliel to study Greek wisdom because they had close associations with the Government. (*Sotah* 49b)

According to the Talmud, a Jewish education under Gamaliel was not limited to the Hebrew Scriptures. Although a Jew by birth, Paul would have had opportunity to learn Greek philosophy both in Tarsus and in Jerusalem at the feet of Gamaliel.

Greek philosophy encompassed all branches of learning, including theology. The evaluation and rejection of traditional Greek religion was among topics of theological debate. The subject had elicited no small discussion among Greeks for hundreds of years. What are the gods like and how are they to be worshiped? Are they really as Homer and Hesiod described? The Classical Period was thought of as an age of enlightenment and, as such, great minds began to generate scientific explanations for the world while eschewing much of the mythology surrounding the gods. The gods exist, yes, but they are not as Homer and Hesiod depict them. These were the sentiments shared by many; hence, a variety of outlooks emerged. This subject was fodder for both Stoic and Epicurean schools.

Was traditional religion a sham? Some of the literary giants wrote pointed critiques of popular thought about the gods. The critique of traditional religion was not a passing fancy but, rather, a theme woven through the literary fabric of the dramatists, the philosophers, and the popular writers for hundreds of years preceding the arrival of the gospel. Xenophanes, a pre-Socratic philosopher of the sixth century B.C., expressed serious misgivings about idolatry and the religious perception of his time (*Fragments* 11–16; Broadie, 1999:209–210). Plato, in the fourth century B.C., decried many of the stories of Homer and Hesiod as inappropriate for children's ears. He advocated censorship, not because of the ribald nature of the content but because he considered that the stories, themselves, were false (*Republic* 377C–380C; Irwin, 1999:53; Kroeger, 1987:15–16). Epicurus, in his *Letter to Menoeceus*, affirms his belief in the gods but also deemed public opinion about the gods to be in grave error (*Lives* X.123). Zeno, founder of the Stoic school, issued sentiments to the effect that temples and cult statues were "unworthy of the real god" and should be abolished (Algra, 2003:177). Seneca, Stoic thinker of the first century A.D., sought to redefine what true worship should look like: "We do not honor the gods by bloody offerings, but by our right and virtuous intention" (*De Beneficiis* I.6.3 [Algra, 2003:177]). Both Stoic and Epicurean schools had sharp criticisms of traditional religion.[5] Craig Keener (2014:2587) notes an increase in the criticism of traditional religion in the Hellenistic era.[6] Keener (2014:2594) also posits that Stoics imposed allegorical interpretations on Homer and other Greek mythology in order to make the stories more congruent to their doctrines.[7]

Paul's words of critique of idolatry may well have resonated with his Stoic and Epicurean hearers. Paul was not the first to speak against superstition (Acts 17:22). The rejection of superstition was a hallmark of Epicurean thought. Nor was Paul the first to speak against idolatrous worship. Perhaps, the concept that God "does not dwell in temples made by human hands nor is he served by human hands as needing anything" (Acts 17:24–25) had already reached public awareness. With respect to philosophical thought regarding idolatry, Paul's ideas would not have been entirely foreign (Creamer, 2011:49).

---

5. For a fuller discussion of primary sources on the topic of the Greek rejection of traditional religion, see my previous work: "Making known the unknown God: an exploration of Greco-Roman backgrounds related to Paul's Areopagus speech" (Creamer, 2011:45–49).

6. Contra Bertil Gärtner (1955:204–205) who suggested that such criticism was not widespread.

7. Cornutus's work, *Epidrome*, is an example of a Stoic text that utilizes an allegorical hermeneutic.

4.4 ORIGINS OF THE COSMOS

While both Stoic and Epicurean schools may have agreed that the deity (or deities) were not as the ancients had taught, the differences in their understanding of the Creator and creation were stark. While they may have had some agreement regarding what God was not like, the question—What then, is God like?—remained. The Stoics responded one way to this question; the Epicureans responded another way.

The Stoic and Epicurean schools were deeply divided on the topic of cosmology. With regard to the beginnings of the physical world, the Stoics maintained belief in a divine Craftsman who ordered the universe while the Epicureans, on the other hand, repudiated such an idea. Conversely, the Epicureans insisted on a natural explanation for the origin of the universe that excluded the possibility of a divine cause.

4.4.1 Stoics: divine origins

For the Stoics, the very existence of the natural order of the universe stood as proof of the existence of a god. Their reasoning may be summarized as follows. Everything that exists has a maker. Every house has a builder. Without a builder there is no house. Human beings cannot create the world. Therefore, the cosmos has a builder that is not of human origin. The builder of the world is greater in nature to humans. In other words, if not human, then divine in nature.

The centrality of Socrates's teachings to the Stoic school was so fundamental that Philodemus commented several hundred years after Zeno's time that the Stoics are "willing also to be called Socratics" (Philodemus, *De Stoicis XIII* 3 [Sedley, 2003:11]). David Sedley also traces Stoic cosmology to the teachings of Socrates. Since the Stoics had a keen interest in the teachings of Socrates, we will begin our discussion with selections from Plato and Xenophon: our two primary sources for Socrates.

4.4.1.1 *Classical antecedents to Stoicism*

This section offers an analysis of works by Plato and Xenophon, important philosophers for the later development of Stoicism.

God as Creator in Acts 17:24

4.4.1.1.1 PLATO

While Plato's *Republic* may be the title better known to us today, it is his *Timaeus* that became foundational in the development of Stoic cosmology. How is this? Zeno, founder of the Stoic school, had been a student at Plato's Academy for many years as a young man. The study of the *Timaeus* was a core component of the curriculum of the Academy during this period of time (Sedley, 2009:206). The Stoic school also incorporated the *Timaeus* as a foundational part of their curriculum but, it seems, they applied a different hermeneutic than that of the Old Academy (Reydams-Schils, 2013:58). Concepts from the *Timaeus* appear regularly in Stoic cosmological thought from Zeno onwards, but are frequently presented in modified or amplified form. The Stoic philosophers often exercised great liberties with Plato's thought—so much so, that the Platonists considered Stoic philosophy a "degenerate regression from the insights of Plato" (Boys-Stones, 2013:128). Nonetheless, in the words of David Sedley, "the single most significant ancestor of Stoic physics is Plato's *Timaeus*" (Sedley, 2009:209).[8]

The *Timaeus*, then, constitutes an important starting point for our study of Stoic views. Since the Stoics appropriated material from the *Timaeus* in their view of the origins and nature of the world we, too, should consider this text.

With respect to its location within Plato's corpus, the *Timaeus* follows the *Republic*. The *Timaeus* was intended as the first work of a trilogy—a trilogy that was never completed. The second book, *Critias*, follows the *Timaeus*. Only a fragment remains of *Critias*. The third, and final intended work, *Hermocrates*, is missing altogether. The *Timaeus* narrates a dialogue between Socrates and three others. Timaeus, Critias, and Hermocrates are the three main speakers around whom the narrative is structured. In the end, Timaeus is the only speaker whose narrative is preserved in its entirety (Plato, 1929:3).

The *Timaeus* begins with an introduction and the character of Critias relaying the first part of the story of Atlantis, allegedly as told by Solon (21D). After giving the first installment of the Atlantis story, Critias introduces Timaeus as "our best astronomer" who has studied the origin of the world and the origin of humans (27A). A monologue by Timaeus on these topics occupies the rest of the book. Timaeus speaks first of the origin of the cosmos (27C–69A). His attention is then turned to the origin of humans (69A–92C).

---

8. See also Ademollo (2012:217–243); Bryan (2013:59); Long (2010:37–53); and Sedley (2002:41–83).

Greek Views of the Creation of the Universe

It is the middle section of the book (27C–69A), in particular, which has captured the imagination of philosophers and thinkers throughout the ages (Bury, 1928:5). For it is in this section that the speaker, Timaeus, recounts the formation of the world by a divine Craftsman. This Craftsman (δημιουργός) is not a Creator in the strict sense of the word. He does not create *ex-nihilo* but, rather, brings order to pre-existent materials in order to build the universe, which is patterned after a pre-existing model (Bury, 1928:7; *Timaeus* 29A–C).

It is near the beginning of this middle section of the *Timaeus* that our passage is situated. After asserting that the cosmos has "come into existence" (28B), Plato has the character of Timaeus state his case for divine cause for creation:

> And that which has come into existence must necessarily, as we say, have come into existence by reason of some Cause. Now to discover the Maker (ποιητήν) and Father (πατέρα) of this Universe were a task indeed; and having discovered Him, to declare Him unto all men were a thing impossible. However, let us return and inquire further concerning the Cosmos (τοῦ παντὸς), —after which of the Models did its Architect (ὁ τεκταινόμενος) construct it? Was it after that which is self-identical and uniform, or after that which has come into existence? Now if so be that this Cosmos (κόσμος) is beautiful and its Constructor (δημιουργός) good, it is plain that he fixed his gaze on the Eternal. (*Timaeus* 28C–29A)

What is Plato's view of a Creator? In this passage, several words are used to depict the Creator of the universe: Maker (ποιητήν), Father (πατέρα), Architect (ὁ τεκταινόμενος), and Constructor (δημιουργός). These may be understood as synonymous terms that all depict the Creator of the universe. The adjective, good (ἀγαθός), appears in apposition to Constructor (δημιουργός). The passage presents a Creator, good in essence, who builds a Cosmos, beautiful (καλός) in appearance.

Plato utilizes forms of δημιουργός in a number of contexts within the *Timaeus*. First, the word may be used of human artisans or craftspeople. An example of this usage is found within the immediate context of the passage quoted above: "but when the artificer (δημιουργός) of any object, in forming its shape and quality ... uses a created model" (28A, Loeb). A second usage of δημιουργός occurs shortly after, but with the meaning of a divine Craftsman. This is seen in 29A and is quoted above. The comparison that Timaeus is making in this context is between that of a human artisan who works from a pattern as a model and that of a divine Craftsman who also, in the speaker's estimate, uses a model for the construction of the universe. References to a divine Craftsman (δημιουργός) also include 41A (with πατέρα [father] in apposition to δημιουργός), 68E, and 69C. The context in 69C shows the Craftsman crafting not only the universe, but also crafting immortal creatures: gods. It is these gods, and not the Craftsman, who fashion human beings:

> He constructed this present Universe, one single Living creature containing within itself all living creatures both mortal and immortal. And He Himself acts as the Constructor (δημιουργός) of all things divine, but the structure of mortal things He commanded His own engendered sons to execute. And they, imitating Him, on receiving the immortal principle of soul, framed around it a mortal body, and gave it all the body to be its vehicle. (*Timaeus* 69C, Loeb)

The work of the Craftsman, then, is limited to the formation of the universe and the formation of gods. This task completed, the Craftsman delegates the remaining work to the deities he has made: "He delivered over to the young gods the task of moulding mortal bodies, and of framing and controlling all the rest of the human soul" (42D, Loeb; Plato, 1929:7; Reynolds, 2009:179). A third usage of δημιουργός, then, refers to the created deities themselves. In 75B, we have an example. These created deities are referred to as "Constructors of our being." The monologue continues to detail how the deities fashioned the human structure: head, hair, limbs, fingernails, respiration, and blood are among specifics mentioned (75C–81E).

The matter of whether Plato intended his divine craftsman as a literal or figurative entity has been the subject of scholarly debate.[9] There are sound arguments on both sides of the debate over whether Plato intended the *Timaeus* to be read literally or figuratively. Francis Cornford, in his commentary on the *Timaeus*, interprets the demiurge as a mythical figure (1997:26). Classicist Sarah Broadie, in her monograph, *Nature and Divinity in Plato's Timaeus*, constructs her research on the presupposition that Plato did, indeed, intend the demiurge to be understood literally: "My approach ... starts by accepting at face value the account Plato has given, and then attempts to understand why he wanted a Demiurge separate from the world" (2012:7). In *Christ as Creator*, Sean McDonough (2009:109) states: "the idea of a fully

---

9. For an overview of the discussion, see McDonough (2009:101–109); O'Brien (2015:20–35); Sedley (2009:99–107); and Sorabji (1983:268–275).

personal creator strictly parallel to the God of the Bible is probably foreign to Plato. He did, however, affirm with many others that the world was ordered by some type of intelligence." David Sedley (2009:100–101) argues for degrees of deliteralization of the text: at the least, the text explains the "teleological structure of the world." Some readers may lean toward an interpretation that highlights divine causation of the universe in the broadest sense. Others read the narrative as demanding not only divine causation, but causation that produces creation at a specific point in time.

Carl O'Brien, in his monograph, *The demiurge in ancient thought: secondary gods and divine mediators,* argues for a figurative reading of the *Timaeus*: "The bulk of Plato's immediate successors, whom we might imagine to be in a better position to know the views of the master, saw the myth as allegorical and as a feature of Plato's paideutic method" (2015:24). Perhaps omitted here is Aristotle. Aristotle studied at Plato's Academy for twenty years, departing shortly before Plato's demise. It is true that he was not a successor of the Academy, for he had left and started his own school, the Lyceum, also in Athens. Of Aristotle, Diogenes Laertius remarks that he "was Plato's most genuine disciple" (*Lives* V.1). If Plato's "most genuine disciple" (although a dissenting voice after leaving the Academy), it is difficult to imagine that he would have misunderstood Plato's language and intention in the *Timaeus*, even if he disagreed with the premise of the book. On the contrary, Aristotle would have been in a good position to understand precisely what Plato meant in his writings. Aristotle read the *Timaeus* through a lens of a literal view of a divine Craftsman and responded accordingly, as did the Stoics, Epicureans, Galen, and Plutarch (Plutarch, 1976:137; Sedley, 2009:107; O'Brien, 2012:34). Aristotle's cosmology denied a divine Creator or demiurge, positing instead, an uncreated universe (Sedley, 2009:169–170). O'Brien suggests that Aristotle may have taken a literal interpretation mainly for polemical purposes, as an opportunity to defeat Plato's logic. In his view, Aristotle strikes at what he perceived to be one of Plato's weaker arguments: world formation at a datable time (O'Brien, 2015:24–25). While it is true that Aristotle's views on cosmology dissented from those of Plato, it is difficult to prove that he took such a stance solely for the purpose of academic debate. Nevertheless, Aristotle did take a stand against what he understood to be Plato's teaching on cosmology, a teaching that he interpreted as a literal creation at a fixed point in time, in the manner described in the *Timaeus*. Since many philosophers did address the matter of a demiurge, what we can say with certainty is that the question of the demiurge was by no means a settled matter in the ancient world.

Those who argue in favor of a figurative reading cite internal inconsistencies, which would render a literal reading untenable (Sedley, 2009:103). Sedley notes that in *Timaeus* 29D, the speaker, himself, comments of his narrative that it is "the likely story." This remark, Sedley (2009:104) argues, helps the reader to excuse any internal inconsistencies.[10] Sedley continues to argue that Plato believed that there was, "at some determinate past time a discrete process of cosmic creation" (2009:106). The possibility that Plato believed in a universe that came into being at a specific point in time is consistent within the context of ancient philosophy as well as with the context of *Timaeus* 29D. We would do well to consider the immediate context in which the "likely account" is embedded:

> [Timaeus]: Wherefore, Socrates, if in our treatment of a great host of matters regarding the Gods and the generation of the Universe we prove unable to give accounts that are always in all respects self-consistent and perfectly exact, be not thou surprised; rather we should be content if we can furnish accounts that are inferior to none in likelihood, remembering that both I who speak and you who judge are but human creatures, so that it becomes us to accept the likely account of these matters and forbear to search beyond it.
>
> Socrates: Excellent, Timaeus! We must by all means accept it, as you suggest. (*Timaeus* 29D, Loeb)

In favor of a more literal reading, we may consider that this passage reads like a disclaimer to cover imperfections in a plausible narrative rather than an admission that he has been spinning a fable. Timaeus does not appear to be dogmatic about his theories but, rather, of sober mind. "Likely account" seems to mean, here, that the narrative was possible (Broadie, 2012:33), rather than the opposite. Unlike our modern colloquialism, "a likely story" (that means precisely the opposite in today's vernacular) the speaker in this passage uses the phrase to bolster the plausibility of the subject of his lecture. Further, Timaeus proposes that the accounts detailed thus far are "inferior to none in likelihood." In other words, he views his narrative of the generation of the world as the top candidate for likelihood. In response, Socrates urges acceptance of the narrative.

---

10. O'Brien (2012:19) also uses the phrase "the likely story" from *Timaeus* 29D as evidence for a figurative reading.

Greek Views of the Creation of the Universe

For the purpose of this study, we will follow Aristotle, the Stoics, the Epicureans, Galen, Plutarch, (and Broadie) in a "face value" reading of Plato's account in the *Timaeus*. In working toward a plausible worldview for the Stoic and Epicurean hearers of Acts 17, it will be important to attempt to read the *Timaeus* as they might have read it. As this chapter unfolds, we will see specific examples of Stoic and Epicurean philosophers who interacted with, and responded to, the concept of the divine Craftsman as portrayed in the *Timaeus*.

Next, we turn our attention to the use of κόσμος in the *Timaeus*. This is a key term in the book. Timaeus, the speaker, has the cosmos as the primary subject of his speech. So, then, how is κόσμος defined in the *Timaeus*? As already mentioned, the κόσμος is a work produced by the divine Craftsman, δημιουργός (29E) and is built as a copy of a model (29B). The cosmos is constructed with four elements: earth, fire, air, and water (32C). There exists only one cosmos, or universe (31B; 55C). The word κόσμος is used in apposition to heaven (οὐρανός) in 28B, so the terms may be synonymous. Κόσμος is also used in close context with τοῦ παντὸς, literally: "the all," used to denote the whole of creation or the universe (BDAG, 2000 §5722) in 28C as well as 92C. The passage in 92C comprises a summary of the study of the cosmos in the *Timaeus*, and is the concluding paragraph of the book:

> And now at length we may say that our discourse concerning the Universe (τοῦ παντὸς) has reached its termination. For this our Cosmos (κόσμος) has received the living creatures both mortal and immortal and been thereby fulfilled; it being itself a visible Living Creature embracing the visible creatures, a perceptible God made in the image of the Intelligible, most great and good and far and perfect in its generation —even this one Heaven sole of its kind. (*Timaeus* 92C, Loeb)

This paragraph sums up our discussion of cosmos thus far: the cosmos is the universe, the all (τοῦ παντός), and defined also as the heaven. This paragraph also brings up one aspect of the cosmos not yet discussed: the cosmos is both a "Living Creature" and "a perceptible God." Other passages that refer to the cosmos as a "Living Creature" include 30B, "This Cosmos has verily come into existence as a Living Creature (τὸν κόσμον ζῶν)," and 30D, "He constructed it as a Living Creature." Plato's craftsman endows the universe with a soul, thus begetting a god: "And in the midst thereof he set Soul, which He stretched throughout the whole of it, and therewith He enveloped also the exterior of its body . . . And because of this He generated it to be a blessed God" (34B). This concept of the cosmos as god is one that will be picked up and discussed at length by later philosophers. Finally, we should mention that Plato's cosmos is indissoluble, except by the will of its Maker. But this would present an impossible scenario, according to the text, since the dissolution of the universe would be "the deed of a wicked one" (41B) and not that of a good and provident Maker. This contradiction demonstrates the eternal nature of the created order, a point that will be contested and modified by later philosophers.

4.4.1.1.2 XENOPHON

The second Classical philosopher we will discuss as an antecedent to the Stoics is Xenophon (426–354 B.C.). Xenophon's *Memorabilia* begins with a defense for Socrates, who went to trial with charges of impiety and corrupting youth. The verdict was the death sentence (Ferguson, 2003:330; Xenophon, 1979:viii). Book I of *Memorabilia* describes the life of Socrates, and then proceeds to narrate some of Socrates's dialogues, in which certain of his key teachings are preserved. In the fourth section of Book I, Xenophon presents some of Socrates's views on theology. Socrates believed in a deity who created human beings. He argued that the creation itself is evidence of a Creator. Xenophon records a dialogue between Socrates and Aristodemus:

> "Which, think you, deserve the greater admiration, the creators of phantoms without sense and motion, or the creators of living, intelligent, and active beings?"
> "Oh, of living beings, by far, provided only they are created by design and not mere chance."
> "Suppose that it is impossible to guess the purpose of one creature's existence, and obvious that another's serves a useful end, which, in your judgment, is the work of chance, and which of design?"
> "Presumably the creature that serves some useful end is the work of design."
> "Do you not think then that he who created man from the beginning had some useful end in view when he endowed him with his several senses, giving eyes to see visible objects, ears to hear sounds? Would odours again be of any use to us had we not been endowed with nostrils? What perception should we have of

Greek Views of the Creation of the Universe

> sweet and bitter and all things pleasant to the palate had we no tongue in our mouth to discriminate between them?
> ... With such signs of forethought in these arrangements, can you doubt whether they are the works of chance or design?"
> "No, of course not. When I regard them in this light they do look very like the handiwork of a wise and loving creator (σοφοῦ τινος δημιουργοῦ καὶ φιλοζῴου τεχνήματι)." (*Memorabilia* I.4.3-7, Loeb)

Here, Socrates describes the purposefulness of humans as evidence of design. The logic in this passage establishes that the very design of creation proves the existence of a Creator, an argument known as the Argument from Design. The Argument from Design is defined as "any argument that purports to demonstrate, by citing evidence of rational design in the natural world, the existence of *a creator god*" (Sedley, 2009:86). This passage from Xenophon provides a foundational concept on which Stoic philosophers continued to build and elaborate on throughout the centuries.

Writing in the second or third century A.D., hundreds of years after Xenophon's time, Sextus Empiricus gives a version of Xenophon's Argument from Design:

> To the same effect is the argument which is put in this form: — "If you saw a statue which was well wrought would you be in doubt as to whether an artistic intelligence had made it? Or would you not be so far from having any such suspicions that you would actually admire the excellence of its workmanship and its artistic quality? If then, in such cases, when you behold the external form you take it as evidence of a constructor and assert that there exists a craftsman (δημιουργόν) who made it, —when you see the mind within yourself, which is so far superior in its intricacy to any statue or any painting, do you suppose that it came into being as the creation of chance and not by some craftsman (δημιουργοῦ) possessed of power and intelligence to a superlative degree? And he can dwell nowhere else save in the Universe, governing it and generating and increasing the things that are therein. And this person is a God; therefore Gods exist." (*Against the Physicists* 1.99-100, Loeb)

The passage appropriates material from Xenophon's *Memorabilia*, showing the canonical status of Socratic texts in the Stoic schools throughout the Hellenistic era (Sedley, 2009:210-218). The inclusion of this passage in *Against*

God as Creator in Acts 17:24

the Physicists also shows that the doctrine of the divine Craftsman continued to circulate throughout the lifetime of Sextus Empiricus (c. A.D. 200).[11]

4.4.1.2 *Zeno (according to Diogenes Laertius)*

As we transition to Stoic thought on the topic of the origins of the universe, we will begin with Zeno. We will see that Zeno, the founder of the Stoic school, builds on Socratic thought. Zeno appropriates Socratic thought in his teachings with particular regard to a divine Craftsman. Biographer Diogenes Laertius presents the Stoic belief in a Creator in his section on Zeno in *Lives of Eminent Philosophers*. A providential deity is named as "an artificer of the universe":

> The deity, say they, is a living being, immortal, rational, perfect or intelligent in happiness, admitting nothing evil [into him], taking providential care of the world (κόσμου) and all that therein is, but he is not of human shape. He is, however, the artificer (δημιουργὸν) of the universe and, as it were, the father of all. (*Lives* VII.147, Loeb)

This passage is not the first time Diogenes Laertius details Stoic theology of divine origins. A few pages earlier, he identifies god as the Craftsman/artificer, also to be understood as the cosmos itself:

> The term universe or cosmos (κόσμον) is used by them in three senses: (1) of God (θεὸν) himself, the individual being whose quality is derived from the whole of substance; he is indestructible and ingenerable, being the artificer (δημιουργὸς) of this orderly arrangement. (*Lives* VII.137, Loeb)

The concept of a divine Craftsman (here, translated "artificer") appears to be an important facet of Stoic cosmology. Zeno's thought, here, is not his own, but echoes Plato's words from the *Timaeus*: the artificer of the universe is the father. Zeno, as the original Stoic, may have established a precedent for interaction with the *Timaeus* that was emulated by his followers

---

11. In book one of *Against the Physicists*, Sextus Empiricus conducts a methodical examination of the teachings of several philosophers on the topic of gods and the universe, including Aristotle (I.20–23), Epicurus (I.25), Cleanthes (I.88–92), Xenophon (I.92–100), and Zeno (I.101–107). Sextus Empiricus was a director of the Skeptic school. His works contain little original information. Rather, Sextus Empiricus compiled texts from other authors (Sextus Empiricus, 1967:xlii). As a Skeptic philosopher, his aim was to find the flaws in the various schools of philosophical thought.

in generations to come. As our discussion continues, we will see that the Platonic concept of a divine craftsman, or artificer, emerges repeatedly in teachings by later Stoics, all the way up through the first century A.D.

4.4.1.3 Chrysippus (according to Cicero)

Cicero, in his work *De natura deorum*, outlines the basic tenets of the Stoic, Epicurean, and Academic schools of thought in the form of an extended dialogue. Book One of this work features Epicurean arguments presented by the character Vellius. Book Two features Stoic arguments presented by the character Balbus. The third, and final book, outlines views of the Academic school of philosophy as expounded by Cotta (Cicero, 1972:xiv–xv).

Cicero has his Stoic character, Balbus, interact with the words of Stoic founder, Chrysippus, as he outlines representative Stoic logic in a well-reasoned proof of the existence of god. His rationale emanates from natural theology:

> (1) For if, says Chrysippus, there is something in nature which man's mind, reason, strength and power cannot make, that which makes it must be better than man. But the things in the heavens and all those whose regularity is everlasting cannot be created by man. Therefore that by which these are created is better than man. But what more suitable name for this is there than 'god'? (2) Indeed, if the gods do not exist, what can there be in nature better than man, seeing that he alone possesses that highest mark of distinction, reason? But that there should be a man who believes there to be nothing in the whole world better than himself is crazy arrogance. Therefore there is something better. Therefore god really does exist. (*De natura deorum* II.16, Long & Sedley)

Like Socrates, in our passage from *Memorabilia*, Chrysippus is noted for using an Argument from Design as a proof of the existence of god. To the Stoic, the very existence of creation is undeniable evidence of a Creator. Cicero depicts the Stoics as reasoning that atheism is "crazy arrogance." Since it is impossible for the universe to have been created by humans, so Balbus reasons, god must exist.

God as Creator in Acts 17:24

4.4.1.4 Epictetus

Epictetus's *Discourses* provide for us a window into representative Stoic thought in the first century A.D. Socrates had always been a figure central to Stoicism, and this is no less so with Epictetus. Epictetus, in fact, "appropriates Socrates more deeply than any other philosopher after Plato" (Long, 2004:8). Theology was also an important component of learning and knowledge for philosophers in the ancient world. Theological themes are especially prominent in the *Discourses*. Epictetus is noted for developing theological themes in a greater manner than that of other philosophers of the Stoic school. In particular, he gives great attention to the subject of providence (Epictetus, 1998:xxiii).

In the first book of *Discourses*, Epictetus identifies god as Maker and Creator: "But to have god (θεὸν) as our maker (ποιητὴν), and father (πατέρα), and guardian, —shall this not suffice to deliver us from griefs and fears?" (*Discourses* I.9.7, Loeb). The vocabulary of Epictetus's identification of god as Maker, with the words ποιητὴν and πατέρα, is identical to the vocabulary of *Timaeus* 28C, where Plato has "Now to discover the Maker (ποιητὴν) and Father (πατέρα) of this Universe were a task indeed." It seems that Epictetus was alluding to the *Timaeus* with a casual tone, as if such an identification of god were familiar to the reader and needed no further explanation.

Epictetus's designation of god also uses two words that are in common with Paul's identification of God in Acts 17:24 (ὁ θεὸς ὁ ποιήσας). Although the *Discourses* were written, likely, several decades after Paul's speech in Athens, the lexical similarity leaves us with the impression that it may not have been uncommon for Stoics to refer to god as Maker during the first century A.D. Paul may have been aware of this.

In the second book of *Discourses*, Epictetus defines god both as Zeus and as a Craftsman:

> But as it is, because Zeus has made you, do you on that account not care what manner of person you show yourself to be . . . but the works of God (θεοῦ) are capable of movement, have the breath of life, can make use of external impressions, and pass judgement upon them. Do you dishonor the workmanship of this Craftsman (δημιουργοῦ), when you are yourself that workmanship? (*Discourses* II.8.19–21, Loeb)

This passage mirrors the Socratic Argument from Design, as seen in *Memorabilia* I.4. Epictetus, here, uses this Argument from Design as a foundation

Greek Views of the Creation of the Universe

for a moral lecture. Upon this foundation, originally propounded by Socrates, Epictetus builds a further argument in an effort to persuade his hearers toward living an ethical life. Further, Epictetus also utilizes the concept of a divine Craftsman, also found in the *Timaeus*. The *Timaeus*, then, continued to be an important text for Stoic philosophers. Epictetus's reference to Socratic thought in this passage provides evidence for us that Socratic thought remained central for Stoic argumentation well throughout the period of time crucial to our study: the time of Paul's visit to Athens and of Luke's writing of Acts.

Epictetus's use of Maker (ποιητήν) in *Discourses* I.9.7 bears similarity to Paul's use of Maker (ὁ ποιήσας) in Acts 17:24, but his identification of god as Zeus and as a Craftsman (δημιουργός) in *Discourses* II.8.19–21 does not. In this way, we see an instance in Paul's speech where there is, perhaps, the careful use of a term that finds precedence in both the Septuagint of Genesis 1:1 as well as in philosophical thought.

4.4.2 Epicureans: natural origins

The Epicureans, in contrast to the Stoics, regarded the concept of a divine Craftsman as unfathomable. Theirs was the realm of natural explanations. To them, the gods had nothing to do with the formation of the world.

4.4.2.1 Lucretius

Despite being an ardent venerator of Epicurus, who had low regard for poetry (Blank, 2010:216–233; Boys-Stones, 2009:144), Lucretius writes his treatise on Epicureanism in poetic verse of fantastic length. *De rerum natura* (*On the nature of things*) is an extended poem, divided into six books. These six books comprise an entire volume in the Loeb library. Lucretius's poem is the lengthiest extant work on Epicureanism (Nichols, 1976:13). In his poem, Lucretius takes sharp exception to the views of the Stoics and refutes them systematically. In his view, the concept of a divine Craftsman is ludicrous. In his fifth book, he writes:

> (1) Now to say that they [the gods] conceived the wish to create a world wonderful in nature for the sake of men, and that for that reason the gods' work is praiseworthy, so that it is proper for us to sing its praises and consider that it will be everlasting and imperishable, and that it is wrong that what was built by an ancient plan

> of the gods for the sake of mankind, in perpetuity, should ever be disturbed from its foundations by any force, or assailed with words and turned upside down—to elaborate such a fiction, Memmius, is folly. (2) For what profit could imperishable and blessed beings gain from our gratitude, to induce them to take on any task for our sake? What novelty could have tempted hitherto tranquil beings, at so late a stage, to desire a change in their earlier lifestyle? . . . (4) Also, from where did the gods get a model for the creation of the world, and from where was the preconception of men first ingrained in them, to enable them to know and see in their mind what they wished to create, or how did they come to know the power of the primary particles and what they were capable of when their arrangement was altered, if nature itself did not supply a blueprint of creation? (*De rerum natura* 5.156–188, Long & Sedley)

Whereas the Stoics believed in gods who created the world, the Epicureans did not. Lucretius, faced with the age-old question, "If God is good, how can we account for evil in the world?" reasoned that a good and kind god could not have created the world since the world contains evil:

> But even granting that I did not know what are the first-beginnings of things, thus much at least I would dare to affirm from the very ways of heaven, and to show from many other facts, that the world certainly was not made for us by divine power: so great are the faults with which it stands endowed. (*De rerum natura* 5.195–199, Loeb)

Perhaps it was for this reason that the Epicureans sought a natural explanation for the universe, rooted in science rather than theology. Just as the Stoics used the Argument by Design as proof for a Creator, Lucretius references the material world as evidence against the suggestion of a Creator. How could a divine Creator make a world rife with problems and faults? After making this assertion, Lucretius then details the manifold faults with the natural world in the lines that follow, lines 200–221. It did not stand to reason that a good and kind god would have created a world prone to floods, droughts, disease, and death.

After asserting that the world was not made by a divine cause and detailing the many shortcomings of the natural world, Lucretius turns to the subject of how the cosmos came into being:

> But next in order I will describe in what ways that assemblage of matter established earth and sky and the ocean deeps, and the courses of sun and moon. For certainly it was no design of the first-beginnings that led them to place themselves each in its own order with keen

intelligence, nor assuredly did they make any bargain what motions each should produce; but because many first-beginnings of things in many ways, struck with blows and carried along by their own weight from infinite time up to the present, have been accustomed to move and to meet in all manner of ways, and to try all combinations, whatsoever they could produce by coming together, for this reason it comes to pass that being spread abroad through a vast time, by attempting every sort of combination and motion, at length those come together which, being suddenly brought together, often become the beginnings of great things, of earth and sea and sky and the generation of living creatures.

Then, in these circumstances, was not to be seen the sun's wheel soaring aloft with generous light, nor the constellations of the great firmament, nor sea nor sky nor indeed earth nor air nor anything like to our things, but a sort of strange storm, all kinds of beginnings gathered together into a mass, while their discord, exciting war amongst them, made a confusion of intervals, courses, connexions, weights, blows, meetings, motions, because, on account of their different shapes and varying figures, not all when joined together could remain so or make the appropriate motions together. In the next place parts began to separate, like things to join with like, and to parcel out the world, to put its members in place and to arrange its great parts—that is, to set apart high heaven from earth, and to make the sea spread with its water set apart in a place of its own, apart from the pure fires of ether set in their own place.

For in plain fact firstly all the bodies of earth, being heavy and entangled, came together in the midst and all took the lowest place; and the more entangled they came together, the more they squeezed out those particles which could make sea, stars, sun, and moon and the walls of the great world; for these were all made of seeds more smooth and more round and far smaller elements than the earth. (*De rerum natura* 5.416–457, Loeb)

The views of Lucretius were, then, opposed to those of Plato and the Stoics. There was no pattern after which the universe was designed. There is no mention of the involvement of deity. Lucretius's presentation of origins underscores scientific theory and omits any mention of divine cause. The cosmos is represented as beginning as a result of a sudden and cosmic convergence of pre-existent matter. The elements were pieces of a great cosmic puzzle that assembled perfectly into a completed product, of their own accord. The universe, then, was a cosmic accident of infinite proportion, generated by remote chance and not by the will of the gods.

4.4.2.2 Cicero

Cicero's Epicurean character, Vellius, is staunchly opposed to Stoic views of creation. He makes direct reference to Plato's *Timaeus* as he attempts to debunk the Stoic view of a builder of the world:

> (1) Listen to no ungrounded and fictitious doctrines: no creator and builder of the world like the god from Plato's *Timaeus*; no prophetic hag like the Stoics' Providence... no world which is itself an animate, sentient, spherical, glowing, rotating god. These prodigies and marvels are the work of philosophers who dream, not argue. (2) By what kind of mental vision could your Plato have envisaged that great building enterprise by which he has god construct the world? What were the building techniques, the tools, the levers, the machines, the labourers, for such an enterprise? How were the air, fire, water and earth capable of complying with and obeying the architect's wishes?
>
> ... To crown it all, having introduced a world which was not merely born but virtually hand-made as well, he said that it would be everlasting. Do you suppose that this man had so much as sipped at the cup of natural philosophy—that is, of the rationale of nature—when he thinks that something with an origin can be everlasting? What compound is not capable of dissolution? What is there that has a beginning and no end? (3) As for your [the Stoics'] providence, Lucilius... why did it make the world perishable, and not everlasting, as the Platonic god did? (4) A question for both of you [Plato and Stoics] is why the world-builders suddenly appeared on the scene, after sleeping for countless centuries... (5) Was it for the sake of men, as you [the Stoics] are in the habit of saying, that all this world was assembled by god? For wise men? In that case this massive feat of world-building was accomplished for just a handful of people. For foolish men? But, first, god had no reason to do the bad a favour. And second, what did he achieve, seeing that all fools are beyond doubt utterly wretched, above all because they are fools (for what can be called more wretched than folly?), but also because there are so many disadvantages in life that, whereas the wise mitigate them with compensating advantages, fools can neither evade those still to come nor bear those which are present. (*De natura deorum* I.18–23, Long & Sedley)

Greek Views of the Creation of the Universe

Vellius pummels the hearer with a series of rhetorical questions. These questions undermine the Stoic view. Vellius directly engages the *Timaeus* in accordance with Stoic theology, demonstrating the relevance of this text for discussion in the philosophical schools during the Hellenistic period. Further, Vellius's tone is sharp and incorporates undertones of sarcasm towards the Stoics. Stoic views are denounced for their lack of empirical evidence and rational sense. The words "fictitious" and "ungrounded" at the start of Vellius's tirade reveals the Epicurean attitude that not only is their view the superior and correct view, but also the attitude that their view is based on scientific evidence whereas the Stoic view is not. The Epicureans were proponents of empirical evidence (Asmis, 2009:84; Sedley, 2009:141). Vellius harpoons Plato's teaching of a world without end as violating a principle of symmetry: everything that had a beginning must have an end. The Stoics, by this time, however, had parted ways with Plato on the matter of an everlasting world. It is likely that they modified Platonic cosmology because it did not fit with the principle of symmetry. The Stoics, as seen in this passage, taught that the world is perishable. Vellius also harpoons the Stoics for deviating from Plato on this matter. There is no escape from the criticism of Vellius.

After a litany of objections against various philosophers, Vellius pummels, once again, the Stoic notion of world-formation with divine cause:

> For the man to whom we owe all our other teaching taught us too that the world is the product of nature, that there was no need for it to be manufactured, and that so easy was that process, the one which you call impossible without divine expertise, that nature will make, is making, and has made infinitely many worlds. Just because you don't see how nature can do this without some mind, finding yourselves unable to work out the denouement of the argument you resort, like the tragedians, to a *deus ex machina*. (*De natura deorum* I.53, Long & Sedley)

Not only did the Epicureans have a very different view of cosmology than their Stoic counterparts but, here, they are also portrayed as engaging in contentious debate on the topic.

4.4.3 Comparison/contrast with Acts 17

In this section, we have seen that arguments regarding creationism are not unique to our modern era. Such debates reach far back into antiquity. Creationism was a topic of great contention between the Stoic and Epicurean

God as Creator in Acts 17:24

schools of philosophy well into, and beyond, the first century A.D. when Paul gave his message on the Areopagus. Essentially, the Stoics claimed divine participation in the building of the cosmos while the Epicureans did not. Paul made a decisive statement regarding God as Maker of the cosmos in his speech, catapulting his words squarely within the battlefields of a highly controversial topic.

In order to gain some insight into how the Stoics in Paul's audience may have understood his words, we will compare and contrast some of their views of god and the origins of the universe, as well as those of their antecedents, with views of Paul. The following table presents the Stoic and Socratic views in side-by-side format with Paul's views, as expressed in Acts 17.

Table 13.
Some views of the Stoics, their antecedents, and of Paul on the origins of the cosmos

Stoic and antecedent views of origins	Paul's view of origins (Acts 17)
ποιητήν used for Maker	ὁ ποιήσας used for Maker
The Maker is Zeus	The Maker is the supreme God
The Maker is the divine Craftsman	The Maker is the supreme God
Divine craftsman creates cosmos; lesser gods create humans	The supreme God creates both the cosmos and humans
Divine craftsman does not create *ex-nihilo* but, rather, builds the world with pre-existent materials	God is Creator of all
Cosmos modeled after a pattern	No pattern
Creation proves existence of a Creator	Existence of God assumed

Perhaps the most striking similarity between the Stoic view and Paul's view is the use of words related to the verb ποιέω. The Stoics used a noun form, ποιητήν, while Paul used a substantive participle form, ὁ ποιήσας. Both terms refer to the Maker of the cosmos. Both the Stoics and Paul ascribe the origin of the universe to divine cause. The Stoic use of ποιητήν reaches back to Plato, who used the same term in *Timaeus* 28C in his identification of the maker of the cosmos. Paul's use of ὁ ποιήσας reaches back to the Septuagint of Genesis 1:1 (ἐν ἀρχῇ ἐποίησεν ὁ θεὸς τὸν οὐρανὸν καὶ τὴν γῆν).

Greek Views of the Creation of the Universe

It follows that Greek thought informs the Stoic concept of a Maker-while Paul's concept of a Maker is informed by Jewish thought. The Stoics view god as simply arranging pre-existent material. Paul views God as the Creator of all, "who made the universe and all the things in it . . . he himself (αὐτὸς) giving to all life and breath and all things" (Acts 17:24, 25b). The reflexive use of αὐτός in Acts 17:25b underscores the truth that the God who made the cosmos is the same God who gives life to all humans. It is one God who creates both the cosmos and humankind; there are no intermediary deities involved. As discussed in chapter three, Paul's understanding of Creator of all emanates from the Old Testament. Paul's Maker is maker of the farthest reaches of the universe as well as the maker of human beings. Stoic thought, rooted in Plato's *Timaeus*, ascribes the making of human beings to lesser gods, identified as Zeus by Epictetus. Stoic thought, also from the *Timaeus*, consistently cites the Maker using a model after which the universe is patterned, much as a builder of structures might use a blueprint today. This, also, is quite different from the Judeo-Christian view articulated by Paul in Athens. Plato's demiurge is not to have "the status of the omnipotent Creator of Jewish-Christian theology" (Cornford, 1997:36).

In summary, we may conclude that although Paul uses ποιέω, a word in common use by the Stoics to identify God as Maker, the way he defines the Maker is quite different from the way the Stoics might define the Maker. To the Stoics, then, it might have been a familiar thought that God is the Maker of the cosmos. Paul clearly presents a literal view of a Creator, a view that would have fit well, thus far, with Stoic ideas. The new thought might have been that the one God is Maker of both humans and the cosmos. Furthermore, any Stoic familiar with the *Timaeus* might recall that Plato stated that not only is it difficult to discover the Maker, but also, to declare him to all humans is impossible (*Timaeus* 28C). With audacity, then, Paul makes known the God whom Plato taught was essentially unknowable.

With respect to the Epicureans in Paul's audience on the Areopagus, Paul's statements contradicted a closely held doctrine of theirs regarding the origin of the universe. Since the Epicureans denied any form of divine participation in the formation of the cosmos, they may not have welcomed Paul's identification of God as Maker. The table below shows the contrast between the Epicurean view and Paul's view.

Table 14. Some views of the Epicureans and of Paul on the origins of the cosmos

Epicurean view of origins	Paul's view of origins (Acts 17)
God creates nothing	God creates both the cosmos and humans
The cosmos comes about by accidental convergence of pre-existent materials	God is Creator of all

Paul's identification of God as Maker may have seemed ludicrous to the Epicureans. The same objections that they presented to the Stoics may also have applied to their perception of Paul's view. Paul's bold statement about God as Maker was antithetical to their view of an accidental formation of the universe when a cosmic confluence of atoms and pre-existent materials happened, randomly, to converge into the cosmos. Paul makes no mention of scientific theory but, rather, discusses divine cause. This was not common ground to the Epicureans.[12] It was, however, a common controversy.

4.5 RELATIONSHIP OF THE GODS TO THE COSMOS

Next, we turn to Stoic and Epicureans theologies regarding the relationship of the divine to the ordered universe. Luke records Paul making the point that the Creator of the cosmos is also the Lord of the cosmos (Acts 17:24). The Creator that Paul declares as Lord is also provident and superintendent over his creation. What, then, about the views of the Stoics and Epicureans with regard to the jurisdiction, or lack thereof, of the deities to the created order? Topics of philosophical debate between the Stoics and Epicureans included, among others, the nature of the gods, providence, and the presence of the divine. Stoics maintained that providential gods superintend the affairs of humans. Epicureans, on the other hand, maintained that since the gods maintain a state of perpetual tranquility they must, therefore, be unconcerned with troublesome matters on earth—or any matters on earth, for that matter.

---

12. But Beverly Gaventa (2003:252) suggests that Paul says little that would have been unwelcome to the philosophers until Acts 17:30–31, when he calls all to repentance and mentions the resurrection.

Greek Views of the Creation of the Universe

4.5.1 Stoics: gods watch over the cosmos

The Stoics embraced a theology that affirmed an omnipotent and omnipresent god. To the Stoics, god was understood as a deity who attends and oversees creation with providence (Schnabel, 2012:732). The theme of divine providence runs throughout many works of Stoic philosophy. The line between the divine and the cosmos become blurred, however, when it comes to the doctrine of the presence of god. The Stoic god is not only present with all creation; he *is* all creation. The Stoics believed in pantheism (Algra, 2003:165–170; Lightfoot, 2014:232).

4.5.1.1 Cleanthes

In the opening lines of his *Hymn to Zeus*, Cleanthes names Zeus as the omnipotent prime mover who orders the disordered and loves the unloved:

> (1) Most majestic of immortals, many-titled, ever omnipotent Zeus, prime mover of nature, who with your law steer all things, hail to you. For it is proper for any mortal to address you: we are your offspring, and alone of all mortal creatures which are alive and tread the earth we bear a likeness to god. Therefore I shall hymn you and sing forever of your might. (2) All this cosmos, as it spins around the earth, obeys you, whichever way you lead, and willingly submits to your sway. Such is the double-edged fiery ever-living thunderbolt which you hold at the ready in your unvanquished hands. For under its strokes all the works of nature are accomplished. With it you direct the universal reason which runs through all things and intermingles with the lights of heaven both great and small ... (3) No deed is done on earth, god, without your offices, nor in the divine ethereal vault of heaven, nor at sea, save what bad men do in their folly. But you know how to make things crooked straight and to order things disorderly. You love things unloved. For you have so welded into one all things good and bad that they all share in a single everlasting reason. (*Hymn to Zeus* 1–3, Long & Sedley)

The reference to Zeus is not original thinking on the part of Cleanthes but, rather, reaches back to Homeric texts. Zeus is named as "father" in *Illiad* 3.320 (Meijer, 2008:71). In Cleanthes's understanding, god pervades all. His view is earth-centric: all the cosmos spins around earth. Zeus is depicted as a dynamic and powerful god who interacts closely with—and directs—both planetary and human affairs. It is under the fiery thunderbolt of Zeus that acts of nature are produced. All deeds done on earth are produced by Zeus, but with a caveat: "save what bad men do in their folly." Zeus may not be blamed for the deeds of the wicked. This passage reflects a belief in a god who is responsible for all the good and rules over the earth with cosmic jurisdiction.

4.5.1.2 Aratus

A contemporary of Cleanthes, Aratus also identifies Zeus as the omnipotent deity. What was the early Stoic notion of the nearness of god? In his poem, *Phaenomena*, Aratus writes of the presence of Zeus everywhere:

> From Zeus let us begin; him do we mortals never leave unnamed; full of Zeus are all the streets and all the market-places of men; full is the sea and the havens thereof; always we all have need of Zeus. For we are also his offspring; and he in his kindness unto men giveth favorable signs and wakeneth the people to work, reminding them of livelihood. (*Phaenomena* 1–7, Loeb)

This Stoic perception of Zeus was a positive one. Aratus's Zeus is a kind god. This god is both far off and nearby. He dwells in the sea and in the markets and in the very neighborhoods where humans live. Aratus's Zeus is omnipresent, the Maker of humans ("We are also his offspring"), and also shows evidence of his providence in his signs and interactions with mortals. In comparison, Paul's speech quotes directly from Aratus's *Phaenomena*: "for we also are his offspring" (Acts 17:28), showing similarity of thought. Paul's statement that "he is not far from each one of us. For in him we live and move and exist" in Acts 17:27b–28a also finds some similarity in thought with Aratus's words regarding the presence of the divine in the streets and in the market-places and in the sea. The primary difference lays in the identification of who God is. To Aratus, Zeus is god. To Paul, the Creator of the cosmos is God.

4.5.1.3 Cicero

Cicero depicts Stoicism as affirming not only the existence and presence of the gods, but also their involvement with creation. Stoic teachings on the cornerstone doctrines of theology are explained by Balbus:

> The topic of the immortal gods which you raise is divided by our school into four parts: first they prove that the gods exist; next they explain their nature; then they show that the world is governed by

Greek Views of the Creation of the Universe

them; and lastly that they care for the fortunes of mankind ... and not only as Jove but as sovereign of the world, ruling all things with his nod, and as Ennius likewise says—father of gods and men, a deity omnipresent and omnipotent. (*De natura deorum* II.3-4, Loeb)

Cicero, in this presentation of Stoic theology, subsumes Stoic doctrines of the nature of god as detailed by earlier philosophers such as Cleanthes and Aratus. His purpose is to summarize the teachings of the school on the gods. This he does by highlighting the four-part question concerning the immortal gods and by naming Jove (the corresponding god to Zeus in Roman mythology) as the omnipresent, all-powerful, "sovereign of the world." Cicero's presentation demonstrates the enduring character of these doctrines regarding the nature of the gods, as they flourished from the early days of the school until the days of Cicero in the first century B.C. and beyond.

Paul covers some topics related to this four-part question regarding the nature of God in his speech in Acts 17:22-31. Relating to the first and second parts of the Stoic question, that there is a God and what his nature is like, Paul identifies the God he proclaims and describes his character: God "made the universe and all the things in it" (v. 24a), "does not dwell in temples" (v. 24b), and is "not far from each one of us" (v. 27). Along the lines of the third part of the Stoic question, that the "world is governed by them," Paul states, "he who is Lord" (v. 24a), and that "he commands all people everywhere to repent, because he has fixed a day in which he intends to judge the world in righteousness" (vv. 30-31). Finally, aspects of the fourth part of the Stoic question regarding divine superintendence over human affairs can be seen in Paul's speech: "From one he made every nation of people to dwell on all the face of the earth, having designated fixed times and the boundaries of their dwelling places to search for God" (vv. 26-27). It seems that Paul may have been well aware of Stoic concerns. God is indeed involved in the affairs of humankind and will bring all to account. The Christian God is both omnipotent and omnipresent.

4.5.1.4 Seneca

Seneca echoes the sentiments of previous Stoics when it comes to the topic of the kindness and providence of god. In his *Epistles*, Seneca depicts the gods as kind and in control of the universe:

> Although a man hear what limit he should observe in sacrifice, and how far he should recoil from burdensome superstitions, he

> will never make sufficient progress until he has conceived a right idea of God—regarding Him as one who possesses all things, and allots all things, and bestows them without price. And what reason have the gods for doing deeds of kindness? It is their nature... The first way to worship the gods is to believe in the gods; the next to acknowledge their majesty, to acknowledge their goodness without which there is no majesty. Also, to know that they are supreme commanders in the universe, controlling all things by their power and acting as guardians of the human race, even though they are sometimes unmindful of the individual. They neither give nor have evil; but they do chasten and restrain certain persons, and impose penalties, and sometimes punish by bestowing that which seems good outwardly. Would you win over the gods? Then be a good man. Whoever imitates them, is worshipping them sufficiently. (*Epistles* XCV.48–50, Loeb)

Thus, the Stoic view of the nature of the gods affirmed a powerful force in the cosmos. This passage makes clear that throughout the centuries, Stoics continued to regard the gods as having jurisdiction over all creation. Seneca portrays the gods as "supreme commanders" who control everything, and act as guardians. These gods, as overseers, are not indifferent to the affairs of humans but do intervene to bring discipline. In light of this, Seneca advocates being a "good man" as adequate worship. Seneca's work is a verification that Stoics continued to discuss topics related to theology well into the first century A.D., the time period of particular interest to this study, since it was during this century that Paul stood in the Areopagus and spoke to philosophers in Athens. From this, we may know that the jurisdiction of the gods, or "lordship," also may have been a pertinent topic for Stoics in Paul's audience in Athens.

Up to this point, we have discussed Stoic views on the nature of the gods in relation to the created order. We have observed texts that show the Stoic view of an omnipresent, omnipotent deity who manages the cosmos and manages humankind. All of this, the Stoic deity does with kindness. Our discussion, however, would be incomplete if we ended here. Stoics affirmed not only the presence of god in the cosmos but also that god *is* the cosmos.

4.5.1.5 Chrysippus (according to Cicero, Plutarch, and Diogenes Laertius)

According to Cicero, Chrysippus made a bold assertion of the nature of god:

> For he [Chrysippus] says that divine power resides in reason and in the mind and intellect of universal nature. He says that god is the world itself, and the universal pervasiveness of its mind; also that he is the world's own commanding-faculty, since he is located in intellect and reason; that he is the common nature of things, universal and all-embracing; also the force of fate and the necessity of future events. In addition he is fire; and the aether of which I spoke earlier; also things in a natural state of flux and mobility, like water, earth, air, sun, moon and stars; and the all-embracing whole; and even those men who have attained immortality. (*De natura deorum* I.39, Long & Sedley)

Chrysippus's god is a pantheistic god. Although Chrysippus makes a bold assertion that god is the world, it is not an idea unique to his own thought. Rather, it echoes the *Timaeus*, a text that he—along with other students of philosophy—would have studied. It appears that Plato's view of an ensouled cosmos lent itself to pantheism. Plato viewed the cosmos as a living, eternal creature with soul and reason. Plato also calls the created order "god" in *Timaeus* 34B and 92C. Likewise, in Chrysippus's teaching, all of the cosmos is god. God is the universal intellect. God includes, but is not limited to, the elements of planet earth (fire, water, earth, air). He is everything in the universe, including the sun, moon, and stars. Not only that, but "men who have attained immortality" are part of the "all-embracing whole." Such thought has nothing, whatsoever, in common with the God Paul preaches.

Plutarch (c. A.D. 50–120) reiterates the sentiments of Chrysippus on the nature of the cosmos. According to Plutarch, Chrysippus taught that the cosmos would never come to an end since Zeus was continually growing and absorbing the material world:

> In the first book on Providence he [Chrysippus] says that Zeus goes on growing until all things have been consumed in his growth: "For, since death is the separation of soul from body and the soul of the universe is not separated but goes on growing continually until it has completely absorbed its matter, the universe must not be said to die." (*Moralia* 1052C–D, Loeb)

God as Creator in Acts 17:24

Chrysippus's teachings on pantheism were, then, still under discussion for many centuries past his demise. This creates for us a scenario of Stoics and other philosophers continuing to interact with these topics during the time of the early church—the time when Paul stood in the Areopagus.

The ideas generated by Chrysippus and Zeno were not short-lived. Diogenes Laertius wrote his *Lives of Eminent Philosophers* no earlier than the third century A.D., many hundreds of years after the days of the early founders of the Stoic school. In the seventh chapter of *Lives*, Diogenes Laertius explains Zeno's thought regarding the nature of the universe:

> The term universe or cosmos (κόσμον) is used by them in three senses: (1) of God himself, the individual being whose quality is derived from the whole of substance; he is indestructible and ingenerable, being the artificer (δημιουργὸς) of this orderly arrangement, who at stated periods of time absorbs into himself the whole of substance and again creates it from himself. (2) Again, they give the name of cosmos (κόσμον) to the orderly arrangement of the heavenly bodies in itself as such; and (3) in the third place to that whole of which these two are parts. Again, the cosmos (κόσμος) is defined as the individual being qualifying the whole of substance, or, in the words of Posidonius in his elementary treatise on *Celestial Phenomena*, a system made up of heaven and earth and the natures in them, or, again, as a system constituted by gods and men and all things created for their sake. By heaven is meant the extreme circumference or ring in which the deity has his seat. The world (κόσμον), in their view, is ordered by reason and providence: so says Chrysippus in the fifth book of his treatise *On Providence*. (*Lives* VII.137–138, Loeb)

Zeno, as the original Stoic, is described as affirming the Platonic notion of the cosmos as god. God himself, at times, was thought to indwell the substance of his creation. Diogenes Laertius presents the Stoic artificer of the universe as the same god who, on occasion, consumes all he has created in the past and continues the process of creation into the present.

A few lines later, also in *Lives* VII.148, Diogenes Laertius traces pantheism to Zeno, as founder of the Stoic school, as well as to Chrysippus, "The substance of God is declared by Zeno to be the whole world and the heaven, as well as by Chrysippus in his first book, *Of the Gods*." Diogenes Laertius goes on next to state that several other authors wrote of similar ideas, showing the prevalence of pantheism in the Stoic school.

Greek Views of the Creation of the Universe

4.5.1.6 Cornutus

A text of particular note is one by first century Stoic philosopher Lucius Annaeus Cornutus. Among Cornutus's extant works, we have the text of his volume, *Epidrome*. This was his primary work of philosophy—a work that has been neglected by scholars, despite a resurgence of interest in Hellenistic philosophy (Boys-Stones, 2007:77). The *Epidrome* contains an allegorical interpretation of Greek mythology, with the intent of motivating the reader to base worship on piety rather than superstition (Boys-Stones, 2007:77–78, 88; Torres, 2011:44). From the early pages of the *Epidrome*, we have the following statement regarding the soul of the cosmos:

> Just as we are governed by a soul, so the cosmos has a soul which holds it together, and this is called "Zeus"—who is pre-eminently *alive* and *lives* through all things that *live*. Because of this, Zeus is said to rule the universe—just as our soul and nature might be said to rule us. And we call him "Dia" because *through* him everything comes to be and is sustained ... Zeus is said to live in Heaven, since Heaven is the most important part of the cosmic soul. (*Epidrome* 2.1–8, Boys-Stones)[13]

Cornutus references Zeus, as did Cleanthes and Aratus, several centuries prior. His assertions also reflect the teachings of Chrysippus, as we observed in Cicero's work, *De natura deorum* I.39. Further, Cornutus's statement that "the cosmos has a soul" alludes to Platonic thought (as discussed earlier) in passages such as *Timaeus*, 34B and 92C. Pantheism was, then, pervasive in Stoic thought from the time of Zeno well through the first century A.D. With respect to pantheism, Stoic thought is completely incongruent to the Judeo-Christian God presented in Acts 17:24–31.

4.5.2 Epicureans: gods are unconcerned with the cosmos

We have already seen that the Epicureans refuted Stoic notions of the beginning of the world. Epicurean disagreement with Stoic theology did not end there. Epicureans also contended against the veracity of Stoic arguments on other topics. Here, we will examine Epicurean thought regarding the nearness of god, providence, and pantheism.

---

13. Corresponds with 3.3–14 in Thesaurus Linguae Graecae (TLG).

4.5.2.1 Epicurus

The Epicureans, despite their denial of a divine artificer of the universe, had a founder who affirmed the existence of gods—with the caveat that they are not anything like the portrayal given by the general public. Epicurus, in his *Letter to Menoeceus,* affirms the existence of deities. In this letter, Epicurus attributes two main characteristics to the gods, immortality and blessedness:

> First believe that God is a living being immortal and blessed, according to the notion of a god indicated by the common sense of mankind; and so believing, thou shalt not affirm of him aught that is foreign to this immortality or that agrees not with blessedness, but shalt believe about him whatever may uphold both his blessedness and his immortality. For verily there are gods, and the knowledge of them is manifest; but they are not such as the multitude believe, seeing that men do not steadfastly maintain the notions they form respecting them. Not the man who denies the gods worshipped by the multitude, but he who affirms of the gods what the multitude believes about them is truly impious. For the utterances of the multitude about the gods are not true preconceptions but false assumptions; hence it is that the greatest evils happen to the wicked and the greatest blessings happen to the good from the hand of the gods, seeing that they are always favourable to their own good qualities and take pleasure in men like unto themselves, but reject as alien whatever is not of their kind. (*Lives* X.123–124, Loeb)

Although Epicurus wrote of the existence of gods, he refuted the popular concept of divine guardianship: "they are not as many believe, for they do not keep watch over them as they think" (*Lives* X.123). The gods of Epicurus were distant from humanity. What might be the rationale for this statement? For Epicurus, the gods could not be concerned with the oversight of the cosmos since to be so would be inconsistent with their nature of blessedness. It would be impossible for the gods to retain their state of blessedness should they be concerned with earthly affairs, for earthly affairs are troublesome. Epicurus asserted his view of the nature of the divine in the first of his *Maxims*: "A blessed and eternal being has no trouble himself and brings no trouble upon any other being; hence he is exempt from movements of anger and partiality, for every such movement implies weakness" (*Lives* X.139, Loeb). For Epicurus, the gods are not engaged with the affairs of humans because to do so would disturb their perpetual state of tranquility (O'Keefe, 2010:157).

Greek Views of the Creation of the Universe

These immortal and blessed deities are not shown as completely disengaged with the human race but, rather, as showing favor to those like themselves and not to others. The formula in this passage is that evils come to the wicked and blessings come to the good "from the hand of the gods." The gods, then, reward good and punish evil, but are not watching over humanity as closely as the Stoics purport.

4.5.2.2 *Lucretius*

Echoing the teachings of Epicurus, Lucretius also bases his understanding of the distance of the gods from mortals on an understanding of the fundamental nature of the gods. The gods are peaceful in their very nature, and maintain that peace by staying far away from humankind:

> For the very nature of divinity must necessarily enjoy immortal life in the deepest peace, far removed and separated from our affairs; for without any pain, without danger, itself mighty by its own resources, needing us not at all, it is neither propitiated with services nor touched by wrath. (*De rerum natura* 2.646–651, Loeb)

There is not much original thought in these lines, as they reflect the words of Epicurus discussed above. Lucretius does underscore the distance of the gods, "far removed and separated from our affairs." What these lines do show us is that the teachings of Epicurus regarding the distance of the gods from the cosmos remained unchanged in Lucretius's thought: in the first century B.C. Epicurean thought, like Stoic thought, maintained consistency over time. Epicurus sought to free his followers from fear of angry gods. It is in this vein that Lucretius also sought to persuade his readers to follow the way of Epicureanism.

4.5.2.3 *Cicero*

Cicero has Vellius expound the Epicurean view of the nature of the gods with respect to the cosmos. Vellius's remarks echo Epicurus's writings. Vellius refutes the Stoic ideas of pantheism and divine guardianship. True to form, Vellius adorns his arguments with a flourish of satire:

> [Speaker: the Epicurean Vellius] (1) We can rightly call this god of ours blessed, and your [the Stoics'] extremely overworked. For if the world itself is god, what can be less tranquil than rotating

about an axis without a moment's break at the heaven's amazing speed? And yet nothing is blessed if it is not tranquil. Or if god is some being within the world, there to rule, to control, to maintain the orbits of the heavenly bodies, the succession of seasons, and the variations and regularities of things, to watch over land and sea and guard men's well-being and lives, he is surely involved in a troublesome and laborious job. We, on the other hand, place the blessed life in peace of mind and in freedom from all duties. (*De natura deorum* I.52, Long & Sedley)

This portion of Vellius's argument against pantheism and divine guardianship is based upon a definition of blessedness as tranquility. Tranquility mandates the absence of responsibility. How could the gods be blessed, Vellius reasons, if they are burdened with the efforts of propelling the earth, causing the seasons, and overseeing the affairs of humans? Blessedness, then, in the Epicurean view, requires freedom from responsibility and freedom from work. Since the gods are blessed they are, therefore, also free from the oversight of the universe. Thus, the Epicureans define the nature of their gods in terms quite different from the Stoics.

4.5.3 Comparison/contrast with Acts 17

The Stoics and Epicureans espoused opposing views on nearly every facet of thought related to the topic of the relationship of the gods to the cosmos. As with the topic of the origins of the cosmos, Paul's views find some commonality with Stoics but not much with Epicureans on the topic of the relationship of the divine to the ordered universe. The following table outlines the views of the Stoics with regard to the relationship of the gods to the cosmos in comparison and contrast to the views Paul presented on the Areopagus.

Table 15. Views of the Stoics and of Paul on the relationship of the divine to the cosmos

Stoic view of relationship of gods to cosmos	Paul's view of relationship of God to cosmos (Acts 17)
The gods rule and have jurisdiction over creation	The Maker is also the Lord over creation
The gods are omnipresent	God is omnipresent
The cosmos is the same as God	The cosmos is separate from God

Greek Views of the Creation of the Universe

The Stoics affirmed that the gods kept careful watch over creation. In their providence, they also rule and govern over the created order. This affirmation comports with Paul's view that the God who made the world is also the God who is Lord of heaven and earth. Some aspects of Stoic doctrine, however, lean in favor of fatalism, which would be an extreme view not endorsed by Paul. The words of Paul's speech might have rung true to the ears of his Stoic hearers on the topic of the Maker also being Lord. The words of Paul's speech on the topic of the presence of God, "he is not far from each one of us. For in him we live and move and exist" (Acts 17:27–28a), also bear some similarity to Stoic thought, particularly as we have read in Aratus's *Phaenomena*.

While Paul does affirm the presence of God in the cosmos, he makes no affirmation, whatsoever, of pantheism. God created the world, yes, but the substance of the world is not the substance of God's being. The created order of the universe and all that is in it is presented as the work of God, but not *as* God. Paul defines the cosmos as the same as the heaven and the earth. Although Luke records Paul using κόσμος, a word common to the vocabulary of Greek philosophers, Paul's definition of the word was not the same as the Stoic's definition.[14] Although pantheism has no place in Judeo-Christian thought, Paul does not speak directly against it in his speech, as he does with idolatry. It may be that Paul limited his negative comments to idolatry because he knew that the philosophers in his audience, both Stoic and Epicurean, had already reached the conclusion that idolatry was inherently wrong. Or, perhaps he limits his critiques to idolatry in response to those who had suggested that he was trying to introduce new gods. Whatever the case, he makes his point clear: the God who made the world is near to his creation.

What about the Epicureans? How might they have understood Paul's declarations? Once again, the Epicureans would have taken exception to points made by Paul in his speech. The following table outlines the Epicurean view of the relationship of the divine to the cosmos in comparison and contrast with the views preached by Paul in Acts 17.

---

14. See also Dibelius (1956:41); Gärtner (1955:174); Haenchen (1971:522); Marshall (1980:286); Pervo (2009: 434); Polhill (1992:372); Williams (1990:305); and Witherington (1998:525).

God as Creator in Acts 17:24

Table 16.
Views of the Epicureans and of Paul on the relationship of the divine to the cosmos

Epicurean view of relationship of gods to cosmos	Paul's view of relationship of God to cosmos (Acts 17)
The gods do not watch over creation	The Maker is also the Lord over creation
The gods are far away	God is near
The cosmos is separate from the gods	The cosmos is separate from God

The Epicurean concept of god was in stark opposition to the Judeo-Christian view presented by Paul. The Epicureans thought of the gods as maintaining their state of perpetual tranquility and blessedness by keeping far from the human race, since humans have continual trouble and discord. In their view, the gods had to keep their distance in order to keep their peace. Accordingly, because of their distance, the gods are not guardians of humankind. Paul's remarks about the nearness of God were, as Derek Thomas puts it, "in direct contradiction to the Epicureans" (Thomas, 2011:502). On one point the Epicureans would agree with the Judeo-Christian worldview: the cosmos is separate from God. This point is implied but not explicitly stated in the Areopagus speech.

4.6 SUMMARY

In this chapter, we have examined sources for the Stoic and Epicurean understanding of the divine, as it exists with reference to the cosmos. The Stoics and Epicureans were at loggerheads against one another on multiple issues of theology and cosmology. The Stoics embraced a belief in a divine Craftsman that fashioned the cosmos after a pattern. The Epicureans rejected this notion as nonsense. They posited, instead, that the formation of the universe was the result of sheer chance: the elements made a random and sudden cosmic convergence that resulted in the appearance of the earth and all planetary bodies. The Stoics had a well-developed theology of providence. They believed that not only are the gods provident over all in their nearness but, also, that the cosmos is god. The Epicureans repudiated the concepts of providence and pantheism as wholly inconsistent with the nature of the divine, for their gods were blessed. Blessedness, in the view of Epicurus and those who followed him, mandated tranquility. And how, then, would it be possible for a tranquil

Greek Views of the Creation of the Universe

god to engage with an un-tranquil world? No, in their minds, it was impossible. Therefore, the Epicureans believed in gods who maintained blessedness by keeping far from humanity. Regarding matters of theology and cosmology, the Stoics and Epicureans could not have disagreed more completely.

In his speech, Paul makes use of two words, ποιέω and κόσμος, which were also common to writings by Greek philosophers. Paul identifies God as Maker (ὁ θεὸς ὁ ποιήσας). Ποιέω was used to identify god in Plato's *Timaeus* as well as in various Stoic authors. In this respect, Paul chose vocabulary that was endemic to both the Old Testament and to Greek literature in order to identify the God he was proclaiming. The terms were familiar to Paul's audience, but his definition of terms would have been new to them, since his understanding derived from the Judeo-Christian tradition and not from pagan philosophy. Paul identifies the Maker of the cosmos as the supreme God, the God of the Old Testament and not as the maker in Plato and other Stoic or Epicurean writers. The Maker presented in the Areopagus speech is the God who created not only the universe, but also everything in it—including human beings. Therefore, Paul uses a familiar word but introduces a new understanding of what that word means.

Similarly, Paul uses κόσμος, another word common to Greek literature. The Stoics would have understood κόσμος not only as the handiwork of a Maker, but also as God himself, since they were known to ascribe to pantheism. Paul's definition of κόσμος includes the handiwork of the Maker but in no way affirms pantheism. God is separate from that which he has made. The Epicureans understood the κόσμος as the product of natural processes and not the work of a Maker. In this respect, while Paul used words familiar to his Stoic and Epicurean hearers, he defined them strictly according to the Judeo-Christian worldview—and not according to the worldview of the Greeks to whom he was preaching. The common ground was in the vocabulary choice; the new ground was in the definition of words chosen. Paul, then, relates to his audience with familiar concepts but challenges the understanding of his hearers by presenting new content. Paul redefines words for his audience.

The Stoics in Paul's audience might have found much to agree with: God as Maker, as ruler of creation, and as omnipresent. The Epicureans, on the other hand, would have found much to disagree with. They denied a Creator God, denied divine governance, and denied omnipresence. In his foray into the domain of philosophical discussion, Paul's assertions on the Areopagus did not find universal commonality with the particular beliefs of those in his audience. Paul's assertions did, however, find a common controversy on the topic of the origins of the cosmos and the relationship of God to the cosmos.

Chapter 5

Conclusion

5.1 SUMMARY OF FINDINGS

THE RESULTS OF THIS study show that the identification of God as Maker of the universe and Lord over his creation in the Areopagus speech (Acts 17:24) both engaged and confronted the contemporary worldview of Paul's Stoic and Epicurean audience in Athens. Paul engaged the audience by employing words and themes that were familiar to Greek philosophers. Paul defined these words and themes in such a way that he communicated a new message to them: a message rooted in the Jewish understanding of the Creator God. In their commentaries, F.F. Bruce (1990:382) and C.K. Barrett (1998:840) have noted the presence of words familiar to Greek culture in the speech within the context of the proclamation of the Old Testament theme of God as Creator. The constraint of space in commentaries, however, prohibits detailed explanation. This study attempts to bridge the gap.

The primary aim of this study has been to investigate Paul's methods of contextualization of the topic of God as Creator in Acts 17:24. To arrive at an understanding of Paul's methods of cross-cultural communication in Athens, we investigated three specific areas of inquiry as objectives. Each of these three objectives was met through corresponding chapters. Chapter two investigated the literary setting and context of Acts 17:24. Chapter three investigated the semantic context for the identification of God as Maker of heaven and earth in the New Testament, the Septuagint, and other Jewish writings. Chapter four investigated the Greek views of the creation of the

Conclusion

universe, with particular attention to the Stoic and Epicurean schools of thought in various philosophical writings. Paul's approach in Acts 17:24 was compared and contrasted with semantic contexts in Jewish literature identified in chapter three, and, also, with passages of Greek literature on the topic of creation in chapter four.

In chapter two, a study of the literary setting showed that Acts was written by Luke, a Gentile, for Theophilus, also a Gentile. Evidence shows that Theophilus was a man of status and, quite possibly, a Roman official. The prologue to the Gospel of Luke (1:1–4) also showed that Theophilus had received some form of instruction in Christianity. This instruction was likely of an introductory nature. As a member of the aristocracy, Theophilus would have been a person of financial means. As such, it is possible that he could have helped to fund Luke's research. The literary context of the book of Acts illustrates an expanding number of Gentiles embracing faith in Christ. Although the book begins with the birth of the Church in Jerusalem, the geographical parameters of Christendom broaden rapidly. Paul's unique call is to the Gentiles, a call that takes him throughout the Roman Empire and, ultimately, to Rome, where he awaits a hearing from the emperor. The theme of the expansion of the Church illustrates that Christianity is not a sect of the Jews. Christianity is for all who believe, Jew and Gentile alike. There is room for someone like Theophilus in the Kingdom of God. Not only is there room, but there is also a purpose: to be witnesses for Christ to the farthest reaches of the earth (Acts 1:8).

In the speech, Paul uses an identification of God as Creator as the foundation from which he proclaims the message of the true God to a culture steeped in idolatry. The speech has a decidedly anti-idolatry tone. Paul deconstructs the thought system undergirding idolatry by illustrating how illogical it is to think that gods made by the hands of humans could have made the universe. He also uses a quotation from Aratus, "we are also his offspring" (Acts 17:28) to demonstrate that God could not possibly be like idols. How can idols have offspring?

Paul's speech in Athens starts with a reference to creation (Acts 17:24), as does his speech in Lystra (Acts 14:15). Both of these speeches are oriented towards Gentile audiences. This approach contrasts with Paul's approach in Pisidian Antioch, where he begins with the exodus as a reference point. Through this comparison, the observation may be made that Paul adjusted his style when speaking to Gentiles. He starts with creation each time. But why?

God as Creator in Acts 17:24

In chapter three, the semantic study of the phrase led us to a plausible answer to this question of why Paul starts with creation when speaking to Gentiles. Passages meeting specific semantic criteria were classified into six types of literary context: core material (Genesis 1:1), liturgical, oath, prophetic oracle, cross-cultural communication, and philosophical or historical treatises. Passages for investigation originated from the New Testament, the Septuagint, the Apocrypha, the Pseudepigrapha, Josephus, and Philo. The findings showed that, while the semantic context of all six types was often within an anti-idolatry setting, the two types that show the highest level of correlation with Acts 17:24 are prophetic oracle and cross-cultural communication. Specific to prophetic oracle, Acts 17:24 showed similar themes with Isaiah 45:18, an oracle calling the nations (Gentiles) to salvation and Jeremiah 10:12, an anti-idolatry oracle to Israel. Acts 17:24–31 also was seen to be similar in structure to Isaiah 45:18–22 and Jeremiah 10:12–16. There are four common elements to the structure of each passage. First, God is identified as Creator. Second, the nature of God is described. Third, idolatry is deemed useless. Fourth, the Lord is not like idols. The passages in Acts 17:24–31 and Isaiah 45:18–22 both end with a call to repent. Specific to cross-cultural communication, Acts 17:24 showed similar context with Jonah 1:9. In both passages, a person of faith in the God of Israel identifies their faith in the one God to persons of Gentile origin who worshiped a multiplicity of gods. The progression of Acts 17:19–34 may also be compared with the progression of Jonah 1:6–16. Three common elements are observed in both passages. First, Gentiles request spiritual information. Second, God is identified as Creator. Finally, Gentiles fear the Lord. This evidence leads us to conclude that Paul was following the example of the Old Testament prophets as he communicated to Gentiles in Acts 17:24. This is seen not only in the reference to God as Creator but also in the structure of his oratory. Paul, then, uses a well-established Jewish technique in his communication about God to the philosophers in Athens when he identifies the God whom he proclaims as the Maker of the cosmos.

There is one significant variant in Paul's use of this Jewish technique. Whereas the usual formula was "The God who made the heaven and the earth" (or similar wording), Paul uses "The God who made the universe (κόσμον) . . . he who is Lord of heaven and earth." Paul injects κόσμον as the direct object where "heaven and earth" normally would be expected. Paul, indeed, uses an established Jewish approach, but he does so with a twist. This twist is intentional. So doing, Paul used a word common to the

Conclusion

Greek vocabulary, κόσμος. This word is immediately defined by the Jewish phrase, "heaven and earth." The κόσμος is defined as the craftsmanship of God and as the totality of the universe, including planetary bodies and human beings. Of all the passages considered, a similar example with κόσμος as the direct object was seen only in works by Philo—also a Jew communicating with a Greek audience.

Next, in chapter four, evidence was gathered from Greco-Roman authors in order to gain a semblance of what the Stoic and Epicurean worldview might have been with regard to a deity, creation, and the jurisdiction of the deity over the world. Passages were selected from philosophical writings leading up to, and through the second century A.D. All philosophers had a connection with Athens: most had lived and studied there, and all had studied the masters of Greek philosophy. The search took us back to Plato's seminal work on cosmology, the *Timaeus*. Evidence from *Timaeus* 28C showed the use of ποιητής (maker) and κόσμος within the context of a creation account involving a demiurge who forms the universe with pre-existent materials, using a pattern as a model. This demiurge created the planetary bodies and the lesser gods. The creation of human beings is left for the lesser gods and is not the work of the primary demiurge. A study of κόσμος in the *Timaeus* showed that the cosmos was defined as the universe. Not only that, the κόσμος was thought to be an ensouled being.

Years after Plato's time, the *Timaeus* became part of the standard curriculum in the Stoic school. The Stoics expounded the *Timaeus*, re-interpreted the *Timaeus*, and disagreed with the Epicureans about the *Timaeus*. The Stoic doctrine of creation essentially emanates from the interpretation of the *Timaeus*. The Stoics believed in a Creator, in the creation of the world at a datable time, and in pantheism.

The Epicureans, in contrast, were proponents of creation by chance and not by design. To them, the formation of the world was simply a matter of atoms suddenly coalescing after an infinite period of kinetic dissonance. They believed in gods, but not in gods who participated in the architecture of the cosmos.

The Stoics and Epicureans were, likewise, divided on the topic of the nearness of God. Stoics asserted divine providence and accountability. The Epicureans viewed gods as able to maintain their tranquility only by remaining distant from the affairs of humans. To the Stoics, god was everywhere and in everything: they were pantheists. Naturally, the Epicureans dissented with wry sarcasm: your God is "extremely overworked" (*De natura deorum* I.52).

The matter of God and Creation, then, was a matter of no small debate between the Stoics and Epicureans. By identifying God as the Maker of the universe, Paul engages the controversy. In some respects his speech would have resonated with Stoics: God is the maker of the universe, and God is provident. But with respect to pantheism, Paul makes no affirmation. Neither is God akin to their demiurge. Κόσμος is defined, in Acts 17:24, within the framework of a Judeo-Christian understanding (the sum total of the work of God, as detailed in Gen. 1), and not within the framework of a Greco-Roman understanding (the sum total of the creation of both a demiurge and lesser gods, also considered a god by the Stoics). Paul's redefinition of terms shows that he was adept in the skill of using words familiar to Greek philosophers but reframing the meaning of those words in order to convey his message.

Paul's speech in Acts 17 may have been intended as an example for Theophilus to consider. Theophilus, as a Roman official, was likely to have received a Greek education. The Areopagus speech is an example of how Paul used his knowledge of Greek culture in order to present the message of Christianity, with its Jewish roots, to a people learned in Greek philosophy. Theophilus, with his government office and training in Greek literature, would have been in a unique position to communicate accurately the message of Christianity to other members of the aristocratic class, who also would have been of Greek background.

5.2 THEOLOGICAL REFLECTION

Throughout this study, two themes emerge time and again. The first of these is the use of references to God as Creator as an argument against idolatry. This theme appears in the Jewish Scriptures of the Old Testament, in extrabiblical Jewish writings, and in the New Testament. In chapter two, the study noted that the contrast of Paul's approach to Jewish and Gentile audiences shows a deliberate addition of God as Creator when he spoke to Gentiles in Lystra and Athens. The setting of polytheism in both locales gave rise to the need to answer the question, "What God do you proclaim?" The response, "the God who made the universe" establishes not only the subject of each speech, but also establishes the Creator as superior to idols. This technique of using creation as a basis for an anti-idolatry polemic was not a new invention. Rather, it reflects ancient Jewish practice. From the first pages of Genesis and throughout the centuries, Jewish writers presented the God

Conclusion

who made the world as supreme over the created order. This was examined in the third chapter of this study. The Lord, the one God, is rivaled by none in his ability to form the world and fashion humankind. Creation is material evidence of the power, the knowledge, the wisdom, the providence, and the uniqueness of God. No other god in antiquity could make the claim to have made the heavens and the earth and everything it.

The doctrine of creation would have begged the question, "Why worship idols created by humans (or anything in the created order) rather than the Creator himself?" The use of references to God as Creator figures prominently in anti-idolatry oracles in the prophetical books of Isaiah and Jeremiah. The structural similarities between Acts 17:24–30, Isaiah 45:18–22, and Jeremiah 10:12–16 suggest that Luke, in his record of the speech in Athens, depicts Paul as speaking in a manner known to the great prophets who fought idolatry in days long past. Such a style was also emulated by Jewish apologists writing up to and through the days of Paul's missionary journeys. *Sibylline oracle* 3, the *Testament of Job*, and Philo's *Creation* exhibit the continued use of a declaration of the supremacy of the God who made the world in their arguments denouncing false gods.

But what might the Stoics and Epicureans in first century Athens thought of the concept of God as Maker of the universe and everything in it? Certainly, the Areopagus speech hits a nerve. This would have been particularly true for the Epicureans who denied any participation of the divine in the formation of the world. For the Stoics, the thought would not have been as much of a stretch since they readily discussed—and redefined—Plato's demiurge. Still, the Stoic concept of creation and a Creator was a far cry from the Creator proclaimed in Acts 17. The demiurge of Plato's *Timaeus*, well known to Stoics and Epicureans alike, makes claim only to building the world, not to creating the elements. This demiurge also retires from his work after the world is built, delegating the formation of humans to lesser gods of his own creation. Even with their modifications to Plato's demiurge, the Stoic description of the Maker remains one rooted in paganism and not identical to the one proclaimed in Acts 17. This is further seen in the philosophical doctrine of divine "ensoulment" of the world—pantheism. The declaration of God as Creator in Acts 17 engages the philosophers at the crux of their debate over creation and presents ideas that would have been new, and contrary, to their preconceived ideas. Paul's methods of contextualization, then, were rooted in Jewish tradition—and included bold statements that we may classify as cultural confrontation.

God as Creator in Acts 17:24

A second theme that has emerged in this study is that of the use of references to God as Creator or Maker in cross-cultural communication. Certainly, in Acts 17, Paul was preaching to an audience of individuals who were culturally different from him. They were steeped in philosophical teachings. Paul was steeped in the Scriptures from his youth. They embraced various gods. Paul embraced a single, omnipotent God. They were Greeks. Paul was of Jewish descent. Again, Paul embraces an age-old technique when he presents his God as the Maker of the universe to Gentiles. Jonah demonstrated this practice when he identified himself and his religion to the sailors on the ship when the seas turned turbulent (Jonah 1:9). Daniel, similarly, used phrases that identified the God he worships as "God of heaven" or "Lord of heaven" in dialogue with Nebuchadnezzar. These phrases occur so frequently in Daniel's interactions with the Babylonian king that when the king finally acknowledges God, it is with the appellation "God of heaven" (Dan 4:31, 33–34, 37). Similar titles are used to identify the God of the Jews also by Persian kings in the book of Ezra. Cyrus uses the phrase "the Lord, the God of heaven" in his decree (Ezra 1:2). Later in the book of Ezra, the phrase "God of heaven" is utilized in correspondence both to and from King Darius (Ezra 5:11–12, 6:9–10). Another example of Jewish literature that employs "heaven and earth" language to identify the one God to a cross-cultural, polytheistic audience is *Bel and the dragon*, in which Daniel is portrayed as defying the king by not worshiping the idol, Bel (Bel 1.5).

When speaking cross-culturally to Gentiles, the Jews in the literature we have explored did not completely identify with them. What we have, instead, is a declaration of a key difference. These Jews were by no means reticent to identify themselves as followers of the God who made the world. Indeed, their worship of the Lord, the one God, is what made them distinctive as a people, in contrast to those of other ethnicities. Paul, also, speaks with boldness in identifying the God who made the universe and everything in it as the subject of his proclamation in Acts 17:24.

This study has unearthed several counts of potential disagreement between Paul and his audience, focusing on Acts 17:24, the identification of God as Maker. The Epicureans would have been ready with a retort. Even the Stoics had a very different concept of the Maker. The demiurge from Plato's *Timaeus* is certainly not the same as the Creator God of the first chapter of Genesis. Although Paul used familiar terms, he did not pander to the audience. He engaged on topics that had the potential to generate internal dissent among his hearers. He also gave them something new: the gospel.

Conclusion

In Acts 17, we learn that contextualization does not mean communicating in such a way that the audience will necessarily agree but, rather, communicating in such a way that the audience can understand. In this study, we have seen how the speaker of the Areopagus speech builds bridges of cognition in order to communicate with a culturally different people. And, also in the case of Acts 17, the contextualization of the message meets with a familiar topic by referencing a common controversy: did God really make the world? This statement had the potential to ignite the emotions of the Stoic and Epicurean from the outset. Paul, then, moves from "common ground" (the altar to the unknown god) to common controversy in the same breath.

In the final analysis, we find that contextualization, in Acts 17, has to do with the use and redefinition of familiar vocabulary in order to convey a new concept. Paul, as a Jew, presented the God of the Old Testament to his audience of philosophers with careful choice of vocabulary that would have been familiar for those in his hearing. He communicates his message by reinterpreting for his audience the meaning of these familiar terms according to Judeo-Christian thought, rather than according to Greco-Roman thought. He uses familiar terms to introduce unfamiliar ideas to his audience. Paul was bold to proclaim the message even when the audience might not agree. Paul does not bend the gospel to fit the culture. Rather, he bends the culture to fit the gospel. The task for the church today is to evaluate its practices of communication with the population at large. Can we, like Paul, put our specialized vocabulary aside while retaining the full content of our message and express it with vocabulary our hearers understand?

Appendix

Greek Text and Translation of Acts 17:16–34

TEXT (UBS/4)

[16] Ἐν δὲ ταῖς Ἀθήναις ἐκδεχομένου αὐτοὺς τοῦ Παύλου παρωξύνετο τὸ πνεῦμα αὐτοῦ ἐν αὐτῷ θεωροῦντος κατείδωλον οὖσαν τὴν πόλιν.

[17] διελέγετο μὲν οὖν ἐν τῇ συναγωγῇ τοῖς Ἰουδαίοις καὶ τοῖς σεβομένοις καὶ ἐν τῇ ἀγορᾷ κατὰ πᾶσαν ἡμέραν πρὸς τοὺς παρατυγχάνοντας.

[18] τινὲς δὲ καὶ τῶν Ἐπικουρείων καὶ Στοϊκῶν φιλοσόφων συνέβαλλον αὐτῷ, καί τινες ἔλεγον, Τί ἂν θέλοι ὁ σπερμολόγος οὗτος λέγειν; οἱ δέ, Ξένων δαιμονίων δοκεῖ καταγγελεὺς εἶναι, ὅτι τὸν Ἰησοῦν καὶ τὴν ἀνάστασιν εὐηγγελίζετο.

[19] ἐπιλαβόμενοί τε αὐτοῦ ἐπὶ τὸν Ἄρειον Πάγον ἤγαγον λέγοντες, Δυνάμεθα γνῶναι τίς ἡ καινὴ αὕτη ἡ ὑπὸ σοῦ λαλουμένη διδαχή;

[20] ξενίζοντα γάρ τινα εἰσφέρεις εἰς τὰς ἀκοὰς ἡμῶν· βουλόμεθα οὖν γνῶναι τίνα θέλει ταῦτα εἶναι.

[21] Ἀθηναῖοι δὲ πάντες καὶ οἱ ἐπιδημοῦντες ξένοι εἰς οὐδὲν ἕτερον ηὐκαίρουν ἢ λέγειν τι ἢ ἀκούειν τι καινότερον.

[22] Σταθεὶς δὲ [ὁ] Παῦλος ἐν μέσῳ τοῦ Ἀρείου Πάγου ἔφη, Ἄνδρες Ἀθηναῖοι, κατὰ πάντα ὡς δεισιδαιμονεστέρους ὑμᾶς θεωρῶ.

Appendix

²³ διερχόμενος γὰρ καὶ ἀναθεωρῶν τὰ σεβάσματα ὑμῶν εὗρον καὶ βωμὸν ἐν ᾧ ἐπεγέγραπτο, Ἀγνώστῳ θεῷ. ὃ οὖν ἀγνοοῦντες εὐσεβεῖτε, τοῦτο ἐγὼ καταγγέλλω ὑμῖν.

²⁴ ὁ θεὸς ὁ ποιήσας τὸν κόσμον καὶ πάντα τὰ ἐν αὐτῷ, οὗτος οὐρανοῦ καὶ γῆς ὑπάρχων κύριος οὐκ ἐν χειροποιήτοις ναοῖς κατοικεῖ

²⁵ οὐδὲ ὑπὸ χειρῶν ἀνθρωπίνων θεραπεύεται προσδεόμενός τινος, αὐτὸς διδοὺς πᾶσι ζωὴν καὶ πνοὴν καὶ τὰ πάντα·

²⁶ ἐποίησέν τε ἐξ ἑνὸς πᾶν ἔθνος ἀνθρώπων κατοικεῖν ἐπὶ παντὸς προσώπου τῆς γῆς, ὁρίσας προστεταγμένους καιροὺς καὶ τὰς ὁροθεσίας τῆς κατοικίας αὐτῶν

²⁷ ζητεῖν τὸν θεόν, εἰ ἄρα γε ψηλαφήσειαν αὐτὸν καὶ εὕροιεν, καί γε οὐ μακρὰν ἀπὸ ἑνὸς ἑκάστου ἡμῶν ὑπάρχοντα.

²⁸ Ἐν αὐτῷ γὰρ ζῶμεν καὶ κινούμεθα καὶ ἐσμέν, ὡς καί τινες τῶν καθ᾽ ὑμᾶς ποιητῶν εἰρήκασιν, Τοῦ γὰρ καὶ γένος ἐσμέν.

²⁹ γένος οὖν ὑπάρχοντες τοῦ θεοῦ οὐκ ὀφείλομεν νομίζειν χρυσῷ ἢ ἀργύρῳ ἢ λίθῳ, χαράγματι τέχνης καὶ ἐνθυμήσεως ἀνθρώπου, τὸ θεῖον εἶναι ὅμοιον.

³⁰ τοὺς μὲν οὖν χρόνους τῆς ἀγνοίας ὑπεριδὼν ὁ θεός, τὰ νῦν παραγγέλλει τοῖς ἀνθρώποις πάντας πανταχοῦ μετανοεῖν,

³¹ καθότι ἔστησεν ἡμέραν ἐν ᾗ μέλλει κρίνειν τὴν οἰκουμένην ἐν δικαιοσύνῃ, ἐν ἀνδρὶ ᾧ ὥρισεν, πίστιν παρασχὼν πᾶσιν ἀναστήσας αὐτὸν ἐκ νεκρῶν.

³² Ἀκούσαντες δὲ ἀνάστασιν νεκρῶν οἱ μὲν ἐχλεύαζον, οἱ δὲ εἶπαν, Ἀκουσόμεθά σου περὶ τούτου καὶ πάλιν.

³³ οὕτως ὁ Παῦλος ἐξῆλθεν ἐκ μέσου αὐτῶν.

³⁴ τινὲς δὲ ἄνδρες κολληθέντες αὐτῷ ἐπίστευσαν, ἐν οἷς καὶ Διονύσιος ὁ Ἀρεοπαγίτης καὶ γυνὴ ὀνόματι Δάμαρις καὶ ἕτεροι σὺν αὐτοῖς.

TRANSLATION

16. And while Paul was waiting for them in Athens, his spirit was greatly distressed within himself when he saw (that) the city was full of idols.

17. So he kept on debating in the synagogue with the Jews and the worshippers of God, also in the marketplace everyday, with those who happened to be present.

18. But also some of the Epicurean and Stoic philosophers were debating with him, and some were saying, "What could this scavenger of information possibly be trying to say?" But others, "He seems to be a proclaimer of foreign gods," because he was preaching the good news about Jesus and the resurrection.

19. So after they took (him), they brought him to the Areopagus, saying, "May we know what this new teaching is that you are proclaiming?

20. For you are bringing foreign things to our ears; therefore we would like to know what these things mean."

21. Now all (the) Athenians and the foreigners staying there had time for nothing but to say or to hear the latest thing.

22. Then Paul, after he stood in the middle of the Areopagus said, "Fellow Athenians, I perceive that in everything you are most devout.

23. For while going through [the city] and observing your objects of worship carefully I also found an altar in which had been inscribed, 'To an unknown god.' Therefore, that which you worship without knowing, this I proclaim to you.

24. The God who made the universe and all the things in it, he who is Lord of heaven and earth, does not dwell in temples made by human hands

25. nor is he served by human hands as needing anything, he himself giving to all life and breath and all things.

26. And he made from one every nation of people to dwell on all the face of the earth, having designated fixed times and the boundaries of their dwelling places

27. to search for God, if perhaps they might grope for him and find him, even though he is not far from each one of us.

28. For in him we live and move and exist, as also some of your poets have said, 'for we also are his offspring.'

29. Since being offspring of God, we ought not to think the deity is like gold or silver or stone, an image made by the skill and imagination of a person.

Appendix

30. Therefore, indeed, while God overlooked the times of ignorance, now he commands all people everywhere to repent,

31. because he fixed a day in which he intends to judge the world in righteousness by a man whom he appointed, having shown proof to all, having raising him from the dead."

32. But when they heard of the resurrection of the dead some were scoffing, but others said, "We will hear from you concerning this also again."

33. So Paul went out from their midst.

34. But some people, having joined him, believed, among them also Dionysius the Areopagite and a woman named Damaris, and others with them.

Bibliography

PRIMARY SOURCES

Aratus. 1969. Phaenomena. (*In* Callimachus: hymns and epigrams. Lycophron. Aratus. Vol. 2. Translated from the Greek by G. Mair. Cambridge, MA: Harvard University Press. p. 185–299). (Loeb classical library, 129).
Bible. 1986. The Septuagint with apocrypha: Greek and English. Peabody: Hendrickson.
Bible. 1989. The Holy Bible: new revised version. New York: Oxford University Press.
Bible. 1994. The Greek New Testament. 4th rev. ed. Stuttgart: United Bible Societies.
Bible. 1998. Novum Testamentum Graece. 27th ed. Stuttgart: Deutsche Bibelgesellschaft.
Brenton, L. 1851. The Septuagint with Apocrypha: Greek and English. London: Samuel Bagster and sons. Available: BibleWorks 9.
Cicero. 1972. De natura deorum. Vol. 19. Translated from the Latin by H. Rackham. Cambridge, MA: Harvard University Press. (Loeb classical library, 268).
Cleanthes. 1921. Hymn. (*In* The hymn of Cleanthes: Greek text translated into English. Translated from the Greek by E.H. Blakeney. New York: Macmillan.)
Cornutus. 2014. Epitome of the things handed down in Greek theology. Translated from the Greek by G. Boys-Stones. (Unpublished).
Demosthenes. 1966. De corona. (*In* Demosthenis orationes, Vol. 1. Greek text edited by S.H. Butcher. Oxford: Clarendon.) Available: Thesaurus Linguae Graecae.
Diogenes Laertius. 1991. Lives of eminent philosophers. Vol. 1. Translated from the Greek by R.D. Hicks. Cambridge, MA: Harvard University Press. (Loeb classical library, 184).
Diogenes Laertius. 1995. Lives of eminent philosophers. Vol. 2. Translated from the Greek by R.D. Hicks. Cambridge, MA: Harvard University Press. (Loeb classical library, 185).
Epictetus. 1998. Discourses, books 1–2. Vol. 1. Translated from the Greek by W. Oldfather. Cambridge, MA: Harvard University Press. (Loeb classical library, 131).
Epstein, I., *ed.* 1985. Tractates Nazier. Sotah. Translated from the Hebrew by A. Cohen and B. Klein. London: Soncino. (Hebrew-English edition of the Babylonian Talmud).

Bibliography

Eusebius. 2007. The church history. Translated from the Greek by Paul Maier. Grand Rapids: Kregel.
Freeman, K. 1978. Ancilla to the pre-Socratic philosophers. Cambridge, MA: Harvard University Press.
Holmes, M., *ed.* 1989. The apostolic fathers. 2nd ed. Translated from the Greek by J.B. Lightfoot and J.R. Harmer. Grand Rapids: Baker.
Josephus. 1926. Works. Translated from the Greek by H.J. Thackeray and R. Marcus. 13 vols. Cambridge: Harvard University Press. (Loeb classical library).
Long, A.A. & Sedley, D., *trans.* 1999. The Hellenistic philosophers: translations of the principal sources, with philosophical commentary. Vol. 1. Cambridge: Cambridge University Press.
Lucian. 1959. How to write history. Translated from the Greek by K. Kilburn. Vol. VI. Cambridge: Harvard University Press. (Loeb classical library, 430).
Lucretius. 1982. De rerum natura. Translated from the Latin by W. Rouse & M. Smith. Cambridge, MA: Harvard University Press. (Loeb classical library, 181).
Lucretius. 2008. On the nature of the universe. Translated from the Latin by R. Melville. Oxford: Oxford University Press. (Oxford world's classics).
Philo. 2005. The Philo concordance database, in Greek, with lemmatization. Bodø: Bodø University College. Available: BibleWorks 9.
Pietersma, A. & Wright, B., *eds.* 2007. A new English translation of the Septuagint. New York: Oxford University Press.
Plato. 1929. Timaeus. Critias. Cleitophon. Menexenus. Epistles. Vol. 9. Translated from the Greek by R. Bury. Cambridge, MA: Harvard University Press. (Loeb classical library, 234).
Plato. 1981. Plato in twelve volumes. Translated from the Greek by R. Bury. 12 vols. Cambridge: Harvard University Press. (Loeb classical library).
Plato. 2013. Republic. Books 1–5. Vol. 5. Translated from the Greek by C. Emlyn-Jones. Cambridge, MA: Harvard University Press. (Loeb classical library, 237).
Plutarch. 1976. Moralia. Part 2. Stoic essays. Vol. 13. Translated from the Greek by H. Cherniss. Cambridge, MA: Harvard University Press. (Loeb classical library, 470).
Plutarch. 1998. Parallel lives. Vol. 1. Translated from the Greek by B. Perrin. Cambridge, MA: Harvard University Press. (Loeb classical library, 46).
Polybius. 1889. Histories. Translated from the Greek by E. Shuckburgh. New York: Macmillan. Available: Perseus.
Rahlfs, A. & Hanhart, R., *eds.* 2006. Septuaginta. Editio altera. Stuttgart: Deutsche Biblegesellschaft.
Seneca. 1925. Epistles 93–124. Vol. 6. Translated from the Latin by R. Gummere. Cambridge, MA: Harvard University Press. (Loeb classical library, 77).
Sextus Empiricus. 1968. Against the physicists. Against the ethicists. Vol. 3. Translated from the Greek by R. Bury. Cambridge, MA: Harvard University Press. (Loeb classical library, 311).
Strabo. 1960. Geography. Vol. 6. Translated from the Greek by H. Jones. Cambridge, MA: Harvard University Press. (Loeb classical library, 223).
Suetonius. 1970. The lives of the caesars. Vol. 2. Translated from the Latin by J. Rolfe. Cambridge, MA: Harvard University Press. (Loeb classical library, 38).
Tacitus. 1937. Annals. Vol. 4. Translated from the Latin by J. Jackson. Cambridge, MA: Harvard University Press. (Loeb classical library, 312).
Whiston, W., *trans.* 1987. The works of Josephus. Peabody: Hendrickson.

Bibliography

Xenophon. 1979. Memorabilia. Oeconomicus. Vol. 4. Translated from the Greek by E. Marchant. Cambridge, MA: Harvard University Press. (Loeb classical library, 168).
Yonge, C., *trans*. 1993. The Works of Philo. Peabody: Hendrickson.

SECONDARY SOURCES

Ademollo, F. 2012. The Platonic origins of Stoic theology. *Oxford studies in ancient philosophy*, 43(2):217-243.
Alexander, L. 1993. The preface to Luke's gospel. Cambridge: Cambridge University Press. (Society for New Testament Studies monograph series, 78).
Algra, K. 1999. The beginnings of cosmology. (*In* Long, A.A., *ed*. The Cambridge companion to early Greek philosophy. Cambridge: Cambridge University Press. p. 45-65).
Algra, K. 2003. Stoic theology. (*In* Inwood, B., *ed*. The Cambridge companion to the Stoics. Cambridge: Cambridge University Press. p. 153-178).
Andrews, D. 1964. Yahweh the God of the heavens. (*In* W. McCullough, *ed*. The seed of wisdom. Toronto: University of Toronto. p. 45-57).
Asmis, E. 2010. Epicurean empiricism. (*In* Warren, J., *ed*. The Cambridge companion to Epicureanism. Cambridge: Cambridge University Press. p. 84-104).
Barclay, J. 2007. Against Apion: translation and commentary. Leiden: Brill. (Flavius Josephus: translation and commentary, 10).
Barrett, C. 1963. The Pastoral Epistles. Oxford: Clarendon. (The new clarendon Bible).
Barrett, C. 1998. Acts. Vol. 2. Edinburgh: T&T Clark. (International critical commentary).
Bauckham, R. 1993. Theology of the book of Revelation. Cambridge: Cambridge University Press. (New Testament theology).
Bauer, W. 2000. A Greek-English lexicon of the New Testament and other early Christian literature. 3rd ed. (BDAG). Danker, F., *ed*. Chicago: University of Chicago Press. Available: BibleWorks 9.
Bauman, M. & Klauber, M. 1995. Historians of the Christian tradition. Nashville: Broadman & Holman.
Beale, G. 1999. The book of Revelation. Grand Rapids: Eerdmans. (The new international Greek testament commentary).
Beale, G. 2012. Handbook on the New Testament use of the Old Testament. Grand Rapids: Baker.
Beale, G. & Carson, D.A. 2007. Commentary on the New Testament use of the Old Testament. Grand Rapids: Baker.
Béchard, D. 2001. Paul among the rustics: the Lystran episode (Acts 14:8-20) and Lucan apologetic. *Catholic Biblical Quarterly* 63(1):84-101, January.
Betegh, G. 2006. Epicurus' argument for atomism. *Oxford studies in ancient philosophy*, 30(2):261-284.
Blank, D. 2010. *Philosophia* and *technē*: Epicureans on the arts. (*In* Warren, J., *ed*. The Cambridge companion to Epicureanism. Cambridge: Cambridge University Press. p. 216-233).
Blomberg, C. 2006. From Pentecost to Patmos: an introduction to Acts through Revelation. Nashville: Broadman & Holman.
Bock, D. 1994. Luke. Grand Rapids: Baker. (Baker exegetical commentary on the New Testament).

Bibliography

Bock, D. 2007. Acts. Grand Rapids: Baker. (Baker exegetical commentary on the New Testament).

Bock, D. 2012. A theology of Luke and Acts. Grand Rapids: Zondervan. (Biblical theology of the New Testament).

Bosma, C. 2013. Jonah 1:9—an example of elenctic testimony. *Calvin Theological Journal* 48(1):65–90, April.

Bovon, F. 2006. Luke the theologian. 2nd ed. Waco: Baylor.

Boys-Stones, G. 2007. Fallere sollers: the ethical pedagogy of the Stoic Cornutus. (*In* Sorabji, R. & Sharples, R., *eds*. Greek and Roman philosophy 100 B.C.–200 A.D. Bulletin of the institute of classical studies, supplement 94. London: Institute of Classical Studies, University of London. p. 77–88).

Boys-Stones, G. 2009. Cornutus und sein philosophisches umfeld: der antiplatonismus der *Epidrome*. (*In* Nesselrath, H. *ed*. A. Cornutus: die griechischen götter. Ein überlick über namen, bilder und deutungen. Tubingen: Mohr Siebeck. p. 141–161).

Boys-Stones, G. 2013. Seneca against Plato: letters 58 and 65. (*In* Long, A.G., *ed*. Plato and the Stoics. Cambridge: Cambridge University Press. p. 128–146).

Braun, R. 1986. 1 Chronicles. Waco: Word. (Word biblical commentary).

Brayford, S. 2007. Genesis. Boston: Brill. (Septuagint commentary).

Broadie, S. 1999. Rational theology. (*In* Long, A.A., *ed*. The Cambridge companion to early Greek philosophy. Cambridge: Cambridge University Press. p. 205–224).

Broadie, S. 2012. Nature and divinity in Plato's Timaeus. Cambridge: Cambridge University Press.

Brotzman, E. 1994. Old Testament textual criticism. Grand Rapids: Baker.

Brown, F., Driver, S. & Briggs, C. 1997. Hebrew-Aramaic and English lexicon of the Old Testament (Abridged BDB-Gesenius lexicon). Ontario, Canada: Online Bible Foundation. Available: BibleWorks 9.

Bruce, F.F. 1976. Is the Paul of Acts the real Paul? *Bulletin of the John Rylands University Library of Manchester*, 58(2):282–305, Spring.

Bruce, F.F. 1988. The book of the Acts. Grand Rapids: Eerdmans. (The new international commentary on the New Testament).

Bruce, F.F. 1990. The Acts of the apostles: Greek text with introduction and commentary. 3rd ed. Grand Rapids: Eerdmans.

Bryan, J. 2013. Chrysippus and Plato on the fragility of the head. (*In* Long, A.G., *ed*. Plato and the Stoics. Cambridge: Cambridge University Press. p. 59–79).

Buitenwerf, R. 2003. Book III of the Sibylline Oracles and its social setting. Leiden: Brill. (Studia in Veteris Testamenti pseudepigrapha).

Cadbury, H. 1920. The style and literary method of Luke. Vol. 1. Cambridge: Harvard University Press.

Cadbury, H. 1922. Commentary on the preface of Luke. (*In* Jackson, F. & Lake, K., *eds*. The beginnings of Christianity. Part 1: The Acts of the Apostles. London: Macmillan. p. 489–510).

Charlesworth, J., *ed*. 2009a. Apocalyptic literature & testaments. New York: Doubleday. (The Old Testament pseudepigrapha, 1).

Charlesworth, J., *ed*. 2009b. Expansions of the "Old Testament" and legends, wisdom and philosophical literature, prayers, psalms and odes, fragments of lost Judeo-Hellenistic Works. New York: Doubleday. (The Old Testament pseudepigrapha, 2).

Clay, D. 2010. The Athenian garden. (*In* Warren, J., *ed*. The Cambridge companion to Epicureanism. Cambridge: Cambridge University Press. p. 9–28).

Bibliography

Collins, J. 1972. The Sibylline Oracles of Egyptian Judaism. Missoula, MT: University of Montana. (Dissertation—PhD).
Collins, J. 1993. Daniel. Minneapolis: Fortress. (Hermeneia).
Conzelmann, H. 1987. Acts of the apostles. Philadelphia: Fortress. (Hermeneia).
Cornford, F. 1997. Plato's cosmology: the Timaeus of Plato. Indianapolis: Hacket.
Craigie, P., Kelley, P., & Drinkard, J. 1991. Jeremiah 1-25. Dallas: Word. (Word biblical commentary).
Creamer, J. 2011. Making known the unknown God: an exploration of Greco-Roman backgrounds related to Paul's Areopagus speech. *Africanus journal*, 3(2):43-55.
Dahle, L. 2001. Acts 17:16-34 an apologetic model then and now? Oxford: Whitefield Institute. (Thesis—PhD).
Dancy, J., *ed.* 1972. The shorter books of the Apocrypha. New York: Cambridge University Press.
deSilva, 2000. Honor, patronage, kinship & purity: unlocking New Testament culture. Downers Grove: InterVarsity.
Dibelius, M. 1956. Studies in the Acts of the apostles. Translated from the German (1951) by Mary Ling. London: SCM.
Dibelius, M. & Conzelmann, H. 1972. The Pastoral Epistles. Philadelphia: Fortress. (Hermeneia).
Dillard, R. 1987. 2 Chronicles. Waco, TX: Word. (Word biblical commentary).
DiTomasso, L. 2012. Pseudepigrapha notes IV: 5. The Testament of Job. 6. The Testament of Solomon. *Journal for the Study of the Pseudepigrapha* 21(3):313-320. March.
Dover, K. 2010. Greek word order. New York: Cambridge University Press.
Dunn, J. 2009. Beginning from Jerusalem. Grand Rapids: Eerdmans.
Erler, M. 2010. Epicureanism in the Roman Empire. (*In* Warren, J., *ed*. The Cambridge companion to Epicureanism. Cambridge: Cambridge University Press. p. 46-64).
Fee, G. 1988. 1 and 2 Timothy, Titus. Peabody: Hendrickson. (New international biblical commentary, 13).
Fensham, F. 1982. The books of Ezra and Nehemiah. Grand Rapids: Eerdmans. (New international commentary on the Old Testament).
Ferguson, E. 2003. Backgrounds of early Christianity. 3rd ed. Grand Rapids: Eerdmans.
Fitzmyer, J. 1981. The gospel according to Luke. Garden City: Doubleday. (The anchor Bible, 28).
Free, J. 1992. Archaeology and Bible history. Grand Rapids: Zondervan.
Friberg, T., Friberg, B. & Miller, N. 2000. Analytical lexicon to the Greek New Testament. Grand Rapids: Baker. Available: BibleWorks 9.
Garland, D. 2011. Luke. Grand Rapids: Zondervan. (Zondervan exegetical commentary on the New Testament).
Garrison, R. 2004. The significance of Theophilus as Luke's reader. Lewiston: Edwin Mellen. (Studies in the Bible and early Christianity, 62).
Gärtner, B. 1955. The Areopagus speech and natural revelation. Lund: Gleerup.
Gaventa, B. 2003. The Acts of the apostles. Nashville: Abingdon. (Abingdon New Testament commentaries).
Gempf, C. 1988. Historical and literary appropriateness in the mission speeches of Acts. Aberdeen: University of Aberdeen. (Thesis—PhD).
Gempf, C. 1993a. Public speaking and published accounts. (*In* Winter, B. & Clarke, D., *eds*. The book of Acts in its first century setting. Vol. 1. Ancient literary setting. Grand Rapids: Eerdmans. p. 259-303.)

Bibliography

Gempf, C. 1993b. Athens, Paul at. (*In* Dictionary of Paul and his letters. Hawthorne, G., Martin, R., Reid, D., *eds*. Downers Grove: Intervarsity. p. 51–54.)

Gempf, C. 1995. Mission and misunderstanding: Paul and Barnabas in Lystra (Acts 14:8-20). (*In* Billington, A., Lane, T. & Turner, M., *eds*. Mission and meaning: essays presented to Peter Cotterell. Carlisle: Paternoster. p. 56–69.)

Gendy, A. 2011. Style, content and culture: distinctive characteristics in the missionary speeches in Acts. *Swedish missiological themes*, 99(3):247–265.

Gerhardsson, B. 1998. Memory and manuscript: oral tradition and written transmission in rabbinic Judaism and early Christianity. Grand Rapids: Eerdmans. (Biblical resource).

Gill, C. 2003. The school in the Roman imperial period. (*In* Inwood, B., *ed*. The Cambridge companion to the Stoics. Cambridge: Cambridge University Press. p. 33–58).

Glerup, M., *ed*. 2010. Commentaries on Genesis 1–3: Severian of Gabala and Bede the Venerable. Downers Grove: InterVarsity. (Ancient Christian texts).

Goldingay, J. 1989. Daniel. Dallas: Word. (Word biblical commentary).

Green, J. 1997. The gospel of Luke. Grand Rapids: Eerdmans. (The new international commentary on the New Testament).

Gruen, W. 2009. Seeking a context for the testament of Job. *Journal for the Study of the Pseudepigrapha* 18(3):163–179. March.

Guthrie, D. 1990. New Testament introduction. 4th ed. Downers Grove: InterVarsity.

Haenchen, E. 1971. The Acts of the apostles: a commentary. Philadephia: Westminster.

Hanson, A. 1982. The Pastoral Epistles. Grand Rapids: Eerdmans. (The new century Bible commentary).

Hartley, J. 2000. Genesis. Grand Rapids: Baker. (Understanding the Bible commentary).

Hayward, R. 1987. The targum of Jeremiah: translated, with a critical introduction, apparatus, and notes. Wilmingon, Delaware: Michael Glazier. (The Aramaic Bible, 12).

Hemer, C. 1977. Luke the historian. *Bulletin of the John Rylands University Library of Manchester*, 60(1):28–51, Autumn.

Hemer, C. 1989a. Speeches of Acts II. *Tyndale bulletin*, 40(2):239–259, November.

Hemer, C. 1989b. The book of Acts in the setting of Hellenistic history. Tübingen: Mohr. (Wissenschaftliche Untersuchungen zum Neuen Testament).

Hengel, M., 2012. The Lukan prologue and its eyewitnesses: The apostles, Peter, and the women. Translated from the German by N. Moore, (*in* M. Bird & J. Maston, *eds*. Earliest church history. Tübingen: Mohr. p. 533–587*).*

Hesselgrave, D. & Rommen, E. 1989. Contextualization. Grand Rapids: Baker.

Holden, J. & Geisler, N. 2013. The popular handbook of archaeology and the Bible. Eugene, Oregon: Harvest House.

Holladay, W. 2000. A concise Hebrew and Aramaic lexicon of the Old Testament: based upon the lexical work of Ludwig Koehler and Walter Baumgartner. Leiden: Brill. Available: BibleWorks 9.

Howard, D. 1998. Joshua. Nashville: Broadman & Holman. (The new American commentary).

Huey, F. 1993. Jeremiah Lamentations. Nashville: Broadman. (The new American commentary).

Hutchinson, G. 2013. Greek to Latin: frameworks and contexts for intertextuality. Oxford: Oxford University Press.

Inwood, B. 2003. The Cambridge companion to the Stoics. Cambridge: Cambridge University Press. (Cambridge companions to philosophy).

Irwin, T. 1999. Plato: the intellectual background. (*In* Kraut, R., *ed.* The Cambridge companion to Plato. Cambridge: Cambridge University Press. p. 51-89).

Japhet, S. 1993. I & II Chronicles. Louisville: Westminster/John Knox. (The Old Testament library).

Johnson, L. 1991. Luke. Collegeville: Liturgical. (Sacra pagina, 3).

Jones, A. 2003. The Stoics and the astronomical sciences. (*In* Inwood, B., *ed.* The Cambridge companion to the Stoics. Cambridge: Cambridge University Press. p. 328-344).

Judge, E. 2009. Antioch of Syria. (*In* The Zondervan pictorial encyclopedia of the Bible, 1:210-213).

Kaiser, W. 2012. Mission in the Old Testament: Israel as a light to the nations. Grand Rapids: Baker.

Keener, C. 2012. Acts: an exegetical commentary, introduction and 1:1—2:47. Vol. 1. Grand Rapids: Baker.

Keener, C. 2014. Acts: an exegetical commentary, 15:1—23:35. Vol. 3. Grand Rapids: Baker.

Kidd, D. 2004. Aratus: phaenomena. Cambridge: Cambridge University Press. (Cambridge classical texts and commentaries).

Kittel, G. *ed.* 1965, Theological dictionary of the New Testament. Grand Rapids: Eerdmans. 10 vols.

Knibb, M., & Van der Horst, P., *eds.* 1989. Studies on the testament of Job. Cambridge: Cambridge University Press. (Society for New Testament studies monograph series, 66).

Knight, G. 1992. The Pastoral Epistles: a commentary on the Greek text. Grand Rapids: Eerdmans. (New international Greek Testament commentary).

Kraus, H. 1993. Psalms 60-150. Minneapolis: Fortress. (Continental commentary).

Kraut, R. 1999. Introduction to the study of Plato. (*In* Kraut, R., *ed.* The Cambridge companion to Plato. Cambridge: Cambridge University Press. p. 1-50).

Kroeger, C. 1987. The 'nachleben' of Euripides' Antiope: the heroine's transformation into a mystagogue and an element in the justification of Zeus. Ann Arbor: University of Minnesota. (Dissertation—PhD).

Kurz, W. 2013. Acts of the apostles. Grand Rapids: Baker. (Catholic commentary on sacred scripture).

Larkin, W. 1995. Acts. Downers Grove: InterVarsity. (IVP New Testament commentary).

Liddell, H., & Scott, R. 1996. A Greek-English lexicon. 9th ed., with new supplement. Oxford: Clarendon.

Lightfoot, J. 2014. The Acts of the apostles: a newly discovered commentary, edited by B. Witherington and T. Still. Downers Grove: InterVarsity. (The Lightfoot legacy set, 1).

Limburgh, J. 1993. Jonah. Louisville, Kentucky: Westminster/John Knox. (The Old Testament library).

Litwak, K. 2004. Israel's prophets meet Athens' philosophers: Scriptural echoes in Acts 17,22-31. *Biblica*, 85(2):199-216.

Long, A.A. 2004. Epictetus: a Stoic and Socratic guide to life. Oxford: Oxford University Press.

Long, A.A. 2010. Cosmic craftsmanship in Plato and Stoicism. (*In* Mohr, R. & Sattler, B., *eds.* One book, the whole universe: Plato's Timaeus today. Las Vegas: Parmenides. p. 37-53).

Bibliography

Long, A.G. 2013. Plato and the Stoics. Cambridge: Cambridge University Press.

Louw, J. & Nida, E. 1989. Greek-English lexicon of the New Testament based on semantic domains, 2nd ed. New York: United Bible Societies. Available: BibleWorks 9.

Lucas, E. 2002. Daniel. Downers Grove: InterVarsity. (Apollos Old Testament commentary).

Lüdemann, G. 2005. The Acts of the apostles: what really happened in the earliest days of the church. Amherst: Prometheus.

Marshall, I. H. 1980. Acts. Grand Rapids: Eerdmans. (Tyndale New Testament commentaries).

Marshall, I. H. 1988. Luke: historian & theologian. Downers Grove: InterVarsity.

Marshall, I. H. 1993. Acts and the 'former treatise'. (*In* Winter, B. & Clarke, D., *eds*. The book of Acts in its first century setting. Vol. 1. Ancient literary setting. Grand Rapids: Eerdmans. p. 163–182).

Marshall, I. H. 2004. The pastoral epistles. New York: T. & T. Clark. (International critical commentary).

Mason, S. 2001. Life of Josephus: Translation and commentary. Brill: Leiden.

Mathews, K. 1996. Genesis 1–11:26. Nashville: Broadman & Holman. (New American Commentary).

McDonald, L. 2000. Antioch (Syria). (*In* Dictionary of New Testament Background Downers Grove: Intervarsity. p. 34–37).

McDonough, S. 2009. Christ as creator: origins of a New Testament doctrine. Oxford: Oxford University Press.

McDonough, S. 2015. New Testament cosmology [email]. 14 July, S. Hamilton, MA.

McKane, W. 1986. Jeremiah. Edinburgh: T. & T. Clark. (International critical commentary).

McRay, J. 1991. Archaeology and the New Testament. Grand Rapids: Baker.

Meadowcroft, T. 1995. Aramaic Daniel and Greek Daniel: a literary comparison. Sheffield: Sheffield Academic. (*Journal for the study of the Old Testament*. Supplement series, 198).

Meijer, P. 2008. Stoic theology: proofs for the existence of the cosmic god and of the traditional gods. Delft: Eburon.

Millard, A. 2001. Reading and writing in the time of Jesus. Sheffield: Sheffield Academic. (Biblical seminar).

Miller, S. 1994. Daniel. Nashville: Broadman & Holman. (New American commentary).

Moles, J. 2011. Luke's preface: The Greek decree, classical historiography and Christian redefinitions. *New Testament Studies*, 57(4): 461–482.

Moran, M. 2005. Seneca the younger. (*In* Ballif, M. & Moran, M., *eds*. Classical rhetoric and rhetoricians: critical studies and sources. Westport: Greenwood. p. 343–347).

Morel, P. 2010. Epicurean atomism. (*In* Warren, J., *ed*. The Cambridge companion to Epicureanism. Cambridge: Cambridge University Press. p. 65–83).

Moulton, J. & Milligan, G. 1997. Vocabulary of the Greek Testament. Peabody: Hendrickson.

Mounce, R. 1998. The book of Revelation. Grand Rapids: Eerdmans. (New international commentary on the New Testament).

Mounce, W. 2000. Pastoral Epistles. Nashville: Nelson. (Word biblical commentary).

Moyise, S. 2012. The later New Testament writings and Scripture. Grand Rapids: Baker.

Nichols, J. 1976. Epicurean political philosophy. Ithaca: Cornell University Press.

O'Brien, C. 2012. The middle Platonist demiurge and Stoic cosmobiology. *Horizons* 3(1):19–39.

Bibliography

O'Brien, C. 2015. The demiurge in ancient thought: secondary gods and divine mediators. Cambridge: Cambridge University Press.
O'Keefe, T. 2010. Epicureanism. Berkeley: University of California Press.
Osborne, G. 2002. Revelation. Grand Rapids: Baker. (Baker exegetical commentary on the New Testament).
Pardigon, F. 2008. Paul against the idols: the Areopagus speech and religious inclusivism. Philadelphia: Westminster Theological Seminary. (Dissertation—PhD).
Pentecost, J. 2010. New wine: a study of transition in the book of Acts. Grand Rapids: Kregel.
Pervo, R. 1987. Profit with delight: the literary genre of the Acts of the apostles. Minneapolis: Fortress.
Pervo, R. 2009. Acts: a commentary. Minneapolis: Fortress. (Hermeneia).
Peterson, D. 2009. The Acts of the apostles. Grand Rapids: Eerdmans. (Piller New Testament commentary).
Pietersma, A. & Wright, B., eds. 2007. A new English translation of the Septuagint (NETS). New York: Oxford University Press.
Polhill, J. 1992. Acts. Nashville: Broadman. (The new American commentary).
Pomeroy, S., Burstein, S., Donlan, W., & Roberts, J. 2008. Ancient Greece: a political, social, and cultural history, second edition. Oxford: Oxford University Press.
Porter, S. 1994. Excurses: the 'we' passages. (*In* Gill, D. & Gempf, C., eds. The book of Acts in its first century setting. Vol. 2. Graeco-Roman setting. Grand Rapids: Eerdmans. p. 545–574).
Porter, S. 1999. Idioms of the Greek New Testament. London: Sheffield Academic.
Ramsay, W. 2001. St. Paul the traveler and Roman citizen. Grand Rapids: Kregel. (Revised from the 15th edition by Mark Wilson. London: Hodder & Stoughton, 1925).
Reid, G. 2006. 'Thus you will say to them': a cross-cultural confessional polemic in Jer 10.11. *Journal for the study of the Old Testament*. 31(2):221–238.
Reydams-Schils, G. The Academy, the Stoics and Cicero on Plato's Timaeus. (*In* Long, A.G., ed. Plato and the Stoics. Cambridge: Cambridge University Press. p. 29–58).
Reynolds, J. 2009. When Athens met Jerusalem. Downers Grove: InterVarsity.
Richards, R. 1998. The codex and the early collection of Paul's letters. *Bulletin for biblical research* 8:151–166.
Rist, J.M. 1972. Epicurus: an introduction. Cambridge: Cambridge University Press.
Robertson, A.T. 1934. A grammar of the Greek New Testament in the light of historical research. Nashville: Broadman.
Rosner, B. 1998. The progress of the word. (*In* Peterson, D. & Marshall, I., eds. Witness to the gospel: the theology of Acts. Grand Rapids: Eerdmans. p. 215–234).
Sandnes, K. 1993. Paul and Socrates: the aim of Paul's Areopagus speech. *Journal for the study of the New Testament*, 50:13–26, June.
Schnabel, E. 2004. Early Christian mission. Two vols. Downers Grove: InterVarsity.
Schnabel, E. 2005. Contextualizing Paul in Athens: the proclamation of the gospel before pagan audiences in the Graeco-Roman world. *Religion & theology*, 12 (2):172–190.
Schnabel, E. 2008. Paul the missionary: realities, strategies and methods. Downer's Grove: InterVarsity.
Schnabel, E. 2012. Acts. Grand Rapids: Zondervan. (Exegetical commentary on the New Testament).

Bibliography

Schweizer, E. 1988. Zur frage der gotteserkenntinis in ausserchristlichen religionen. (*In* Mitten im tod-vom leben umfangen. Hesse, J. *ed.* Frankfurt: Verlag Peter Lang, p. 236-239).

Sedley, D. 2002. The origins of Stoic god. (*In* Frede, D. & Laks, D., *eds.* Traditions of theology: studies in hellenistic theology, its background and aftermath. p. 41-83).

Sedley, D. 2003. The school, from Zeno to Arius Didymus. (*In* Inwood, B., *ed.* The Cambridge companion to the Stoics. Cambridge: Cambridge University Press. p. 7-32).

Sedley, D. 2009. Creationism and its critics in antiquity. Berkeley: University of California Press.

Sedley, D. 2010. Epicureanism in the Roman Republic. (*In* Warren, J., *ed.* The Cambridge companion to Epicureanism. Cambridge: Cambridge University Press. p. 29-45).

Sellers, G. 2014. Seneca's philosophical predecessors and contemporaries. (*In* Heil, A., and Damschen, G., *eds.* Brill's companion to Seneca: philosopher and dramatist. Leiden, Netherlands: Brill. p. 97-114).

Selman, M. 1994. 2 Chronicles. Downers Grove: InterVarsity. (Tyndale Old Testament commentaries).

Slee, M. 2003. The church in Antioch in the first century c.e. New York: T & T Clark. (*Journal for the study of the New Testament.* Supplement 244).

Smith, B. & Page, F. 1995. Amos, Obadiah, Jonah. Nashville: Broadman & Holman. (New American commentary).

Smith, G. 2007. Isaiah 1-39. Nashville: Broadman & Holman. (New American commentary).

Smith, G. 2009. Isaiah 40-66. Nashville: Broadman & Holman. (New American commentary).

Sorabji, R. 1983. Time, creation & the continuum. London: Duckworth.

Spencer, A. 1998. Paul's literary style: a stylistic and historical comparison of II Corinthians 11:16—12:13, Romans 8:9-39, and Philippians 3:2—4:13. Lanham: University Press of America.

Spencer, A. 2013. 1 Timothy. Eugene: Cascade. (New covenant commentary).

Stein, R. 1992. Luke. Nashville: Broadman. (New American commentary).

Strelan, R. 2007. A note on ἀσφάλεια in Luke 1:4. *Journal for the study of the New Testament*, 30(2)163-171.

Stuart, D. 1987. Hosea-Jonah. Waco: Word. (Word biblical commentary).

Taub, L. 2010. Cosmology and meteorology. (*In* Warren, J., *ed.* The Cambridge companion to Epicureanism. Cambridge: Cambridge University Press. p. 105-124).

Taylor, C. 1999. The atomists. (*In* Long, A.A., *ed.* The Cambridge companion to early Greek philosophy. Cambridge: Cambridge University Press. p. 181-204).

Thayer, J. 1997. Greek-English lexicon of the New Testament. (Abridged and revised Thayer lexicon.) Ontario: Online Bible Foundation. Available: BibleWorks 9.

Thom, J. 2005. Cleanthes' hymn to Zeus: text, translation, and commentary. Tübingen: Mohr Siebeck. (Studies and texts in antiquity and Christianity, 33).

Thomas, D. 2011. Acts. Phillipsburg: P&R. (Reformed expository commentary).

Thompson, J. 1994. 1, 2 Chronicles. Nashville: Broadman & Holman. (New American commentary).

Torkki, J. 2004. The dramatic account of Paul's encounter with philosophy: an analysis of Acts 17:16-34 with regard to contemporary philosophical debates. Helsinki: Helsinki University Publishing House. (Thesis—PhD).

Bibliography

Torres, J.B. 2011. Roman elements in Annaeus Cornutus's ΕΠΙΔΡΟΜΗ. (*In* Torres, J.B. *ed*. Vtroque sermone nostro. Bilingüismo social y literario en el imperio de Roma / Social and literary bilingualism in the Roman Empire. Pamplona: EUNSA. p. 41–54).

Towner, P. 2006. The letters to Timothy and Titus. Grand Rapids: Eerdmans. (New international commentary on the New Testament).

Van der Horst, P., & Newman, J. 2008. Early Jewish prayers in Greek. Berlin: Walter de Gruyter. (Commentaries on early Jewish literature).

Van Engen, C. 2004. Peter's conversion: a culinary disaster launches the gentile mission. *In* Mission in Acts. Gallagher, R. & Hertig, H., *eds*. Maryknoll: Orbis.

Volk, K. 2010. Aratus. (*In* A companion to Hellenistic literature. Clauss, J. & Cuypers, M., *eds*. Chichester: Wiley-Blackwell. p. 197–210).

Wallace, D. 1996. Greek grammar beyond the basics. Grand Rapids: Zondervan.

Wallace, D. 2000. The basics of New Testament syntax. Grand Rapids: Zondervan.

Walters, P. 2009. The assumed authorial unity of Luke and Acts: a reassessment of the evidence. Cambridge: Cambridge University Press. (Society for New Testament studies monograph series, 145).

Walton, S. 2004. A tale of two perspectives? The place of the temple in Acts. (*In* Heaven on earth: the temple in biblical theology. Alexander, T. & Gathercole, S., *eds*. Waynesboro, GA: Paternoster. p. 135–150).

Ward, G. 1974. The speeches of Acts: Dibelius reconsidered. (*In* Longenecker, R. and Tenney, M., *eds*. New dimensions in New Testament study. Grand Rapids: Zondervan. p. 232–250).

Warren, J. 2010. Removing fear. (*In* Warren, J., *ed*. The Cambridge companion to Epicureanism. Cambridge: Cambridge University Press. p. 234–248).

Watts, J. 2005. Isaiah 34–66. Nashville: Nelson. (Word biblical commentary).

Welch, J., *ed*. 1999. Chiasmus in antiquity. Provo, Utah: Research.

Wenham, G. 1987. Genesis 1–15. Waco, TX: Word. (Word biblical commentary).

Wesselschmidt, Q. 2007. Psalms 51–150. Downers Grove: InterVarsity. (Ancient Christian commentary on scripture. Old Testament).

Williams, D. 1990. Acts. Peabody: Hendrickson. (New international biblical commentary).

Williamson, H. 1985. Ezra, Nehemiah. Waco: Word. (Word biblical commentary).

Williamson, R. 1989. Jews in the hellenistic world: Philo. Cambridge: Cambridge University Press. (Cambridge commentaries on writings of the Jewish and Christian world, 200 BC to AD 200).

Wilson, S. 1973. The gentiles and the gentile mission in Luke–Acts. New York: Cambridge University Press. (Society for New Testament studies monograph series, 23).

Wineland, J. 2006. Syrian Antioch. (*In* The new interpreter's dictionary of the Bible. Nashville: Abingdon. 1:179–180).

Winter, B. 2005. Introducing the Athenians to God: Paul's failed apologetic in Acts 17? *Themelios* 31(1):38–59, October.

Winston, R. 1981. Philo of Alexandria: the contemplative life, the giants, and selections. Mahwah, New Jersey: Paulist.

Witherington, B. 1998. The Acts of the Apostles: a socio-rhetorical commentary. Grand Rapids: Eerdmans.

Witulski, T. 2007. Die Johannesoffenbarung und kaiser Hadrian: studien zur datierung der neutestamentlichen Apokalypse. Göttengen: Vandenhoeck & Ruprecht.

Zweck, D. 1989. The exordium of the Areopagus speech. *New Testament Studies*, 35(1):94–103, January.

Subject Index

Abram, Abraham, 57, 59–60, 62, 64–65, 86, 88, 91
Academy, Plato's, 104, 106, 111–12, 116, 119, 125
Alexander the Great, 10, 111
anti-idolatry
    context, 2–3, 62–63, 65–66, 68–70, 80, 82–83, 88, 91, 95–96, 149–50
    polemic, 40–44, 70, 74, 80–81, 86, 91, 152–53
Aramaic, 69–70, 79
Aratus, 32–33, 102–3, 106, 136–37, 141, 145, 149
Areopagus speech, comparison to speeches in Lystra and Pisidian Antioch, 34–39
Areopagus speech,
    reliability of, 11–18, 95
    structure of, 28
Argument from Design, 123, 125–26, 128
Aristotle, 111–12, 119, 121
Assyria, Assyrian, 58, 63, 78–80, 89–90, 95
ἀσφάλεια, 17, 19, 21–23
atheism, 125
Athenian setting, 98, 102, 106–7, 110–14

Babylon, Babylonian, 10, 38, 57–58, 70, 75, 78, 80–81, 88, 93, 95, 154
blessing, 26, 47, 59–60, 64–65, 88–90, 142–43

Caligula, Gaius, 84–85
chiastic structure, 69, 73–74
Christianity, inclusive nature of in Acts, 25–28
Chrysippus, 101–3, 106, 112–13, 125, 139–41
Cicero, 102–3, 106–7, 112, 125, 130–31, 136–37, 139, 141, 143
Cleanthes, 14, 32–33, 102–3, 105–6, 112, 135–37, 141
communication, cross-cultural, 5, 37–38, 43, 48, 52, 70, 72, 75, 79–80, 86, 92, 96, 154–55
contextualization, 1, 4–6, 148, 153, 155
Cornelius, 26
Cornutus, 102–3, 108, 141
cosmology, 58, 98–100, 115–47, 151; *see also* Epicurean cosmology, Stoic cosmology
Craftsman, divine, 115, 117–19, 121, 123–27, 132–33, 146; *see also* δημιουργός, demiurge
creation texts, Egyptian, 57
creation theology, 43, 53, 57–58, 86, 89
creation myth, Babylonian, 57

Subject Index

Cyrus, 66–67, 70, 78, 80, 88, 154

Daniel, 70, 75–81, 87, 89, 93, 96, 154
Darius, 70, 78–80, 154
δημιουργός, demiurge, 117–21, 126, 133, 140, 142, 151–54
Diogenes Laertius, 13, 101–6, 119, 124, 139–40

Epictetus, 14, 102–3, 108–9, 126–27, 133
Epicurean, 2, 4–5, 29–30, 34, 36, 97–103, 106–10, 114–15, 119, 121, 125, 128, 130–34, 141–49, 151–55
   cosmology, 98, 100, 127
   school, 98, 106, 109, 111–15, 125, 149
   theology, 141–44, 146, 151
Epicurus, 101–3, 105, 107, 112, 127, 142–43
Eusebius, 8–10
exodus, Israelite, 38, 41, 58, 68, 149
eyewitnesses, 8, 10, 13, 15–17
Ezra, 63–64

Felix, 19
Festus, 19, 22–23

Gamaliel, 113
Gentile mission, 61–63, 66, 89
Gentiles, 6, 7, 9, 18, 24–28, 35–41, 46–47, 51–54, 60–63, 66–68, 70, 72–73, 75, 77–78, 80–81, 86–89, 91–93, 95, 149–50, 152, 154
Gentiles, inclusion of, 25–28
γῆ, 31, 44–46, 50–56, 59
Godfearer, 24–26, 28–29, 37, 41
grammatical analysis, 15–18, 28–34
Greek religion, critique of, 113–14

Hadrian, 20, 108
Herodotus, 23, 102
Hesiod, 105, 113–14
Hezekiah, 54, 63–64, 80, 88–91
historian, historiography, 7, 10–15, 23, 40, 111
Holy Spirit, 15, 25–28, 41

Homer, Homeric, 14, 108, 113–14, 135
Huram, King of Tyre, 70–72

idols, 21, 29, 31–33, 35–36, 44, 48–49, 51–52, 59–63, 69–70, 73, 76, 82, 87, 89–90, 92, 95, 97, 149–50, 152–53
idolatry, 2–3, 29, 39–41, 43, 48, 58, 61, 63, 81–82, 87–89, 92, 96, 114, 145, 149, 152–53
imperial worship, 84–85
Irenaeus, 9
Israelites, 38, 57–58, 61–62, 64, 68–72, 78

Jesus, 7–8, 16, 19, 21–23, 25–26, 30, 37–39, 41, 54, 95
Jonah, 70, 72–75, 77–80, 88, 92–93, 96, 154

κατηχέω, 19, 21
κόσμος, 44–46, 50, 52, 56, 81, 84–86, 90, 92–96, 117, 121, 124, 140, 145, 147, 150–52
κράτιστος, 19–21, 40
κύριος, 31, 45–46, 49, 51, 59, 61, 64–67, 69, 71–72, 75–78, 81, 90, 92–93

liturgical, 46–47, 54, 58–59, 79, 81, 86–88, 90, 95, 150
Lucretius, 102–3, 107, 127–30, 143
Lucian, 13–14
Luke, as author, 2, 5–27, 40–41, 95, 149
Lyceum, Aristotle's, 111, 119
Lystra, speech in, 6, 25, 34–41, 51–52, 54, 68, 149, 152

methodology, research, 11, 15, 44–48, 98, 100–110
Mithridatic war, 106, 112

Nebuchadnezzar, 70, 75–80, 88, 93, 154
Nero, 20, 53, 107–8

oath, 46–47, 64–65, 79–80, 85–88, 90–91, 95, 150
optative mood, 30, 32

Subject Index

oracle, prophetic, 65–68, 79–80, 86–88, 91–92, 95–96, 150, 153
Origen, 9
οὐρανός, 31, 44–46, 50–56, 55–57, 59–67, 69, 71–72, 75–78, 81–86, 90, 92–93, 121, 132

pantheism, 75, 106, 135, 138–41, 143–47, 151–53
parallelomania, 57
Paul, ix, 1–6, 8–12, 15, 21–23, 25, 27–43, 48–51, 54, 58, 61, 63, 68, 72, 75, 78, 82, 84, 86, 89–99, 108–10, 112–14, 126–27, 132–34, 136–40, 144–50, 152–55
Pentecost, 26–27
Peter, 26–27, 38, 54
Persia, Persian, 10, 73, 78–80, 88, 93, 95, 154
Pisidian Antioch, speech in, 6, 25, 27, 34–39, 41, 68, 75, 149
Philo, 80, 83–87, 150–51, 153
Philodemus, 115
philosophers, Greek, 13, 28, 33–34, 36, 40, 48, 151–52, 155; *see also* individual names, Epicurean, Stoic.
Plato, 32–33, 94, 96, 99–100, 102, 104, 108, 111–12, 114–22, 124–26, 129, 133, 139–41, 147, 150–51, 153–54
ποιέω, 44–46, 49–50, 52–56, 59–61, 63–64, 66–67, 69, 71–72, 77, 81, 83–86, 90, 92–94, 96, 126–27, 132–33, 147
ποιητής, maker, 85, 117, 125–27, 132–33, 151
pleonasm, 16
Plutarch, 102–3, 108, 119, 121, 139
Polybius, 12–15
polysyndeton, 52
prayer, 47–48, 54–55, 62–64, 79–81, 86, 88–91, 94
providence, 52, 84, 89, 126, 130, 134–37, 139–41, 144–46, 151, 153

Rahab, 70–71, 80
resurrection, 29–30, 33

scholarchs, 113
scholarship, summaries of, 1–4, 7, 11–12, 15, 43–44, 99–100
Seneca, 102–3, 107–8, 114, 137–38
Sennacherib, 63
Sextus Empiricus, 102, 123–24
Socrates, Socratic, 13, 100, 102, 104–5, 109, 111–12, 115–16, 120, 122–23, 126–27, 132
Solomon, 62–64, 71–72, 80, 88–89, 91
σπερμολόγος, 30
Stoic, 2, 4–5, 14, 29–30, 32, 34, 43, 97–116, 119, 121–41, 143–49, 151–55
 cosmology, 98, 100, 115–27
 school, 98, 104–6, 109, 111–16, 123–25
 theology, 99, 124, 131, 135, 137–38, 141, 146, 151
Strabo, 30, 112–13
style, 6–7, 10–11
Syrian Antioch, 9–10

Talmud, 113
Tarsus, 106, 112–13
temple, Jerusalem, 27, 44, 62, 64, 67, 71, 79–80, 88, 91
Ten Commandments, 68, 71
theology, natural, 38, 125
Theophilus, 5–8, 16–26, 28, 40–41, 149, 152
θεός, 44–46, 48–49, 51–52, 55–56, 59, 61–62, 64–68, 71–72, 75–78, 81, 83–86, 90, 92–93, 96, 124, 126, 132, 147
Thucydides, 15, 23, 111

universe, 49–51, 56, 81, 94, 97–99 110, 115, 117–21, 123–26, 128–30, 132–34, 137–42, 144–54
unknown god, 6, 31, 34, 40, 49, 155
ὑπάρχω, 31, 45, 49, 51, 90, 92–93

Subject Index

word order, 17–18, 31, 74
writing and note-taking in the ancient world, 13–14, 104, 108

Xenophanes, 114
Xenophon, 100, 102, 104, 108, 111, 115, 122–23

Zeno, 32, 101–6, 111–16, 124, 140–41
Zeus, 36, 51, 86, 103, 105, 109–10, 132–33, 135–37, 139, 141
zoolatry, 81–82, 87

Ancient Document Index

SEPTUAGINT

Genesis

1	55, 57, 59, 78, 87–88, 152, 154
1–2	64, 77
1:1	3, 44–45, 47, 55–58, 70, 79, 84–85, 89–91, 93, 95, 127, 132, 150
1:1—2:3	56
1:2	55
1:8	55
1:14	55
1:20	55
1:22	55
1:25	55
1:26	55
1:28	55
1:30	55
2:1	56, 94
2:2–3	56
2:4	56
2:4–25	56
2:8	51
14	90
14:1–24	64–65
14:19	47, 59, 88–90
14:22	45, 47, 64–65, 80, 86, 88, 90
14:22–24	86
15:2	51
24	79
24:2–4	91
24:3	46–47, 65, 73
24:3–4	80, 86, 88

Exodus

20:2–3	68
32	58

Deuteronomy

4:19	60, 94
5:6–7	68
6:4	39, 85
30:19	65

Joshua

2:11	46–47, 70–71, 80

Ancient Document Index

1 Samuel

13:14	37

2 Samuel

7:16	38

1 Kings

5:15 [1]	72

2 Kings

17:5–7	58

1 Chronicles

16	60, 89
16:4–6	60
16:7	60
16:8–36	60
16:23	61
16:23–33	60
16:24	61, 89
16:24–26	61, 91
16.26	46–47, 60–61, 79–80, 88
16:31	89
16:33	89

2 Chronicles

2:3 [4]	72
2:11 [2:12]	45, 47, 71–72
6:14	46–47, 62–63, 80, 88–89
6:18	62
6:21	62
6:25	62
6:27	62
6:30	62
6:32–33	91
6:33	62, 89
6:35	62
6:39	62
9:8	71

Ezra

1:1	78
1:2	46–47, 78, 80, 154
5:11–12	78–79, 154
6:9–10	154

Nehemiah

9:6	45, 47, 64, 80, 88

Psalms

2:7	37
16:10	38
89:20	37
95 [96]	60–61, 88–89
95:1	61
95:3	61
95:4	61
95:5	61
113	60
113:11	59
113:11–12	60
113:13–15	60
113:20–22	59
113:23 [115:15]	45, 47, 59–60, 89
114:7	51
133:3 [134:3]	45, 47, 59–60

Isaiah

37:11	80
37:12	63
37:16	45, 47, 54, 63, 88–89

37:16-36	89	2:44	46-47, 75
37:19	63, 91	2:46-47	75
37:20	89-90	2:47	89
37:36	63	2:48	75
37:38	63	3	76
42	91	3:17	46-47, 76
42:5	44-45, 47, 65-66, 88	3:19-95 [19-28]	89
42:6-7	66	4:17	46-47, 76, 89
42:8	66, 91	4:27	46-47, 76
44	91	4:31	46-47, 77, 154
44:24	46-47, 65-66, 88	4:33	46-47, 77
45	65, 91-92	4:33-34	154
45:13	67	4:34	46-47, 77
45:18	42, 45, 47, 65, 67-68, 88, 92, 150	3:34-37	78
45:18-22	92, 150, 153	4:37 [4:1]	45-47, 77, 154
45:18-25	67-68, 88		
55:3	38		

Jonah

1	93
1:4	73
1:4-16	73-74
1:5	72-73
1:6-8	73
1:6-16	93, 150
1:9	42, 45, 47, 72-75, 77-78, 80, 88, 93, 150, 154
1:10-11	73
1:12	73
1:13-14	73
1:15	73
1:16	73-74, 78

Jeremiah

9:11-15 [12-16]	68
10	91-92
10:1-16	68-70
10:11-12	42, 45, 47, 68-70, 88
10:11-16	69
10:12	150
10:12-16	92, 150, 153

Daniel

2-4	75-76
2:28	46-47, 75
2:37	46-47, 75

Habakkuk

1:5	38

APOCRYPHA

Bel and the Dragon

1.5	45, 47, 81, 154

PSEUDEPIGRAPHA

Prayer of Manasseh

1	81
2	45, 47, 81

Sibylline Oracles

3	82, 91
3:10	82
3:11–14	82
3:29–35	82
3:33–35	45, 47, 82

Testament of Job

2.4	45, 47, 83
3.3	83
5.2	83

NEW TESTAMENT

Luke

1:1–4	11, 15–16, 18, 149
1:2	8, 16
1:2–3	16
1:3	8, 16, 19, 22
1:4	16, 19, 22
3:22	37
9:25	95
11:50	95
12:30	95

John

14:6	14

Acts

1–7	26
1:1	7–8, 19
1:8	25–26, 41, 149
2:41	26
4:24	45, 47–48, 54, 62, 89
8–12	26
9:15	27–28
10	27
10:2	24, 26
10:3–7	26
10:10–16	26
10:13–15	26
10:18	26
10:19–29	26
10:22	24
10:35	24
10:44–45	26
11:2–3	27
11:4–18	27
11:25–26	10
13	27, 37
13–14	27
13–28	26
13:1	10
13:2	27
13:4	27
13:7	23
13:16	24, 37
13:16–41	25, 37
13:17	37
13:18	37
13:19	37
13:20–21	37
13:22	37
13:26	24
13:33	37
13:34	38
13:35	38
13:38–39	38
13:43	24

Ancient Document Index

13:47	66		110, 126–27, 133–34, 137, 148–50, 152, 154
13:50	24		
14:8–10	36		
14:8–14	52	17:24–25	32, 114, 133
14:8–17	35	17:24–27	31, 53
14:11–13	35–36	17:24–29	29
14:15	35–36, 38, 45, 47–48, 51–54, 149	17:24–30	92, 153
		17:24–31	97, 141, 150
14:15–17	25, 35–36, 43	17:25	35–36, 49, 89, 91, 97, 133
14:16	35–36, 52		
14:17	36, 52, 89	17:26	49
14:18	52	17:27	32, 137
14:26–28	10	17:27–28	49, 97, 136, 145
15:1	27	17:28	32–33, 106, 136, 149
15:2	27		
15:5	27	17:29	33, 35–36, 49, 91
15:35	10	17:30	35–36, 49, 52
16:11–17	8	17:30–31	29, 33, 35, 97, 137
16:14	23	17:31	37, 82, 89
17	2, 93, 121, 132, 144–45, 152–55	17:32	29, 33
		17:32–34	28–29, 33
17:2–3	37	17:33	33–34
17:4	24	17:34	15, 23, 29, 34
17:10	37	18:4	37
17:12	23	18:7	24
17:16	35	18:12	107
17:16–21	28–31	18:22–23	10
17:16–31	35	18:25	21
17:16–32	27	18:26	21–23
17:16–34	5, 28–34, 44	19:8	37
17:17	24, 28	19:35–41	23
17:18	29–30, 32–33	20:5	8
17:18–19	35	21:17	8
17:19	30–31, 33	21:21	21
17:19–34	93, 150	21:21–24	21
17:20	31	21:25	21
17:21	31	21:27–30	27
17:22	31, 114	21:28–29	27
17:22–23	29	21:31–40	23
17:22–31	28–29, 31–33, 43, 137	21:34	22
		22:3	113
17:23	31, 34, 40, 49, 91	22:21–22	27
17:24	1, 4–6, 25, 31, 34–36, 38, 40, 42–45, 48–54, 56, 58, 63, 68, 80–81, 84–85, 87, 89–90, 92–99,	22:25–29	23
		22:30	22
		23:23	27
		23:26	19
		24:3	19

Ancient Document Index

Acts (*continued*)

24:27	19
25:25–27	23
25:26	22
26:31–32	23
27:42–43	23

Romans

2:18	21

1 Corinthians

14:19	21

Galatians

6:6	21

Colossians

4:11–14	9
4:14	9, 15

2 Timothy

4:6–18	9
4:11	9
4:13	14

Philemon

24	9

Revelation

7:9	53
14:1–5	53
14:6–7	45, 47–48, 53–54
14:7	52

OTHER JEWISH WRITINGS

Josephus

Against Apion

1.1	20
2.121	45, 47, 85–86, 88
2.191	86
2.192	45, 47, 86

Antiquities of the Jews

15.405	20
18.273	20
20.13	20

Jewish War

1.68	20

Life

1.430	20

Talmud

Sotah

49b	113

Philo

Creation of the World

LXI.172	46–47, 83–84

Embassy to Gaius

XVI.115	46–47, 83–85, 87

GRECO-ROMAN WRITINGS

Aratus

Phaenomena

1–7	109–10, 136
5	32

Cicero

De Natura Deorum

I.18–23	109–10, 130
I.39	109–10, 139
I.52	109–10, 144, 151
I.53	109–10, 131
II.3–4	109–10, 136–37
II.16	109–10, 125

Cleanthes

Hymn to Zeus

l.1–3	109–10, 135
l.4	32

Cornutus

Epidrome

2.1–8	109–10, 141

Diogenes Laertius

Lives of Eminent Philosophers

II.48	14, 100, 102, 104
III.5–6	102
VII. 1–160	101
VII.2–6	103
VII.5	111
VII.6	105
VII.137	110, 124
VII.137–38	109–10, 140
VII.147	109–10, 124
VII.148	110, 140
VII.168	105
VII.170	105
VII.174	14, 103
VII.175–76	105
VII.179	103, 106
VII.180	106
VII.183	106
X.1	103, 105
X.2	105
X.9	105
X.16–21	102
X.26	101
X.35–83	102
X.84–116	102
X.122–35	102
X.123	114, 142
X.123–24	109–10, 142
X.139	109–10, 142
X.139–54	102

Ancient Document Index

Epictetus

Discourses

I.9.7	109–10, 126–27
II.8.19–21	109–10, 126–27

Lucian

How to Write History

VI.47	13

Lucretius

De Rerum Natura

2.646–51	109–10, 143
5.8	107
5.156–88	109–10, 127–28
5.195–99	109–10, 128
5.220–21	128
5.416–57	109–10, 128–29

Philodemus

De Stoicis

XIII.3	115

Plato

Apology

17C	111

Republic

377C–380C	114

Timaeus

21D	116
24D	32–33
27A	116
27C—69A	116–17
28A	117
28C	94, 99, 121, 126, 132–33, 151
28C—29A	109–10, 117
29A	117
29B	121
29D	120
29E	121
30B	121
32C	121
34B	121–22, 139, 141
41A	118
41B	122
68E	118
69A—92C	116
69C	109–10, 118
75C—81E	118
92C	121, 139, 141

Plutarch

Moralia

1052.C-D	109–10, 139

Polybius

Histories

12.25	13
12.27	13

Seneca

De Beneficiis

I.6.3	114

Epistles

XCV.48–50	109–10, 137–38

Sextus Empiricus

Against the Physicists

I.99–100	109–10, 123

Strabo

Geography

XIV.5.13	113

Suetonius

Lives of the Caesars

6.7	107
6.35	107

Tacitus

Annals

15.60–64	107

Thucydides

Peloponnesian War

1.22.1	15

Xenophon

Memorabilia

I.4	126
I.4.3–7	109–10, 122–23

EARLY CHRISTIAN WRITINGS

2 Clement

17.1	21

Epistle to Diognetus

1.1	20

Eusebius

Historia Ecclesiastica

3.4	8–9
5.8	9
6.26	9

www.ingramcontent.com/pod-product-compliance
Lightning Source LLC
Chambersburg PA
CBHW062044220426
43662CB00010B/1647